VOICE OF ISRAEL

ISRAEL

0 10 20 30 40 50
MILES

LEBANON

SYRIA

MEDITERRANEAN SEA

Metulla

Lake Hula

Nahariya

Mishmar

Acre

SAFAD

Hayarden

Haifa

Tiberias

SEA OF
GALILEE

Nazareth

GALILEE

Afula

Qeisariya

Hadera

Beit Shean

Natanya

Tulkarm

Nablus

SAMARIA

TEL AVIV
Jaffa

Lydda

Ramallah

Amman

Rishon
le Zion

Ramla

Jericho

Rehovot

Jerusalem

Bethlehem

R. Jordan

Negba

Ashkelon

Yad Mordekhai

JUDEA

Beit Hanun

Niram

DEAD
SEA

Gaza

Lakhish

Hebron

Dorot

Nahaloz

Nirim

Beersheba

Rafiah

Revivim

Sedom

Nitsana

Sede Boqer

NEGEV

JORDAN

EGYPT

SINAI

DESERT

Yotvata

Elath

Aqaba

GULF OF
AQABA

35° East of Greenwich

VOICE OF
ISRAEL

by
S.
ABBA EBAN

FABER AND FABER
24 Russell Square
London

*First published in mcmlviii
by Faber and Faber Limited
24 Russell Square London W.C.1
Printed in Great Britain by
Latimer Trend & Co Ltd Plymouth*

Contents

7

Contents

MAPS

Israel's First Decade
1948-1958

The hour of history which we commemorate this year is only ten years old. But who can doubt its eminence amongst the authentic moments of climax in human history? For this was an hour which re-established the identity of a people; inaugurated the transformation of a land; released the youthful vigour of an ancient culture; opened gates of hope and freedom to hundreds of thousands in distant lands; brought consolation to a people at the moment of its unfathomable grief; gave the community of nations a new dimension, a new link with its oldest spiritual roots.

Nobody who lived that hour will ever forget its mingled sentiment. Israel was no sooner born than her very survival was imperilled. The gust of universal joy which swept the House of Israel and moved men of generous heart in every land, was attended, also, by anguish and suspense. High opportunity and deadly danger, supreme ecstasy and icy fear, came together in that moment side by side. As the spectre of destruction hovered over us, we looked upon our new-born republic with a sense of the awesome fragility of all cherished things.

The danger was surmounted. The tide of conflict rolled away; and Israel set itself to the labours of its first decade. As we look back upon our record of achievement, we need not fear that we have dishonoured the moment of our birth, or that the brave ambitions of that summer morning have played us false.

The festive banners of Israel's birthday year look down upon a rich and varied scene. A people multiplied threefold out of the small community which proclaimed its independence less than one decade

9

ago; a land endowed with deeper grace and broader fertility than it has known since the days of the ancient Hebrew kingdoms; a culture charged with the combined virtues of age and youth, inspired both by a sense of innovation and by pride of descent from a lineage of three thousand years; a citadel of democracy, in a region where political freedom has few other bulwarks; a lively centre of social idealism and technological progress; an arena in which the pent-up energies of immigrants and pioneers still have wide fields to conquer; a focus of pride for all throughout the world who cherish the Jewish faith and tradition as the central impulse of their daily lives; a testimony to the power of the human will to overcome the calculations of material chance; a new banner planted in a family of nations which would lack completeness without its presence—these are amongst the consequences of Israel's rebirth. When we recall the brief time in which these things have been accomplished and the war and siege which have impeded every forward step, we may well greet this anniversary hour in thankfulness and praise.

It is a tragic paradox to find Israel plunged so deeply in preoccupations of defence. We, the authors of mankind's oldest pacific tradition, do not wish our homeland to be forever an armed camp. On days of remembrance there come into our minds the poignant figures of thousands of our fallen sons who consecrated Israel's statehood by giving to it all that a man can give. Would that we might be free from these military burdens. The true genius of our people lies in its visions of social and cultural progress. Despite the stern necessities of defence, we have not betrayed that vision even in recent months. The past years with all their tension, have seen a brave advance in many varied fields. The battle of the plough against the wilderness has celebrated many triumphs. Agricultural development and industrial enterprise have gone forward in swift momentum. Immigration has resumed its beneficent course. Water has been brought down to the dry places of the South. Oil has gushed forth from the coastal plain, not indeed with delirious profusion, but at least with steady promise. A window has been opened through Elath to the continents of the east. A flood of immigration takes it welcome course. New homes and farms, schools and factories have spread a network of life across many a slumbering landscape. Our democratic tradition has deepened its roots and consolidated its hold upon the popular will. The soil has yielded up monuments and relics which remind us of our link with the incomparable Hebrew past. The arts and letters flourish. Our scientific community

10

has played its honourable part in exploring the vistas of the new age in natural power.

The air of Israel is alive with the tumult of creation. A sense of constructive fulfilment pervades the scene. But this potentiality will not be fully realized unless we obtain that physical security which is the condition of all future progress.

There are no obstacles to peace which cannot be overcome in full respect for the independence and territorial integrity of each Middle Eastern State. We look without grudge or envy upon the neighbouring world. Never has the Arab nation commanded such elements of freedom, strength and opportunity as those which now lie in its hand. With its twelve sovereign States, its vast territory, its great resources of manpower and wealth, it has realized ambitions beyond the wildest expectations of recent years. Is the world really asking too much if it demands of this vast empire that it live in peace and harmony with a little State, established in the cradle of its birth, sustaining its life within the narrowest territory in which its national purposes can ever be fulfilled? To live in peace with Israel, as she is today, imposes no sacrifice, inflicts no injury, incurs no grievance for the Arab people in this golden age of its emancipation. Across the futile barriers of conflict can we not discern the abundance and greatness which our region could achieve if belligerency, blockade and non-recognition would but give way to the duty of sovereign States to harmonize their efforts for the regional welfare and the universal peace? But we shall not inherit this fulfilment if Middle Eastern leaders spurn the patient courses of internal development, and go off chasing dreams of hegemony, regional domination, nationalistic prestige and the exploitation of Great Power rivalries for short-term bargaining gains. Surely our region deserves better leadership than this.

Thousands of years ago a people, a land and a language came together in Israel's birth, and the course of man's life and thought was lifted to a new point of elevation. Then, for centuries this pattern was split asunder. The people, the land and the language were separated; and tragedy and danger befell them all. Separated each from the other, none of these three achieved the creative potency which they each knew when they lived together. What is modern Israel, except the reunion of this people, land and language in a sublime fulfilment of history's cycle, a bridge thrown across the gulf of continents and generations, to symbolize the unity of all historic experience?

11

Prologue: Israel's First Decade

Seen in this light, the smallness of our State in area and population is enlarged in the consciousness of men by the vistas of historic memory. The chronicle of a people's rebirth is presented here in the hope that it will be contemplated against the broad perspectives of history and conscience.

CHAPTER I

... Only With the State of Israel*

On 15th May 1948 the armies of five Arab States crossed their frontiers and attempted to overthrow the newly established State of Israel.

On 22nd May 1948 the Security Council voted for an unconditional cease-fire.

On May 26th, as their armies advanced deep into Israel, the Arab governments rejected the cease-fire and delivered an ultimatum demanding that Israel's statehood be abrogated and Israeli forces disarmed.

The answers received from the Arab States are more significant for what they omit than for what they contain. They contain a remarkable array of violent threats. But they omit any sign of willingness to stop making war. They merely define the political objectives for which those States are invading a neighbouring country. Israel is asked to yield her integrity and independence in return for a cessation of the assault upon her.

This interchange with the governments of the Middle East has had a salutary effect in defining the exact nature of our problem. Everything is now clear. All obscurity falls away. Both sides were asked if they would unconditionally stop fighting.

Israel answers: 'Yes.' This is the fifth offer of an unconditional cease-fire from the Israel side, before, during and after the establishment of our State.

The Arab States answer: 'No.' Here is a flat and defiant rejection of the Security Council's cease-fire resolution. In its place we have a proposal for satisfying Arab ambitions by revoking Israel's statehood and independence. The sovereignty regained by an ancient people, after its long march through the dark night of exile, is to be surrendered at pistol point.

It becomes my duty to make our attitude clear, beyond ambiguity or doubt. If the Arab States want peace with Israel, they can have it. If they want war, they can have that too. But whether they want peace or war, they can have it only with the State of Israel.

* Security Council of the United Nations, 26 May 1948.

CHAPTER II

The War Renewed[*]

On 29th May 1948 the Security Council adopted a truce resolution which was accepted by Israel and, for the first time, by the Arab States. Fighting stopped for four weeks, and the United Nations Mediator, Count Bernadotte, strove for an extension of the truce.

The Arab governments, however, insisted on another attempt to destroy Israel by force. They rejected successive appeals by the Mediator, including one for a ten-day extension of the cease-fire. Count Bernadotte flew to United Nations headquarters for the debate in the Security Council.

On July 15th, the Council resolved that the Arab action constituted a breach of the peace and ordered a permanent cease-fire under penalty of sanctions.

There is not a single person in this room or outside it who does not know in the depths of his heart that the Arab States, by resuming their attacks upon Israel, have committed an act of aggression.

Their armed forces are operating beyond their frontiers for purposes which the United Nations Charter specifically forbids. They are using force against the territorial integrity and political independence of Israel. Their object, which they candidly avow, is to secure the violent extinction of the State of Israel, the establishment of which was recommended by the General Assembly. They have rejected the solemn appeal of the Security Council to agree to a prolongation of the truce agreement initiated on May 29th, with the result that this agreement has now become void.

On July 3rd Count Bernadotte, the Mediator appointed by the United Nations, in appealing to all governments concerned for a prolongation of the truce, made the following statement:

'There is little doubt that a decision to resume fighting would be universally condemned and that a party taking such a decision would

[*] Security Council of the United Nations, 13 July 1948.

be assuming a responsibility which will be viewed by the world with the utmost gravity.'

The Arab States have taken that decision. They have assumed that responsibility. They have resumed fighting. Their violence is directed against the recommendation of the General Assembly, against the appeal of the Security Council, against the call of the Mediator, against the very life and survival of the State of Israel, against the principles of world peace. Israel, which is the victim of this renewed aggression, now turns to this organ of the United Nations to ask: Is that decision 'universally condemned'? Is that responsibility 'viewed by the world with the utmost gravity'? Does this Council condemn the decision to resume fighting? And if so, what steps does it propose to take to vindicate the Charter against flagrant aggression; to impose the penalties which aggression incurs; and to place moral and material support behind the State of Israel, defending its independence against aggressive attack?

No elaborate evidence is needed to prove the aggressive character of these warlike movements upon which the armies of the Arab States have embarked—with welcome lack of success—since Friday last. The Charter of the United Nations, with its explicit distinction between the legitimate and illegitimate use of force, provides a spontaneous response to those who would doubt the aggressive character of these acts. Neither Article 51 which allows members of the United Nations the 'right of self-defence' only 'if an armed attack occurs upon them', nor the preamble of the Charter which lays it down that 'armed force shall not be used save in the common interest', can possibly be invoked in support of these attacks. For Egypt, Transjordan, Syria, Lebanon, Saudi Arabia and Yemen have not been individually or jointly attacked; and they have certainly not been invited by the United Nations to storm into territory not their own for purposes of havoc and murder.

Therefore, the principles of the United Nations proclaim these operations as acts of aggression; and the same result is reached if we apply the criterion of responsibility and initiative. For here we are in the unusual position of not being faced with any conflict of views on the origin of the fighting. When the first phase of this aggression began on May 15th, representatives of the Arab States showered documents upon the United Nations, asserting that they had taken the initiative for using armed force outside their frontiers with the purpose of overthrowing a neighbouring State, whose existence they

15

disliked. Under the Charter, they are of course, entitled to dislike the existence of the State of Israel. But they are most categorically forbidden to use armed force against the political independence or territorial integrity of that State; or indeed to use armed force for any purpose whatever, 'save in the common interest' of the United Nations, or in defence of their own territories, if those territories should be attacked without provocation.

Not one of the conditions which would make the use of armed force legitimate exists, or has ever been claimed to exist, in this case.

At a previous meeting of the Security Council, representatives of the Arab States read statements, similar in substance and tone to those which now lie before us, asserting the political ambitions whereby they are animated, and the violent means which they use in their support. On that occasion, the representative of the United States said of those Arab declarations:

'Their statements are the best evidence we have of the international character of this aggression. . . . They tell us quite frankly that their business in Palestine is political and that they are there to establish a unitary State. . . . Therefore, we have evidence of the highest type concerning the international violation of the law, namely the admission by those who commit this violation.'

On May 28th supporting a resolution submitted by the Soviet Union, the representative of the United States succinctly expressed the purposes of Arab aggression in these words: ' "We are there only for the purpose of overwhelming the Government of Israel; we are going to overwhelm it by power, and we are going to determine an international question ourselves." ' Continuing, the representative of the United States said:

'An existing, independent government cannot be blotted out in that way. It cannot be blotted out by just sitting at the Security Council table and ignoring it. The Arab States are taking the only course that can be taken to blot it out—and that is marching in with their armies and blotting it out. That is a matter of international concern, a matter of so great importance that we cannot sit here and say: "Oh, we wash our hands of it. We shall not do anything about it that will be effective. . . . We know, of course, that this is a violation of the Charter." '

At the same meeting, the representative of the United States

16

referring to the Arab claim that their operations were aimed at the maintenance of peace, said:

'This is equivalent in its absurdity to alleging that these five armies are there to maintain peace, and at the same time are conducting a bloody war.'

During the earlier phases of this assault which began on 1st December 1947 and took official form on 15th May 1948, the aggressive character of the Arab invasion was so clear to many members of the Security Council that five of them were already prepared to determine that there existed a threat to the peace. Those members who were unable to support that view at so early a stage, did not deny that an act of aggression might exist. Not one of them—except Syria, whose government has been implicated in every act of aggression that has taken place in the Near East for the last six months—was prepared to assert that the Arab armies had any justification for the military operations which they were carrying out. These members, however, wished to make sure that all methods of pacific settlement had been exhausted. They wished to give a final chance for the counsels of moderation to assert themselves.

To this end, cease-fire resolutions were repeatedly sponsored, accepted by the Government of Israel, rejected by the Arab States, re-examined by the Security Council, and eventually served up on May 29th in the form of a resolution which combined the call for a cease-fire with the satisfaction of what the United Kingdom representative called 'the political demands which the Arabs consider reasonable'. These demands were expressed in a universal arms embargo, which denied arms equally to Israel, engaged in its own defence, and to the Arab States bent upon aggression. This equation between the defending State of Israel and its lawless attackers enabled the invading States to maintain the preponderance of arms which they had built up through their long exercise of sovereign rights, and their military alliance with a Great Power.

For four weeks, an uneasy truce has existed during which the Mediator reports that 'no military advantage was gained by either side'. It was of course, the Mediator's duty to preserve that military equilibrium. But now, faced as we are with open aggression, it does not comfort us to recall that the party which has loyally accepted every honourable means of avoiding bloodshed and the party which now stands guilty of aggression, have, for the past four weeks, been equally impeded in their preparations for defence and attack respectively.

The War Renewed

Addressing the Security Council five weeks ago, I enquired whether any State represented around this table would willingly neglect opportunities of improving its defence for four weeks, if it had complete certainty that at the end of those weeks, the armies of five neighbouring States would sweep down upon it in redoubled fury. I expressed doubts whether any State would submit its immigration policy, a matter of its own internal jurisdiction, to the scrutiny or control of anyone else. Yet Israel did accept those restrictive conditions, which it believes should never have been imposed upon it. It allowed its scanty defence forces to remain unaugmented during a period which we knew to be merely a prelude for further attacks upon our boundaries and our political integrity. We allowed external control to reach into our rights of immigration which are the very essence of our national purpose. We were able to accept these limitations because they were imposed for a period of brief duration; and because Israel, born out of a United Nations' recommendation, has been eager at all times to affirm its fidelity to the principles and processes of the Charter. But when we read documents from the Egyptian Government and the Arab League portraying the period of truce as one of 'Jewish advantage', we lose faith in the integrity of those who formulate such charges, knowing, as they must, that the brunt of the truce restrictions fell heavily on Israel alone.

On the morning of July 9th, the four weeks truce expired. Owing to the Arab refusal to grant a prolongation, it was not renewed. It is, therefore, no longer in force; and no one is bound by any of its provisions or restrictions. The apparatus of observance and supervision has disintegrated. The readiness of Israel to agree to a four weeks continuation was contemptuously rejected on the Arab side. In a last minute effort to keep war at bay while the next step was contemplated, the Mediator turned to both parties and asked them to agree, at the very least, to an unconditional cease-fire for a period of ten days. Here was a searching test of peaceful intention. Here was a request, the refusal of which could be nothing but an avowal of aggression. For what legitimate objectives can anybody have which can be threatened by the preservation of peace for ten days? What are the ambitions which rest upon so flimsy a moral foundation that they cannot endure ten days and ten nights of peace?

Israel accepted this proposal. I know not whether this was our seventh or eighth acceptance. The Arab Governments rejected it.

18

The War Renewed

Before the previous truce had even expired, Egyptian forces in the coastal sector of the Negev launched their assault. Their commanders were found, on capture, to possess operation orders which show conclusively that their Government had planned, not merely to avoid prolongation of the truce, but even to launch aggression anew before the period of the existing truce had expired.

In these circumstances, anybody who will not determine these acts to constitute aggression, must be hard pressed to demonstrate that the word aggression can have any meaning at all. If Governments that are members of the United Nations use armed force outside their frontiers when they have not been attacked, with the avowed aim of overthrowing the political and territorial integrity of a State established by recommendation of the General Assembly; when they do this in defiance of an appeal by the Security Council and of its accredited representative; when they rekindle the flames of war which the whole world passionately wishes to see extinguished; when they decline a respite of ten days during which the hope of peace may still be pursued; when they do all this, how can you say that they do not commit aggression, unless you are prepared to erase the word 'aggression' from your Charter and from the dictionary, and to sign an advance certificate of impunity for any act of aggression that the future may bring?

It is obvious that those who reject proposals for a cease-fire and commit their destiny to military action, must be prepared to take the full military consequences of their acts; and this, the Arab States are now doing in the field.[1] But surely, if the Security Council wishes to retain its authority in the eyes of both parties, it cannot pass over aggression in silence and allow no political consequences to flow from it. It is for that reason that the Government of Israel, in its cable to the Secretary General, concludes with the following words:

'While its armed forces are ready for the most determined action on all fronts, the Provisional Government of Israel is most interested to learn what the Security Council will decide in the present emergency.'

We believe that this interest is shared by peace-loving peoples throughout the world, who regard it as the central function of the United Nations to suppress threats to the peace, breaches of the peace, and acts of aggression.

[1] Having refused to extend the truce and insisted on resuming the fighting, the Arab States suffered one reverse after another on the field of battle.

The War Renewed

We need no repetition of an abortive truce with invading armies poised on Israel's frontiers. We need a deterrent to aggression. We need those invading armies to go home, so that the frontiers of Israel become the frontiers of a durable peace. A truce crystallizes aggression at the point which it has reached. It therefore, carries with it the seed of renewed war. What we must now ensure is that the tide of invasion be ordered back to the territory from which it came.

I should like to pass a few reflections on the Arab replies to the Mediator's proposals.

Running through these answers is a single theme, namely, that the Arab States have political ambitions which cannot be advanced if there is peace. We ask whether this fact is not itself a reflection on those ambitions; whether political aspirations which can only be fostered by successful war do not disqualify themselves from the approval of the world. For we cannot admit that there is a natural equation between the political aspirations of both sides. On the one hand, there is the spectacle of a nation rising up from the ocean of twenty centuries in which it had been submerged, founding a new unit of the human family, embodying a distinctive tradition, spirit and culture whose survival has not been without significance to the life of mankind. This resurgence takes place on the very soil on which that nation first established its identity. It brings a hope of personal deliverance to the victims of the world's greatest tragedy. And this event which, despite its small compass, has made an irresistible appeal to the chivalry and sentiment of the world, rests upon a valid international decision.

This is one process—the establishment of Israel. It can be carried out in peace; though even war does not make it unfeasible. On the other hand, there is the desire of a neighbouring people, sated and replete with an abundance of political and territorial independence, to wipe this little nation off the face of the earth. That is an ambition nurtured in the very spirit of war. The question which lies at the root of this controversy—whether Israel should exist or be extinguished —is, in the last resort, an issue between peace and war; between self-determination for all peoples and the doctrine of regional domination by a single national and cultural element, to the exclusion of national freedom for anyone else. When the Arab States confess that their political aspirations cannot be advanced without war, they do not thereby justify their war. They merely invalidate their political aspirations.

The War Renewed

It is well that all parties to this dispute, and all who hope to help bring it to an end, should focus their attention upon the central issue. That issue is the determination of Israel to exist and survive.

This State of Israel is the product of the most sustained historic tenacity which the ages recall. Somehow this people, in the very climax of its agony, has managed to generate the cohesion, energy and confidence to bring the third Jewish commonwealth into existence. The Jewish people has not striven towards this goal for twenty centuries in order that, having once achieved it with the full endorsement of international opinion, it will now surrender it in response to an illegitimate and unsuccessful aggression. Whatever else changes, this will not. The State of Israel is an immutable part of the international landscape. To plan the future without it is to build delusions on sand. Everything that contributes to an Arab belief in the stability and permanence of Israel brings the prospect of harmony nearer. That is why every recognition of Israel, every voice uplifted against aggression, every manifestation of sympathy for our republic in its gallant fight, is a milestone on the road which may lead us to peace, perhaps more rapidly than we can now expect.

CHAPTER III

Israel Amongst the Nations*

On 11th March 1949 the Security Council had approved Israel's application for membership in the United Nations. But the General Assembly's ratification was still required.

The Arab States violently opposed Israel's admission to membership, and succeeded in blocking it at several procedural stages. On 5th May 1949 the Political Committee of the General Assembly invited the Israel representative to reply to arguments invoked by Arab States against Israel's application.

Following this address, the General Assembly adopted a Resolution on 11th May 1949 admitting Israel to membership in the United Nations.

On 29th November 1948 Israel's application for membership in the United Nations was submitted to the Security Council in accordance with Article 4 of the Charter. This was the anniversary of the General Assembly's original Resolution which had 'called upon the inhabitants of Palestine to take such steps as may be necessary on their part to put the plan (of partition) into effect'. On 14th May 1948—just one year ago yesterday, according to the Hebrew calendar—Israel proclaimed its independence, responding both to its own right of self-determination as a distinctive political and cultural unit, and to the explicit recommendation of the General Assembly. The Resolution of 29th November 1947 had recommended that when either State envisaged by that Resolution had made its independence effective, 'sympathetic consideration should be given to its application for admission to membership in the United Nations in accordance with Article 4 of the Charter of the United Nations'.

A year later Israel had withstood an aggressive onslaught launched against it by seven States, including six members of the United Nations, in an effort to overthrow the Assembly's Resolution by

* General Assembly of the United Nations, 5 May 1949.

22

force. Israel had established the foundations of its government. It had secured recognition by nineteen States. It had made efforts, directly and through the agencies of the United Nations, to negotiate with the neighbouring Arab States for an end of the war and the establishment of peace. Alone amongst the States involved in that war, Israel had undertaken to comply with the Security Council's Resolution of 16th November 1948 calling upon the governments concerned to negotiate an armistice as a transition to lasting peace.

Israel was already a vibrant reality. Rarely in history had a people so small in physical power surmounted so many ordeals and adversities on its path to independence. It had now emerged out of mortal danger into the clear prospect of survival. Having reached this degree of stability, both in its domestic institutions and its international position, Israel came forward to seek the shelter of the United Nations Charter, and to assume its obligations.

This application has thus been before the United Nations for five months. When it was first discussed in December 1948 there was already a considerable body of opinion in the Security Council, represented by the United States, the Soviet Union, Argentina, Colombia and the Ukrainian S.S.R., ready to favour an immediate recommendation. Others, however, counselled a brief delay. They pointed out that no beginning had yet been made in the Arab-Israeli negotiations called for by the Security Council on 16th November 1948, and by the General Assembly on 11th December 1948. Indeed, no formal contact had then been established anywhere at that time. Others invoked the provisional character of Israel's governmental institutions and the restricted basis of its international recognition at that time. We found it difficult to admit that any reading of Article 4 of the Charter made these considerations strictly relevant. Many States had been admitted to membership before, or even without, the establishment of elected governments. If the conciliation effort had not begun by last December, this was no fault of Israel which was the first to propose direct armistice and peace talks as far back as 1st August 1948. Nevertheless, the Security Council is the body which has been entrusted by the members of the United Nations with 'primary responsibility for the maintenance of international peace and security'. Its decisions or hesitations must carry great weight in a matter so closely bound up with international peace.

Accordingly, my Government waited until the early days of March before asking for renewed consideration of its application. Meanwhile, the imagination of the world had been profoundly impressed by the spectacle of Israel's swift consolidation. Israel had now secured recognition by an overwhelming majority of other States, in all the five Continents, in the Old World and the New. It had conducted the only democratic election which this part of the Near East had seen for many years. It had established a legislature based on popular suffrage. It had formed a government dedicated to parliamentary democracy and social reform. It had elected as the head of the State its most respected and venerated citizen, to symbolize both Israel's concern for international prestige and its vision of scientific humanism. It had successfully concluded its first experience in the most crucial task of all. For on February 24th, after direct and intricate negotiations under the skilful direction of Dr. Bunche, the Government of Israel had concluded a general armistice with the leading power in the Arab world. In an official statement the Government of Israel declared that it wished to regard this notable agreement as the prelude to final peace between Israel and Egypt.

These were the circumstances in which the Security Council met on March 3rd and March 4th. By nine votes to one, with one abstention, it adopted the following Resolution:

'THE SECURITY COUNCIL, having received and considered the application of Israel for membership in the United Nations;

'DECIDES that in its judgment Israel is a peace-loving State and is able and willing to carry out the obligations contained in the Charter, and accordingly

'RECOMMENDS to the General Assembly that it admit Israel to membership in the United Nations.'

In every other case of admission such a resolution of the Security Council has had a decisive effect when Assembly confirmation has been sought. But this particular Resolution has a special authority which does not apply to other applications. For Israel's claim for admission to membership was hotly contested within the Security Council itself by one of the States which had felt themselves entitled to make war—violent and brutal war—for the extermination of Israel and the overthrow of a General Assembly Resolution by force. The majority in the Security Council was thus not achieved by any cursory or perfunctory review. A suggestion that residual problems of the war, especially those of the status of Jerusalem and Arab refugees, should be clarified before this admission was recommended, was put forward with force and clarity by the United Kingdom. The Security Council rejected this suggestion by its vote. Remaining with austere fidelity within the terms of Article 4 of the Charter, and in full consciousness of Israel's position on both of these questions, it sent its impressive verdict to this session of the General Assembly.

What has happened since the Security Council gave Israel's application such emphatic support? The significant developments may be briefly summarized. On 23rd March 1949 Israel concluded an armistice agreement with Lebanon by a unilateral withdrawal of its own forces and the establishment of defensive zones. On April 3rd an Armistice Agreement was concluded between Israel and the Kingdom of Transjordan through reciprocal concessions, whereby any serious threat of renewed hostilities was removed from the greater part of the area which had formed the Palestinian battlefield. Under the terms of this agreement, lasting peace has been assured to the City of Jerusalem and its inhabitants. At this moment, armistice negotiations with Syria are approaching what we hope will be a successful conclusion. On April 26th the Government of Israel despatched a delegation to Lausanne where the Conciliation Commission had invited the parties to meet for a preliminary exchange of views.

Eight months have elapsed since my Government formally requested the Arab States to meet with it for a settlement by negotiations of all outstanding military and political questions. Nearly six months have gone by since the Representative of Canada in the Security Council proposed and secured the adoption of the momentous Resolution calling for an armistice—a Resolution supported by my Government and opposed by the Arab States. Hundreds of thousands of people in Israel and in neighbouring areas are denied the prospect of security and welfare so long as the conclusion of a formal peace is delayed. The Government of Israel has accordingly informed the Conciliation Commission that it wishes to regard the Lausanne meetings not as a mere preliminary exchange of views, but as an earnest attempt by both parties to achieve a final and effective peace.

In response to the requests of this Committee I have been asked to state my Government's attitude on the question of Jerusalem and the Holy Places. We believe that the principle of international control must be maintained, but that, in the existing circumstances, it

Israel Amongst the Nations

should be expressed more realistically than was envisaged in the ambitious proposals worked out by the General Assembly last November. We must seek to apply the international principle with some regard to the conditions existing in April 1949; and not in accordance with the conditions which our predecessors might have envisaged in November 1947. The peace of Jerusalem is too precious to be disrupted by reversing the clock of history, even if this could be done. I notice that in the recent Papal Encyclical the principle is laid down that the status of Jerusalem must be one which 'in the present circumstances'—not in the circumstances of November 1947—will ensure the safety and protection of the Holy Places.

One possible way of solving the problem is by limiting the international régime in area, so that it applies not to the entire City but only to that part of it which contains the greatest concentration of religious and historic shrines. This was a proposal put forward by my Government in the earlier part of the current session. On the other hand, it is possible to go further and to envisage an international régime which applies to the whole City of Jerusalem, but which is restricted functionally so as to be concerned only with the protection and control of Holy Places and not with any secular or political aspects of life and government. This is the approach which we favour at our present stage in the consideration of this problem. To this end, the Government of Israel made a statement on April 23rd through the President of the State, expressing its policy in the following words:

'The Government and people of Israel are conscious of the international interest in the safety of the Holy Places and the right of free access to them. We pledge ourselves to ensure full security for religious institutions in the exercise of their functions; to grant the supervision of the Holy Places by those who hold them sacred; and to encourage and accept the fullest international safeguards and controls for their immunity and protection. Just as we are resolved to give complete and practical expression to the universal interest arising from the Holy Places, so we expect that the international community will understand the direct and inescapable responsibility which Israel bears and exercises in the daily life and administration of Jewish Jerusalem. I am satisfied that no real incompatibility exists between the interests and concerns of Christianity, to which His Holiness the Pope has recently given eloquent expression, and the aspirations of the people of Jerusalem to assure their government and security in conformity with their national allegiance. If there is a genuine desire to reconcile these two interests, a harmonious solution can swiftly be secured with international consent.'

This is a far-reaching commitment, offering the international community the right of jurisdiction over Holy Places in Israeli territory. It deserves the closest examination by all parties concerned. No similar pledge has been made by the Arab Government which controls the majority of the Holy Places in Jerusalem. If a commitment similar to ours were elicited from Transjordan, it cannot be doubted that the problem of the Holy Places would be on the way to solution, provided only that the United Nations were to assume even this more modest responsibility in an active and responsible spirit. The sad history of the Jerusalem Statute should have taught us that it is of little value to cede responsibilities to the international community, if the United Nations shows no tendency to take them up.

If the United Nations could secure from the Arab Government concerned a commitment similar to that made by Israel, and were then to establish an international régime in Jerusalem which would confine its jurisdiction and authority to the Holy Places, the Jerusalem problem could be successfully solved.

We are still in an intermediate stage of discussion. We seek the reconciliation of two interests for each of which we have a deep and abiding concern. There is the universal interest arising out of the Holy Places—an interest understandably seeking juridical expression; and there is the necessity of providing the people of Jerusalem with an administration that conforms with their welfare and their national sentiment and allegiance. These two interests are to be reconciled; we do not and should not seek the complete subordination of one to the other.

In coming to discuss the question of Arab refugees, I repeat that all the outstanding political problems between Israel and its neighbours only exist as a direct consequence of the fact that a war was launched for the purpose of overthrowing the General Assembly's Resolution by force. Of no problem is this more true than the refugee question, on which I have been asked to clarify my Government's views. None of these movements of population would have occurred if the Arab world had joined with us in an attempt to give peaceful implementation to the General Assembly's Resolution on Partition. These migrations are a familiar circumstance of war, especially wars affecting countries of mixed populations which become involved in agonizing conflicts of allegiance.

Dr. Malik, the representative of Lebanon, informed us correctly this morning that it was not the intention of the General Assembly for Israel to become free of its Arab inhabitants. But surely it was not the intention of the General Assembly that Lebanon and six other states should make war against the General Assembly's Resolution. Every disturbance of the 1947 plan is a plain result of the fact that a war was launched. The Arab States are responsible for every modification of that Resolution; responsible for every death, for all the bereavement and for all the panic and exile which has resulted from this futile and unnecessary conflict.

The exodus of the Arab population began in the early days of that war during the tenure of the Mandate and had already become irrepressible by the time the Government of Israel assumed its responsibilities. Efforts made by Israel to stem the flood did not avail against the panic of war. A vivid eye-witness account was published in the London *Economist* in October 1948 as follows:

'During the subsequent days, the Jewish authorities . . . urged all Arabs to remain in Haifa and guaranteed their protection and security. . . . Various factors influenced their decision to seek safety in flight . . . far the most potent of these factors was the announcement made over the air by the Arab Higher Committee urging all Arabs in Haifa to quit. The reason given was that upon the final withdrawal of the British, the combined armies of the Arab States would invade Palestine and drive the Jews into the sea. It was clearly intimated that those Arabs who remained in Haifa and accepted Jewish protection would be regarded as renegades.'

So many passions have been aroused by this grave humanitarian issue that we feel compelled to return again and again to the question of initial responsibility. This problem is nothing but a direct consequence of the war proclaimed and launched by Arab States through the action of irregular forces on December 1947, and the invasion of Israel by regular armies on 15th May 1948.

Thus, quite apart from their own ties of kinship with the refugee population the Arab governments are morally obliged, by their own unqualified guilt, to take a full share in the solution of this problem.

Israel Amongst the Nations

The refugee question should be examined and solved during the negotiations for the establishment of peace. I doubt if this proposition can be seriously questioned. The rehabilitation of dispossessed peoples cannot take place when the countries of the Middle East are divided by armistice lines; when no peaceful contact exists; when considerations of military security must still be paramount; when all movements of people, whether refugees or not, are subject to the restrictive requirements of war; and when the economic and social effort required from all governments for such rehabilitation is paralysed by mobilization and a war economy. Indeed, one of the conditions which lend greatest urgency to peace negotiations is the fact that only such negotiations can open the way to the satisfactory solution of this grave humanitarian problem.

In order to clear away all misunderstandings and to place on record the principles which determine Israel's approach, the Government of Israel has authorized me to make the following statement on the refugee problem:

'1. The problem of the Arab refugees is a direct consequence of the war launched by the Arab States which are therefore entirely responsible for this as well as for other forms of suffering inflicted by that war.

'2. However, the ensuing problem has raised a deep humanitarian issue and also has serious implications for the future peace, development and welfare of the Middle East. The Government of Israel believes that a solution of this problem is inseparably linked with a solution of the outstanding issues between it and the Arab States and that no satisfactory solution is possible except by the restoration of peace in the Middle East. A solution can only be found within a final settlement creating conditions of co-operation between Israel and its neighbours.

'3. The Government of Israel is earnestly anxious to contribute to the solution of this problem even though it is not of its making. This anxiety proceeds from moral considerations and from Israel's vital interest in stable conditions throughout the Middle East. Any rehabilitation of Arab refugees in any part of the Middle East, whether in Israel or in the neighbouring countries, involves intricate tasks of resettlement. The two principles most widely advocated are (a) resettlement of the refugees in the places from which they fled, thus creating a large minority problem and a possible menace to internal

29

peace and stability, also placing masses of Arabs under the rule of a Government which, while committed to an enlightened minority policy, is not akin to these Arabs in language, culture, religion or social and economic institutions; (*b*) resettlement of the refugees in areas where they will live under a Government akin to them in spirit and tradition and in which their smooth integration will be immediately possible with no resultant political friction. Moreover, a study of the economic, irrigation and other potentialities of the under-populated and under-developed areas of the Arab States reveals greater possibilities for a stable solution by this method than by re-settlement in Israel. It is for these reasons that the Government of Israel contends that resettlement in neighbouring areas be considered as the main principle of solution. However, Israel will be ready to make its own contribution to a solution of this problem. It is not yet ascertainable either how many wish to return under conditions that may be prescribed by the Assembly, or how many Israel can receive in the light of existing political and economic considerations. Our first objective at Lausanne will be to reach an agreement by direct negotiation on the contribution to be made by each Government to-wards the settlement of this grave problem. The extent of the Govern-ment of Israel's own contribution will depend entirely upon the for-mal establishment of peace and relations of good neighbourliness between Israel and the Arab States.

'4. The Government of Israel has already announced its acceptance of obligations to make compensation for lands abandoned. The entire question of compensation may well be settled by negotiations at Lausanne as well as the general question of reparations and war damage.

'5. Deeply conscious of the humanitarian problems involved, the Government of Israel observes with sympathy the efforts of inter-national, governmental and non-governmental agencies to alleviate the immediate plight of these refugees suffering hardships as a result of the war. The Government of Israel is prepared to lend its assis-tance to these efforts.

'6. The Government of Israel feels that prolongation of this distress without alleviation and final settlement undermines the stability of the Middle East, the maintenance of which is its most vital interest. While thus indicating its readiness to do all possible to contribute to a solution and while welcoming United Nations initiative in that regard, Israel hopes that those States which caused this problem by their action in proclaiming war last year, will face up squarely to their responsibilities and to the undeniable opportunities available to them for settling the problem in a manner beneficial to their own economic needs and those of development in the vast under-populated areas of the Arab States. An immediate declaration by all the Governments concerned of their desires for an early peace settlement would create a favourable atmosphere for the discussion of this problem.'

At this point I digress to state our views on the boundary question which has been raised this morning and which does not seem to us to be a major obstacle on the road to a settlement. The fact that an Arab State did not arise in the part of Palestine envisaged by the 1947 Resolution, as well as the circumstances of war and military occupation, necessitates a peaceful adjustment of the territorial provisions laid down under the Resolution of 29th November 1947. The General Assembly itself has twice endorsed the need of such peaceful settlement; and its representatives have even from time to time made proposals for effecting changes in the territorial dispositions of the November 29th Resolution. The view which my Government expounded at the Paris session was that this adjustment should be made, not by arbitrary changes imposed from outside, but through agreements freely arrived at amongst the Governments concerned. This principle commended itself to the overwhelming majority of the General Assembly, which declined to endorse any specific territorial changes and dealt with this question in paragraph 5 of the Resolution as follows:

'The General Assembly calls upon the Governments and authorities concerned to extend the scope of the negotiations provided for in the Security Council Resolution of 16th November 1948, and to *seek agreement by negotiations* conducted either with the Conciliation Commission or directly, with a view to the final settlement of all questions outstanding between them.'

Israel interprets this as a directive to the Governments concerned to settle their territorial claims, as well as other differences by negotiation.

In this connection, we draw great encouragement from the success of the armistice negotiations which had led to the establishment of agreed demarcation lines between the military forces of the Governments concerned. These agreements were reached by free discussion and reciprocal concession. In some instances, it was necessary for

Israeli forces to withdraw in favour of Arab forces. In other cases, Arab forces withdrew to make way for the forces of Israel. In other cases still, the principle of reciprocity was accepted. One of the parties gave up territory in one sector and gained territory in another. The mediating agencies of the United Nations attempted to lay down no fixed principles but to leave the parties to unfettered negotiation, having in mind the general interest of peace and stability rather than the assertion of unilateral claims. I presume that the same procedures will be followed by the parties in the boundary discussions shortly to take place. I presume further that the General Assembly will rejoice in any territorial dispositions which rest upon the agreement and consent of the parties concerned. Membership in the United Nations, and the consequent protection of the Charter, would enable the Government of Israel to see its prospects of territorial security in a more hopeful light, and would thus help the rapid conclusion of agreements.

I could have wished that this statement of our views might have proceeded without any polemical note. But I should be giving the Committee a false impression of sentiment in Israel if I did not express our indignation at the extraordinary spectacle of our application for membership in the United Nations being challenged by the Arab States.

I envy the easy assurance whereby these representatives come forward today as the advocates of compliance with General Assembly Resolutions. For in the earliest and most tender years of its existence, this United Nations was assaulted at the very foundations of its authority by the first attempt of member States to overthrow a General Assembly Resolution by force. It is not long since these very rooms echoed with dire threats from Arab representatives of their intention to offer armed resistance to the Assembly's policy for the establishment of a Jewish State. 'Any line drawn by the United Nations', declared an Arab representative, 'shall be nothing but a line of fire and blood.'

These threats, which were destined to be translated into destruction and slaughter, rested upon the doctrine of the optional character of Assembly Resolutions. On 24th February 1948 the Representative of Syria declared: 'In the first place, the recommendations of the General Assembly are not imperative on those to whom they are addressed. We have numerous precedents during the short past life

of the General Assembly: the Indo-South African dispute, the Balkan
situation, the Interim Committee, the Korean question, the admission of new members.' He went on to say: 'The General Assembly
only gives advice, and the parties to whom the advice is addressed
accept it when it does not impair their fundamental rights.' Again,
on 19th March 1948 he declared: 'Not every State which does not
apply, obey or execute these recommendations would be breaking
its pledges to the Charter.'

The Representative of Egypt made this theory his own. At meeting
after meeting of the Security Council he consoled his audience for
the violation of the Palestine Resolution by the happy thought that
other resolutions of the General Assembly had not been complied
with. 'No one', he said, 'could say that compliance is imperative or
that the countries which did not comply are acting against the Charter or undermining the structure of the United Nations. We do not
choose to comply with the General Assembly's Resolution on Palestine. This is our privilege under the Charter.'

Even if the exercise of this 'privilege' had been confined to this
contribution to international jurisprudence, the Arab States would
still have been disqualified to lecture to others on the binding force
of Assembly Resolutions. But, as is well known, their defiance went
'further. They took up arms, they crossed their frontiers, they launched
a war for the purpose of overthrowing that Resolution by force. The
next step was to exercise a 'privilege' not to stop fighting when
ordered by the Security Council.

International morality and law in our generation recognize those
who initiate war as solely responsible for the entire sequence of bloodshed and suffering which ensues from that choice. Here sit representatives of the only States which have deliberately used force against an
Assembly Resolution; the only States which have ever been determined by the Security Council to have caused a threat to the peace,
posing as the disinterested judges of their own intended victim in his
efforts to secure a modest equality in the family of nations. It is a
cynical manœuvre. It cannot be allowed to succeed without bequeath-
ing a mood of disillusion to all equitable men. In the name of those
who have been killed, maimed, blinded, exiled or bereaved by the
exercise of that cynicism, we must express our most passionate
resentment at this insincerity.

I do not wish to enter a discussion of the exact degree of legal compulsion inherent in a General Assembly Resolution. Certain it is that the right of a State to appeal against a Resolution or to seek its revision must fall short, very far short, of armed violence. My Government, in the course of its future international career, will never be found amongst those who, by emptying Assembly Resolutions of all compelling moral force, would sacrifice the restraints of international law upon the altar of undiluted sovereignty. A Resolution can be revised; yes, but by argument and renewed examination. A recommendation can be modified, but by agreement. A United Nations policy may be opposed and resisted—but certainly not by the use of force against any state. It was a signal victory for the United Nations when the first forcible attempt to sabotage a solution desired by the General Assembly failed in its objective. In assuring its own establishment and survival, Israel vindicated the supreme international authority.

We are as one who, having been attacked in a dark street by seven men with heavy bludgeons, finds himself dragged into court only to see his assailants sitting on the bench with an air of solemn virtue, delivering homilies on the duties of a peaceful citizen. It is essential for the dignity of international institutions that such a device should not succeed.

The State of Israel, which is now celebrating its first anniversary amidst the applause of its friends throughout the world, is bound to the United Nations by many links of intimacy and strength. Israel is new in the art of practical statecraft. We shall be fortunate if our contribution to the solution of international problems can go much beyond the limited size of our State. Yet Israel is at once the ancestor and the heir of a great universal tradition. The doctrines of the Charter, founded on the hope of international brotherhood, were bequeathed to modern civilization by Israel's Prophetic writings which expressed the longing of mankind for an era when 'nation shall not lift up the sword against nation nor shall they know war any more'. A continuous line of thought and aspiration unites San Francisco to Sinai. In the minds of many contemporary historians Israel represents the modernist element in Near Eastern life, striving for progress by technology and science. But no less potent an influence in the life of our new Republic is its sense of continuous association with the traditions of Israel's past. It is no accident that the coins and stamps of the State revive memories of those early periods of Israel's independence which have left so profound an impression on the course of human civilization. It is no accident that our Hebrew language evokes the memories and associations of the golden period of Israel's literary achievement.

But quite apart from a deep affinity between Israel's ideals and the basic concepts of the United Nations, we can point to a more recent experience of common endeavour. This is the only State in the world which sprang into existence at the summons and behest of the international community. The General Assembly is now called upon by the Security Council to acknowledge a State to whose establishment it gave the sanction and incentive of its own prior approval. The records of Israel's life have a way of entering into eternal history. The story of this brave and unequal struggle for independence of a people, which lost six million of its sons in the cause of the victorious United Nations against Nazi despotism, is enshrined in the documents and archives of this organization. Israel's battle for survival has gone hand in hand with the most successful effort of the United Nations to solve an international conflict by judgment, mediation and conciliation. It would be an extraordinary paradox, not understood by the peoples of the world, if the United Nations were to close its doors upon a State which it helped to quicken into active and vigorous life. And the question whether the United Nations now confirms or defers this application is not a matter of procedure. It is a grave issue of substance. It affects the prospects of peace. It affects the future authority of the United Nations in the solution of outstanding problems. It affects the question whether the Arab world will receive from this Committee the implicit counsel to regard Israel as a permanent international fact with which it has to make peace or whether, by hesitating now, the Assembly will confirm the Arab peoples in their hesitations about Israel's existence, and Israel's rights. The General Assembly could do nothing more calculated to persuade the Arab States to maintain the strife than if it were to rise in an atmosphere of doubt as to Israel's international status. You could do nothing more prejudicial to the prospect of conciliation than to insist on one party going there with an inferior status and prestige to that enjoyed by the other party.

The time has surely come, for the United Nations, if it wishes Israel to bear the heavy burdens of Charter obligations, to confer upon Israel the protection and status of the Charter as well. At every stage of Israel's relations with the Arab world, we have felt equality of status to be the essential conditions of partnership. Until the scars of conflict are healed and Israel becomes integrated with its immediate world, the United Nations may be the only forum in which Israel sits as a colleague and partner of its neighbouring States in the transaction of international business and in the paths of social and economic co-operation. This Committee should not debar us from that precious meeting place. We cannot logically expect the Arabs to recognize Israel if the United Nations hesitates to recognize Israel.

You have it in your hands to expedite the decisive moment when the Arab world will find itself exhorted by the world community to recognize Israel as a partner in its destiny. Do not delay that moment. The responsibility is too grave. The foundations of peace, improvised by skilful mediation, are not so strong that they can easily withstand another period of uncertainty and strife.

I have tried, without obscuring honest difficulties and differences, to reassure the Committee on the issue of Israel's goodwill. We cannot now do more. The banner of Israel is inscribed with the struggle and the achievement of the youngest nation on earth. Its progress has been followed with ardent sympathy by the peoples of the world. Whatever intellectual or spiritual forces Israel evokes are at the service of the United Nations, as a reinforcement of its activity and prestige. You will certainly lose nothing, and you perhaps may gain some modest asset, if you join our banner to your honoured company. Whatever happens, we shall cherish this banner above everything else. We shall dedicate it to the ideals of peace and national independence; of social progress, of democracy and cultural dynamism.

A great wheel of history comes full circle today as Israel, renewed and established, offers itself, with all its imperfections but perhaps with some virtues, to the defence of the invincible human spirit against the perils of nihilism, conflict and despair.

CHAPTER IV

'If I Forget Thee, O Jerusalem'*

In the United Nations between October 1949 and February 1950, Israel argued against a statute for an international régime for Jerusalem, and in favour of international supervision for the Holy Places.

Adevotion to the Holy City has been a constant theme in the history of our people for three thousand years. In our own generation we have seen the ancient link between Israel and Jerusalem fully restored. Assaulted by the violence which threatened their total destruction two years ago, the State of Israel and the New City of Jerusalem have emerged together from mortal danger to deliverance. They now speak with one voice. The views which I shall express on Israel's behalf are upheld with special fervour by 100,000 Israel citizens in Jerusalem of whose security, welfare and freedom my Government is the responsible guardian.

It is urgent that the views of my Government should enter the substance and atmosphere of this debate. In the last resort, any international arrangements for the protection of the Holy Places must depend for their implementation on the consent of Jerusalem's population, and of the Government in which that population reposes its trust. The idea that any régime for the satisfaction of religious interests can endure amidst an aggrieved, disaffected and turbulent population will be instantly rejected by any serious mind.

Unless Jerusalem is politically contented, it cannot be religiously serene.

The issue of implementation is so powerfully influenced by considerations of consent that I feel a special duty to convey a frank impression of the state of opinion in Jerusalem, and throughout the rest of Israel, towards the Statute which now forms the basis of the Council's discussion.

This attitude rests primarily on considerations of moral principle and political rights. But it owes its special vehemence to the dark

* Trusteeship Council of the United Nations, 20 February 1950.

memories which the Statute evokes in the mind of everyone in Jerusalem who recalls its history.

The General Assembly on 29th November 1947 'recommended to the United Kingdom and member States' the adoption and implementation of proposals for Jerusalem which were later specified in the Statute. The objective was 'to protect and preserve the unique spiritual and religious interests located in the city'. The United Nations pledged itself 'to ensure that peace and order reign in Jerusalem'. It undertook 'to promote the security, well-being and any constructive measures of development for the residents'. The Trusteeship Council was instructed to elaborate and approve the detailed Statute of the City by 30th April 1948. A Governor at the head of a large military and administrative staff was to assume authority in time to secure legal succession immediately on the termination of the Mandate.

Not a single one of these provisions was ever carried out. Within a few days and throughout the ensuing months, the Holy City, theoretically protected by an international status, was plunged into brutal violence which shook the foundations of its life and cast the shadow of death over every family and home. As the danger to Jerusalem became increasingly acute, the retreat of the United Nations from the responsibility which it had incurred became swifter and more decisive. In the Trusteeship Council the representative of Iraq sounded the note of unconditional resistance. He declared that the proposal for the Statute 'was illegal and contrary to the Charter and, being in the form of recommendation, was not binding'. He went on to say that the Arab Governments were in no way bound and would reserve complete freedom of action. He stated:

'. . . the prestige of the United Nations could not be served by the enforcement of an unjust plan which could only provoke disorder and bloodshed. . . . Jerusalem deserves independence in the same degree as do the people of Palestine. It can be separated neither geographically nor economically from the rest of the country. The fact that it is a city sacred to three religions provides no legal basis for separation.'

The statement made by the representative of Iraq on 18th February 1948, is a notable and eloquent utterance containing many observations on the juridical weakness of the Statute. No one would seriously doubt the accuracy of his comments on the recommendatory effect

38

of the General Assembly's resolutions. The weakness of the Arab position lay not in the exercise of a legitimate right of non-compliance but in the use of armed force to overthrow the recommendation of the General Assembly. It was at this point alone that the violation of the Charter occurred. Thus in April 1948 the United Nations Palestine Commission, reporting its inability to implement any part of the General Assembly's recommendation, including the Jerusalem Statute, wrote:

'Powerful Arab interests both inside and outside Palestine are defying the Resolution of the General Assembly and are engaged in a deliberate effort to alter by force the settlement envisaged therein. Armed Arab bands from neighbouring Arab States, together with local Arab forces, are defeating the purposes of the Resolution by acts of violence.'

The Arab world had taken up arms not only against the establishment of a Jewish State, but also, with equal fervour and with greater success, against the establishment of an international régime in Jerusalem.

A new phase in the agony of the Holy City was soon to begin as the armies of the Arab States stood poised for invasion to commence at the precise moment when the Mandate would end. By the end of May the Jewish quarter of the Old City had fallen amidst the destruction of its ancient synagogues, and the banishment of its people. At any moment it appeared that the New City must also succumb. Surrounded on four sides by superior forces, its food supplies dwindling towards the point of famine, with artillery directed toward residential areas taking a hideous toll of life, Jerusalem endured the perils of warfare augmented by the horrors of siege. The supreme torment was the forcible denial of the water supply from the coast. Bombardment, starvation, pestilence and thirst haunted the life of the city at the lowest point of its fortunes since the destruction of the ancient Temple. The Jews of Jerusalem amidst the debris of their homes and beside the graves of their sons looked expectantly towards the United Nations which but a few months previously had assumed responsibility for their 'security and welfare, their peace and order and constructive development'.

As the scene shifts from Jerusalem itself to the sessions of the United Nations, we discern a contrast of fantastic proportions between a grave responsibility solemnly assumed—and a resolute determination to do nothing for its fulfilment. The Trusteeship

'If I Forget Thee, O Jerusalem'

Council, having brought the Statute to a point where it could be adopted and applied, met on 19th March 1948 to accept a proposal to postpone any discussion of the Jerusalem question for a further six weeks. Meanwhile our representatives in the Security Council reiterated their urgent appeals to isolate Jerusalem from the general conflict by a specific assertion of United Nations responsibility. Their appeals fell on deaf ears. On 1st April 1948, Mr. Sharett informed the Security Council that if the United Nations abandoned Jerusalem to its fate, its population would naturally take all the measures which they deemed necessary for their survival and defence. Syria and Egypt, who represented the Arab world in the Security Council, reiterated the Iraqi theme that the Statute was illegal, that Jerusalem must take its chance with the rest of the country, and that the siege and denial of water must be maintained not only as a legitimate act of war but even in the event of truce. No action was taken. 'Security, well-being and constructive measures of development' together with the reign of 'peace and order' were clearly not available from the Security Council. Perhaps the General Assembly, as the author of this solemn international commitment, would rise to the occasion and provide these desirable things?

The answer came on the afternoon of 14th May 1948. The General Assembly met in special session to determine whether to assume responsibilities in Jerusalem. The Resolution of 1947 had not in itself created United Nations sovereignty in Jerusalem; it had only recommended certain processes which, had they been duly accomplished, would have resulted in the effective succession of the United Nations to the authority previously exercised in the city by the Mandatory Power. That authority, however, could arise not from the adoption of the Resolution but from its implementation; and more especially from the effective installation of a government to take over by 15th May 1948.

The opportunity was decisive and irrevocable. It was deliberately cast away. The General Assembly accepted the view of the United States and Iraq that it would have to act before the expiration of the Mandate at 6 p.m. that day if it wished to establish a legal basis for United Nations authority in Jerusalem. After a discussion under specially expedited procedure, the General Assembly emphatically rejected *first* a Guatemalan proposal that the Statute be admitted to the Agenda and ratified as it stood; *second* a United States-French proposal establishing an interim 'Government of Jerusalem consist-

40

ing of a United Nations Commissioner and such officers as may be appointed by him or by the Trusteeship Council'; and *third* an Australian proposal described by its author as a last attempt to 'establish a link of any kind between the United Nations and Jerusalem'. This proposal would have empowered a United Nations Municipal Commissioner to undertake executive responsibilities in Jerusalem. By this comprehensive rejection, the General Assembly had repudiated its previous intention in the most specific terms. Knowing that a British Act of Parliament terminating the Mandate would take effect in a matter of hours, the General Assembly refused to step into the breach.

The juridical effect of these events was that the Jerusalem area lost its mandatory government on May 14th and that the General Assembly simultaneously decided not to confer any other international capacity upon it. It was not a passive default, but an active relinquishment of responsibility in a critical hour.

The moral implications are even graver. The General Assembly knew that failing a tangible assertion of its interest in Jerusalem, military invasion from the neighbouring states would converge upon the Holy City and overwhelm its besieged and isolated Jewish population. The question was whether or not the United Nations should implicitly open the gates and pass by on the other side; or whether it should impose at least a theoretical barrier to invasion. The General Assembly decided to open the gates. At six o'clock when the Mandate expired, the representative of Iraq arose exultantly to cry 'the game is up'. The General Assembly had lost its right of succession.

The Jews of Jerusalem, engulfed in death and famine, fighting against dire odds for sheer survival itself, had little time to reflect on the deliberations of those who had promised them 'security, well-being, peace and order', but five months ago. The Security Council, the Trusteeship Council and the General Assembly had left them no room for misunderstanding. Their alternative was now clear. They must either sit back, paralysed and inert, while military conquest, anarchy and starvation engulfed their homes; or they must summon up their own energies to fight for their homes and their future at Israel's side. They chose the latter course. When their prospect of survival hung on a thread, at a time when parents wondered if they would see their children wither from famine before their eyes, the life-line thrown from the State of Israel reached the beleaguered city.

41

'If I Forget Thee, O Jerusalem'

On the first trucks of the convoys reaching the city with water and food were inscribed the Hebrew words 'If I forget thee, O Jerusalem, may my right hand forget its cunning'. The people of Jerusalem were not forsaken or alone.

Once bare survival was assured and the siege heroically broken, there began a rehabilitation which has sustained its momentum ever since. In that process a relationship grew up between the State of Israel and Jewish Jerusalem which has now reached full and organic integration. It is a relationship of duty and sacrifice; of mutual responsibility and common aspiration. The city was cut off from its main route of supply; the Government of Israel built an alternative road under heavy enemy fire. The city was threatened with pestilence and thirst; the Government of Israel renewed its water source. Jerusalem was falling apart in anarchy and dissidence through lack of recognized organs of government; the Government of Israel established a separate military governorship to be succeeded by a civil administration, which later merged in a complete union with the rest of Israel. The economy of the city had been struck a nearly fatal blow; the Government of Israel began to pump its life-blood back. Institutions were restored, buildings repaired, damaged areas cleared, industries established, financial subsidies lavished upon the city by the hard-pressed Israel Treasury. Jerusalem was spiritually darkened by a sense of solitude, insecurity and neglect; the Government of Israel made it the scene of the most solemn and historic moments celebrating the deliverance of Israel and Jerusalem alike. Thus the swift withdrawal of the United Nations from direct governmental responsibility and the advance of the Government of Israel towards the assumption of that responsibility were parallel and simultaneous. Every chance had been given for the United Nations to assume its responsibility and authority. When the opportunity had been irretrievably cast away and further hesitation would have spelled destruction, the vacuum of security and law was swiftly and permanently filled.

Meanwhile the echoes of the Statute for Internationalization continued to die away. The General Assembly in special session had ignored the Statute and the work of the Trusteeship Council. On 29th July 1948, when the Soviet Representative proposed that the Council should proceed with the adoption of the Statute, his one vote alone was available in support of his motion. The Belgian proposal that the Trusteeship Council should forget about the Statute indefinitely was overwhelmingly carried.

'If I Forget Thee, O Jerusalem'

In the ensuing weeks the Mediator and the Palestine Conciliation Commission both regarded the Statute as too obsolete a document to merit their attention. The General Assembly in December 1948, evidently considering the Statute to be neither valid nor relevant, called for the preparation of an entirely new scheme over the period of a year. The Statute, with all its associations of illusion and suffering, receded into oblivion. Nothing was heard of it again until, to the general astonishment, it reappeared abruptly in a draft resolution one November morning last year. The rest is recent history leading to our situation today.

The attitude of the people of Jerusalem to this Statute is powerfully influenced by these experiences which are indelibly engraved upon their hearts. Any idea that they can have security or well-being for themselves and their city without the maintenance of their union with Israel has been banished forever from their minds. They cannot justly be asked to dismantle their free institutions in favour of imposed tutelage. Their allegiance goes out to the flag of their people, around which they fought their way to survival against overwhelming odds. Their natural loyalty is committed to their Government which rescued them from wild carnage and rallied their city with firm and reverent hands into the dignity and peace of Jerusalem's reviving life today. There is no example in history of a people, having once achieved union with its own natural and kindred government, voluntarily turning back to semi-autonomy under outside control. The Charter provides for no contingency whereby a self-governing community can become a dependent territory.

Above all, the people of Jerusalem ask the Trusteeship Council, in the light of the history which I have recalled, to direct to itself a decisive moral question: 'Having been unable to provide Jerusalem with government, security and subsistence when it needed them with desperate urgency, can you now come on the scene to disturb the government, security and subsistence which we have consecrated with our own sacrifice and toil?'

The Council appears already to have noticed the paradox whereby the Arab states that killed the Jerusalem Statute by violence now cry aloud for the resurrection of their victim. When I recall the violence let loose upon Israel and especially upon Jerusalem by the combined power of the Arab League, and when I reflect on the vehemence with which those same States asserted their right to question the mandatory force of General Assembly recommendations, the spec-

43

tacle of Dr. Jamali as the disinterested defender of international virtue becomes much less impressive than it would otherwise be.

The necessity for an agreed solution is dictated not only by the principles of the United Nations 'and by the absence of any alternative within the Charter, but also by the special aims which we all seek to attain. The protection of the Holy Places under United Nations authority is a religious objective sought reverently by countless multitudes throughout the civilized world. It cannot be imagined that such a sublime purpose could ever be secured through political suppression leaving bitterness and rancour in its wake.

But the sentiment of Jerusalem's population, though a primary consideration, is not the only factor which determines whether the Statute is now capable of implementation. The Council is not dealing with abstract principles. We have a project for establishing institutions of government, security, administration and law in a specific territory. Now this territory is not a vacuum. It happens that this territory already contains institutions of government, security, administration and law—institutions deeply rooted, effectively administered and most passionately cherished. When the Statute was drafted it was designed to provide the immediate succession to an expiring régime and thus to establish institutions where none were presumed to exist. Today, however, you cannot establish a governorship or a legislature, a council or a court without somehow accomplishing the disintegration of established institutions. There are no functions unexercised. There are no vacant areas of jurisdiction. The laws, the taxes, the regulations, the judicial processes, the culture, the language, the national and religious customs of Jerusalem are those which it holds in common with Israel as a whole. Indeed, from the earliest days in the development of modern Jewish society in the country, all the concerns and activities of that society have radiated from Jerusalem as their natural centre. Its population of 100,000 occupies exclusively those parts of the city constructed outside the walls of historic Jerusalem during the past eight decades.

The fact that scarcely a brick or a house or a street in the greater part of the Israel area of Jerusalem today even existed eighty years ago makes it difficult to contend that the area is of such venerable significance that it must become an international trust.

There are some who, on first thoughts, might be tempted to suggest that this complex and active pattern of institutional life ought not to have come into existence. These laws and taxes, these councils and courts ought not to be there; for they constitute an obstacle to the arrival of the institutions described in the Statute. I hope that what I have said about the developments in the past two years is sufficient to disprove such a contention. It is not easy to suggest with any seriousness that the people of Jerusalem should have lived in a sort of Nirvana for the past twenty-two months, suspended in a vacuum of chaos without government and order, in case the discarded Statute should one day come to life and claim its jurisdiction. My Government has no doubts whatever concerning the legitimacy of the political and judicial institutions of Jerusalem. International law contains no definition of lawful authority which does not wholly apply to the status of Israel in Jerusalem today. This authority proceeds from the people. It is based on consent. It is freely accepted and voluntarily obeyed. It operates effectively without challenge. It is recognized in a valid international agreement concluded at the behest of the Security Council. Its development did not even compete with any previously existing authority or with any other authority lawfully attempting to assume the burden of government.

When the General Assembly on May 14th voted not to establish any government in Jerusalem, it could not have expected that the people of Jerusalem would therefore live in a jungle. When the Security Council, between February and May 1948, firmly declined to organize the city's defence, it must have expected that the city would see to its own security itself. When the Trusteeship Council repeatedly refused to apply a system of administration and law in the early half of 1948, it cannot have imagined that Jerusalem would go on indefinitely preserving a separation from its environment. In that negative sense the United Nations has contributed to the integration and union which mark Jerusalem's life today.

I therefore submit that the Trusteeship Council should report that the adoption of the Statute would commit the Council to the process of destroying free institutions as a prelude to the imposition, against the popular will, of other institutions which could not even be established two years ago. This would be the precise opposite of the role played by the Trusteeship Council everywhere else in the world, where it seeks to develop tutelary régimes into free institutions inspired by local initiative and consent. Indeed, the spectacle of a principal organ of the United Nations occupying itself, at this crisis of civilization, with the cancellation of liberty, tranquillity and civic order in a modern urban residential area whose people and institutions are doing no harm to any living soul—would excite surprise and, perhaps, even ridicule in world public opinion, which rightly expects our Organization to rise to high levels of rational purpose.

The Charter designates three categories of territory to which the Trusteeship System may ever apply, provided the necessary agreements are drawn up. The first category refers to territories under Mandate. It cannot be contended that the Jerusalem area is now under Mandate, in face of a British Act of Parliament terminating the Mandate nearly two years ago and a simultaneous decision of the General Assembly by its vote on 14th May 1948, not to become the successor régime. It is not necessary to prove that the Jerusalem area does not belong to either of the other two categories referred to in Article 77. This area was not detached from an enemy power in the Second World War; and is not now being voluntarily placed under the Trusteeship System by one or both of the States responsible for its administration.

Since the area is in no way eligible under the Charter for administration by the Trusteeship Council, it is of small importance to reflect that none of the procedures of agreement laid down in Articles 79 and 81 have been carried out. Of greater interest is the comparison between the idea of placing the Jerusalem area under the administration of the Trusteeship Council and the basic objectives of the Trusteeship System as defined in Article 76:

'. . . to promote the political, economic, social and educational advancement of the inhabitants of the trust territories and their progressive development towards self-government or independence as may be appropriate to the particular circumstances of each territory and its peoples and the freely expressed wishes of the peoples concerned. . . .'

The people of Jerusalem may, with all modesty, claim that their development towards self-government and independence is not unduly slow, and does not require the accelerating processes of the Trusteeship System.

Although the Trusteeship Council is not charged with responsibilities for the maintenance of peace and order, it cannot be indifferent to the need for preserving stability and honouring security agreements everywhere in the world. I therefore draw the attention of the Council to the fact that the attempted implementation of the Statute would undermine public order in Jerusalem and would specifically impair the authority of the Israel-Jordan General Armistice Agreement by which the security of the city is organized. Under that Agreement, which can only be modified by the parties themselves, my Government has undivided responsibility towards its own people and towards the Security Council for the maintenance of law and order in the greater part of Jerusalem. My Government would not be entitled to regard itself as released from that responsibility by any action of the Trusteeship Council. However, the adoption of the Statute would impair the security of the area, first by reason of the deep resentment which the Statute evokes in the memory and sentiment of our people; and secondly by the explicit encroachment on the authority, title and prestige of the government on whose influence and forces the peace of the city depends. In taking such action the Trusteeship Council would be counteracting the results of laborious efforts invested by the parties, by the Security Council and by the Mediator in constructing an equilibrium of security which has stood the test of many difficulties. In the light of the Security Council's Resolution of 11th August 1949, appealing for the continued maintenance of all the provisions of the Armistice Agreement, the Trusteeship Council would be prejudicing the maintenance of international peace if it adopted any measures inconsistent with that Agreement.

The sole abiding objective of the United Nations in the Jerusalem question is the protection of the Holy Places and sites by the direct exercise of United Nations responsibility. My Government proposes the fulfilment of that objective in a manner consistent with the peace, freedom and welfare of the city. Any particular statute or régime, devised in the past or in the present, is only a means to that paramount end. The means may change, while the end remains inviolate. The means envisaged in 1947 or 1948 for protecting the Holy Places may be replaced or adapted without the least betrayal of the end. When the Jerusalem question first came before the United Nations, it was not in the context of a specific political régime, but in relation to the Holy Places and sites. Indeed, it is noteworthy that the original proposals put before the United Nations by religious authorities asked nothing but effective measures for the protection of Holy Places and religious rights. Thus, on 15th July 1947, Brother Bonaventura,

47

'If I Forget Thee, O Jerusalem'

Custos of the Holy Land, made requests of the United Nations Special Committee on Palestine which were limited to the international guarantee of religious immunities and which at no point suggested any special political status for the city. He said:

'Should there be a non-Christian State we recommend that measures—international guarantees—be embodied in any arrangement with the new State that may possibly be set up.'

In his original letter to the Secretary-General, the Catholic representative expressed Catholic aspirations exclusively in terms of religious guarantees without mentioning any particular political status for Jerusalem as indispensable to the satisfaction of those needs. He said:

'We are completely indifferent to the form of the régime which your esteemed Committee may recommend, provided that the interests of Christendom, Catholic, Protestant and Orthodox, will be weighed and safeguarded in your final recommendations. Primarily, all our sanctuaries should be respected, not only with cold juridicism but with local reverence, and they should be continuously and unconditionally accessible not only to local inhabitants but also to the Christians of the entire world.'

In order to satisfy that objective, my Government has repeatedly submitted proposals to international organs. It should be borne in mind that the Holy Places of three faiths in Jerusalem which are of universal concern are located within an area of no more than one and a half square miles, within the Walled City and its immediate vicinity. The Statute would establish international rule over an area of one hundred square miles, the greater part of which, including practically all Israel Jerusalem, contains no sites ever defined as Holy Places.

Thus the Statute would attempt to disfranchise, denationalize and subjugate a secular area of ninety-eight and a half square miles for the sake of Holy Places which it does not contain.

It was in order to avoid this obstacle that my Government has at various times been concerned to examine means of establishing an international régime concerned with the Holy Places. In the Third and Fourth Regular Sessions of the General Assembly the Israel delegation drew attention to the feasibility of extending international rule to the area of historic Jerusalem within which the Holy Places are gathered in a unique concentration, leaving the secular urban areas to pursue their life and freedom unimpaired. In order to secure

48

that international responsibility should extend to all sacred sites in whatever area of the city they are located, my delegation later contributed the idea of an international control applied not to any specific territory but to the Holy Places themselves wherever they are. My Government further offered to conclude agreements to this effect and to provide for the United Nations to be represented in Israel for the exercise of its responsibility in the Holy Places. It may be that a majority of the members of the United Nations would prefer to see such an arrangement for the Holy Places embodied in statutory rather than in contractual terms. In that event, my Government would be prepared to consult on the form which might be given to a Statute for the Holy Places. We are prepared to explore with the Council and with other parties concerned any avenue which may lead to the effective fulfilment by the United Nations of its responsibility for the Holy Places.

I reaffirm my Government's readiness, apart from arrangements for the Holy Places, to make binding declarations or agreements with the United Nations assuring religious freedom and full liberty for the pursuit of religious education and protection of religious institutions. The United Nations would not be forgiven by history, if presented with a clear possibility of reconciling its primary objectives with the freedom and peace of Jerusalem today, it were to spurn that opportunity in favour of an extremist project which has been associated with constant failure in the treatment of this problem for over two years.

The people of Israel and the Jewish people throughout the world are deeply inspired by the restoration of Israel's independent life in Jerusalem in fulfilment of ancient prophecy. At the same time the solution of the question of the Holy Places in a universal spirit is a purpose which we ardently uphold. While the Christian and Moslem Holy Places were mercifully spared serious damage, the ancient synagogues in the Old City were wantonly destroyed after the end of hostilities. Whereas the Mosque of Omar and the Masjid al Aqsa are accessible to Moslem worshippers and the Church of the Holy Sepulchre, the Church of the Nativity, Gethsemane, the Church of the Ascension, though in Arab hands, are the scenes of devout Christian pilgrimage, the Wailing Wall, the most hallowed Sanctuary of Judaism and the most ancient shrine in the entire city, is barred to all access by worshippers despite solemn agreements and undertakings. In any final settlement to be developed by negotiations out of the Armistice Agreement, the situation affecting the Jewish part of the Old City will surely have to be adjusted.

I am aware that there are some throughout the Christian world who still sincerely doubt whether the destiny of modern Jerusalem as the centre of Israel's independence can be harmonized with Jerusalem's universal mission. To them I would suggest that the existence of political freedom in Jerusalem side by side with an international authority for the Holy Places is not only a more expedient and practical solution than that envisaged in the Statute. It is also in every sense a higher ideal. It was as the centre of an active political and cultural life, beset by the problems and ordeals of a State, that Jerusalem in antiquity became the home of prophecy and revelation. Only a city alive with movement and ideas could have attracted to its midst the searching minds and spirits who generalized transient events into abiding truths. Prophecy and spiritual searchings have never flourished in a museum. They only arise out of the issues and dilemmas of life. The spiritual heritage which has gone forth from Jerusalem is historically linked with its character as a political centre, and with the ancient people who established Jerusalem on what was an obscure Jebusite hill. Surely any sensitive religious insight cannot fail to see some grandeur in the restoration of this people to the city which its own experience rendered famous in the world.

The spiritual ideals conceived in Jerusalem are the moral basis on which modern democracy rests. Would it not be incongruous if the United Nations were to advance the course of democratic liberty everywhere, and yet prevent self-government from taking root in the very city where the democratic ideal was born? Seen in this light, Jerusalem appears above all other cities as a place where democratic institutions most appropriately belong. Out of Biblical ethics came the Declaration of Human Rights proclaiming in its 21st Article that 'the will of the people shall be the basis for the authority of government'. Less in Jerusalem than anywhere else on earth can this principle be denied fulfilment or set aside.

Our vision is of a Jerusalem wherein a free people develops its reviving institutions, while a United Nations representative, in all tranquillity and dignity, fulfils the universal responsibility for the safety and accessibility of the Holy Places. This is a vision worthy of

50

the United Nations. Our Organization should move at once to realize this harmony and liberate its energies for the issues affecting human survival. Perhaps in this as in other critical periods of history a free Jerusalem may proclaim redemption to mankind.

CHAPTER V

'The Voice of the Trumpet Exceeding Loud'*

In this great arena where you celebrated Israel's Declaration of Independence three years ago, you now assemble to record the events whereby that Declaration was fulfilled.

The words with which our State was founded are a moving document in the annals of freedom. But it is upon the deeds which followed the words that the eye of history will be eternally fixed. A people which continues year by year, across the abyss of succeeding generations, to tell the story of its first emergence to freedom three thousand years back, will never fail to recount the episodes of a liberation, no less heroic, which came upon it but three years ago today.

Here is a people which defended its life, its home and its open gates against the fury of a powerful foe; set up an oasis of democracy, liberty and progress in a wilderness of despotism and squalor extending in vast expanse on every side; received into its shelter 600,000 of its kinsmen coming out of the depth of insecurity and want; multiplied the centres of settlement and cultivation beyond any scale hitherto conceived; began to explore and uncover the hidden resources of its soil which had lain neglected for long centuries past; caused water to gush forth in the most primeval wilderness of recorded time; extended the foundations of its industrial progress; embarked upon one of the great cultural adventures of history, to create out of diverse and remote citizens a unified society in the tongue and the spirit of Israel's past; established its banner in the family of nations and gave utterance to Israel's immemorial yearning for world peace. All this the people of Israel, sustained by Jews throughout the world, has accomplished within this brief spasm of time. Is this not a convincing proof of the courage and vitality, the resilience, the spiritual vigour, the capacities of self-sacrifice which repose in the people of Israel and the Jewish communities throughout the world!

* Israel Independence Day, Madison Square Garden, New York, 10 May 1951.

52

'The Voice of the Trumpet Exceeding Loud'

Yet it is not in order to linger amidst the glories of the recent past that we have come together in a mood of dedication tonight. It is rather to temper our deep and just satisfactions with the thought that the battle is not over, the victory not finally won. Having secured physical survival and political recognition, we see the central point of our concern shifting with emphasis towards the task of economic consolidation. This is the most crucial sector in all our front. If Israel is economically weak, she cannot be militarily strong. If Israel is not militarily and economically strong, she cannot be politically resistant to the pressures still directed against her vital interests.

Our sharpest weapon in this struggle is the Israel Independence Bond Issue whose inauguration we witness tonight. How majestic is the opportunity, how deadly the hazard of this venture! If it succeeds, then within a few years our country will be fruitful in its agriculture, prolific in its industry; both for the home market and for foreign trade; strong in its defences; solid in its social and cultural unity; ingenious and versatile in its scientific energy; and perhaps even at peace with its neighbours, who delay making peace only in the expectation that our economic collapse will save them from that necessity. Remove that illusion of Israel's economic failure, and the last barrier to peace will crumble before their eyes. If we were to fail in this venture, then our population would so far outstrip our production that the standard of life would decline below its present austere level. Our social ideals would encounter disillusion. The ingenuity and skill of our people would be frustrated by lack of the tools necessary for their fruition. The security of the State would be menaced by weakness. The epic achievements of the past three years would appear as a transient flash of lightning, not as an abiding sun. The whole drama of our effort lies in this acute contrast, between the decisive results of success and the unthinkable consequences of failure. Can I not tell my Government with confidence in your name, that you are determined, by everything that you hold dear, in the name of Jewish security, Jewish dignity and honour, not to let the thought or prospect of failure for a single moment cross your minds?

The programme of which this project forms part has other aspects which will doubtless command your enthusiastic support. We still have great need of subsistence funds to carry out the transportation and initial settlement of immigrants. Moreover, we have felt that Israel's role in the defence of democracy at the crossroads of the

53

'The Voice of the Trumpet Exceeding Loud'

eastern hemisphere, and its efforts to remedy suffering caused by war and persecution, make it natural that we should seek inclusion, on a scale commensurate with our needs, in the aid programmes whereby the United States assists friendly countries abroad.

I am deeply conscious of the personal theme in our celebrations tonight as we greet the Prime Minister in our midst; but I also respect his diffidence in the face of personal praise. He cannot, however, quarrel with the Greek historian who said that 'their own deeds are the memorial of great men'. Let me do nothing but recount those deeds. In 1943, David Ben Gurion declared that an independent Jewish State must be established in the Land of Israel. The Great Powers and the world community at that time had as much intention of supporting the idea of a Jewish State as of organizing a voyage to the moon. In the winter of 1947, David Ben Gurion proclaimed that the Jews in the Land of Israel must be ready to resist and defeat the invading armies of all the neighbouring states. No military expert who regarded this as a reasonable prospect would have been credited with professional sanity. In September 1950 David Ben-Gurion declared that Israel for its strength and survival must have a billion dollars from the United States in three years. This time it was the turn of the economists to greet his suggestion with a tolerant but sceptical smile. But the Jewish State was established; the Arab armies were defeated; the billion dollars *will* be obtained. From David Ben-Gurion who proclaimed and directed all these ventures, I have learned this basic lesson of politics and life. First, define your objective; declare your need; say what you want. Then, and then only, consider the obstacles. But even then the obstacles must be subordinated to the objective. Never must the objective be renounced in favour of the obstacles.

Let this moment be for us a moment of supreme confidence, of ecstasy and revelation—a moment of 'thunder and lightning and the voice of the trumpet exceeding loud'. It is for us so to act that a future historian will one day record that this ancient people of Israel, in its long tormented journey on the scene of time, knew no pride and no inspiration like unto the pride and inspiration of being a Jew, and being alive on the third anniversary of Israel's independence, the 10th May 1951.

If you link yourselves with such a cause at such a time, you link yourselves with immortality.

CHAPTER VI

Nationalism and Internationalism in the Middle East*

I shall limit my comments to three aspects of my subject in different planes of international and spiritual experience. First, the confrontation of internationalism and nationalism in the world of political affairs. Second, the implications of internationalism and nationalism in the region where the State of Israel has risen to independent life. And third, the issue of nationalism and internationalism as the pivot of a controversy about the mission of the Jewish people in the world.

The historic debate which has portrayed nationalism and internationalism as opposite concepts is one of the most sterile controversies of all ages. The discussion has been fruitless because it has been rooted in a basic fallacy. The two terms have been wrongly conceived in conflict and antithesis. Yet in the very meaning of the word we are reminded that internationalism is nothing but a relationship between nations. Just as the rights and duties of individual citizenship fit a man for service to the national community, so the rights and duties of nationhood are indispensable for any people which desires to serve the universal cause. This is particularly true of our generation, in which the sovereign nation state is the only recognized unit of international life and therefore the only instrument for expressing universal ideals in the practical sphere of human relations.

The United Nations is based upon the synthesis between these two doctrines, and it therefore comes into conflict with the concept of world federalism or world government, which denies the validity of separate sovereignty and argues that an abandonment of the national framework is an essential prelude to the creation of universal solidarity. The drafters of the United Nations Charter took the contrary view. The universal society must arise, but it should arise as the

* Jewish Theological Seminary, New York, 29 February 1952.

aggregate of sovereign and independent national units. It was to be neither a parliament of man nor a federation of the world, but rather a union of separate peoples representing individual facets of national and cultural experience.

There is a plausible doctrine which ascribes to national sovereignty all the failures which have attended the world in its efforts to create an organization capable of preserving international peace. Yet surely if the peoples of the world are not ready to surrender such degree of their sovereignty as is essential for the preservation of international peace, how much less ready must our generation be to embark upon a total surrender of sovereignty and to entrust the affairs of all the nations to some supernational, Esperantist organization.

The imperfections of international life do not arise from the existence of sovereignty, but rather from defects which have affected its exercise. The concept of a universal society based not on uniformity but on diversity, of a United Nations uniting all the civilizations, traditions, and faiths, is both in the spiritual and political sense a more fruitful concept than that of a vast global society in which national differences are obscured. To aspire to such uniformity of government is to attack the very spark of human culture.

Just as it would be reactionary to abolish those distinctions of language, literature, and art, which give the human mind its infinite variety, so it would be retrograde to abolish the political sovereignties of peoples. A people's political outlook and social organization are just as integral a part of its culture as are its language, art, and music. National differences and linguistic varieties are just as much a part of the cultural landscape of the world as mountains and valleys are part of its geographical fabric. To aspire to any elimination of these differences and varieties is no more intelligent than to wish that the earth would lose all its contours, all its heights, all its depths, and all its oceans.

Insufficient attention has been focused upon the possibilities of international organization as an element in the cultural enrichment of our age. The United Nations, apart from its political and economic functions, provides a challenging opportunity for the contact of all civilizations and traditions. Individual political units representing Christianity, Judaism, Islam, Buddhism, and even the aberrations of materialism, all confront each other with infinite possibilities of creative interaction.

Nationalism and Internationalism in the Middle East

It is significant also that problems of nationalism concern the international mind with special reference to what is called the Middle East. I use this reserve concerning the Middle East because I propose to inject a heresy against the current assumption.that the Middle East is a cultural unit within which Israel should seek its own integration.

The importance of individual sovereignty within the international community is derided too often by those who aspire to the domination of the international scene. The idea of 'one language', for example, can easily be thrown into the world as an abstract conception; but what factors of national pride, what deeply latent impulses of competition arise when the choice of an international language becomes immediate? Is it really too harsh to state that 'universalism' means that all other nations and cultures should accept the cultural domination of oneself? The concept of the sovereign equality of nations, which seems so unreal in the world of power, does possess a certain stature when examined from the point of view of the cultural history of mankind. It is a fact that the original revelations of human culture have come not out of vast continental empires, but out of small, coherent, and well-articulated small states. Some of these considerations will assist us to understand the recent processes of national liberation throughout the Middle East.

Israel came to birth in a region where political nationalism has recorded signal advances in recent years. It would be incongruous for Israel to approach the national movements of our area with anything but a sympathetic spirit. Our own people, which won its liberty after an arduous struggle against colonial rule, would be false to its experience and destiny if, having acquired its own freedom, it were to take a grudging attitude towards the efforts of neighbouring peoples to achieve their independence from foreign control. But having said this, I must enter a reservation against a tendency to accept with uncritical eulogy every sign of effervescent Moslem nationalism. Not everybody who assassinates his Prime Minister, not every student in Cairo who throws a stone through the window of a foreign establishment, is necessarily the spiritual descendant of Thomas Jefferson or Robespierre. To nationalism, as to all other human experience, the critical faculty should be ruthlessly applied.

Does an attitude of grievance and rancour really become the Arab world? Has history in its broad lines of movement dealt harshly with that section of the human race? Four decades ago, every Arab, I might almost say every Moslem, upon the surface of the inhabited globe lived in subjection either to the rule of the Ottoman Empire or to the colonial powers. The great Moslem and Arab cultural traditions were nowhere the centre of independent political and economic life. What a vast and astonishing transformation has come over this scene within a brief space of time! Today eight sovereign Arab states extend over a huge continental expanse of two million square miles, embracing all the centres which owe their historic fame to their connection with the Arab and Moslem traditions. Cairo, Baghdad, and Damascus, the scenes of the Caliphate; Mecca and Medina, the Holy Cities of Arabia, the sources and origins of the Moslem faith—today all are centres of independent Arab societies. The imagination falters at the magnitude of the opportunity which has, almost overnight, been presented to the liberated Arab peoples. This good fortune in their political evolution has come to them less as a result of their own sacrifice and effort than as a consequence of international influence in two world wars, and, more recently, of the revival throughout the world of sympathy for national liberation.

This concept of Arab nationalism as a movement which has acquired unprecedented good fortune is essential if we are to understand the ethical basis of the relationship between the Arab world and Israel, and between the Arab world and the West.

The West, which has many things to apologize for in the past, has no need to stand in an attitude of defensiveness when it confronts the Arabic-speaking world. It is true that for four centuries, under Western control or indifference, the Arabic-speaking world fell behind the best levels of political and technological progress. As far as the Arab world was concerned the French Revolution might never have occurred, for the doctrines of political equality and social justice which spread through Europe and later across the Atlantic made no impression upon the dark hinterland of Arabia, which continued to organize itself upon medieval feudal patterns. Similarly, as far as the Middle East was concerned, the Industrial Revolution might never have occurred. The developments in human technology which had revolutionized material progress made no impress on the squalor and suffering of the teeming millions who dwelt in the subcontinent between the central Mediterranean and the Persian Gulf. Thus, if we were to strike the balance at the end of the nineteenth century, an attitude of grievance and injury by the Arab world toward the West would have had ample justification. But all this has been swept away

58

Nationalism and Internationalism in the Middle East

by the breadth of the liberation which the West has now bestowed upon the Arab world. Nor is there any reason to believe that this process is at an end. Moslem national sentiment continues to beat up against the central and western Mediterranean, where it encounters the imperial power of France. Libya is a recent entry into the international community. Eritrea and Somaliland, both predominantly Moslem states, are to become independent not as a result of rebellion or sacrifice, but through the injunctions of the international community.

If this picture means that Arab nationalism does not have a valid grievance against the Western world, how much more striking is the balance of equity when struck between Arab nationalism and Israel; for in a small corner of this vast domain, within an area of eight thousand square miles, the State of Israel has arisen in a land immortalized by the Jewish people in its previous era of independence. Israel need not envy the Arab world its eight sovereignties, its forty-six million people, its vast subcontinent rich with natural resources. But we need not and shall not apologize for our eight thousand square miles. It is the least debt which history owes us. This planet passed from paganism to civilization at the moment when it was touched in Israel by the lucid radiance of the Hebrew mind. The Land of Israel owes any lustre which history confers upon it to its connection with the Hebrew tradition. No people ever suffered more cruelly from the deprivation of its nationhood, or ever merited its restoration more.

Thus, if we analyse the crises of nationalism in our area, we cannot find in them any conspiracy by the Western powers or by Israel to deny the Arab world its just patrimony. The crisis and tension spring from imperfections in the body of this national movement itself.

The first of such defects is a lack of altruism. A progressive nationalism would acknowledge to other national movements the same prerogatives and rights which it asserts for itself. Arab nationalism concentrates its attention not on the million and a half square miles which it has gained, but on the eight thousand square miles which have been justly withheld; not on the vast gift which has been conferred upon it, but upon the small and single act of denial which Arab nationalism was called upon to assume in the cause of international equity. Israel is the only territory to which Arab nationalism in recent years has ever submitted a claim and seen that claim rejected, not once, but several times—and not by Israel alone but by the conscience of the world.

59

Nationalism and Internationalism in the Middle East

Perhaps this obsession with the negative rather than with the posi-' tive, with the small domain which has been denied rather than with the vast inheritance which has been bestowed, derives from a failure of nationalism throughout the Middle East and Asia to understand the scope of its responsibility. It is a marked attribute of nationalism in the Middle East and Asia that it concentrates exclusively upon the political aspect of national freedom. It aspires to the external emblems of nationhood. It demands with clamouring impatience the removal of foreign control. It sets up the flag of political sovereignty as the final objective of a national struggle. Behind the glittering façade of national freedom, the old social apathy, the old economic inertia, the old squalor, the old poverty, the old illiteracy, the old disease, the old nihilism, the old religious fanaticism, all linger on unaffected by the transition from colonial domination to local sovereignty or sometimes even aggravated by the removal of Western control.

This contrast in the Middle East and Asia between political success and social irresponsibility is the root of the tension which grips so vast a section of the globe. Men are awakened to find that they can be politically free and yet lose the essence of their freedom in the throes of squalor and want. Discovering with shock that the panacea of national liberation has solved none of their individual or social problems, they turn their backs in disillusionment upon the very concept of national freedom, and create an atmosphere of fear, bitterness, and frustration in which anti-democratic slogans make swift headway. This disillusionment with an abstract political freedom has already undermined democracy in the Far East, and unless Middle Eastern nationalism adds social and economic content to its political programmes, the same disillusionment and decay are inevitable there.

It is not within the power of Israel, isolated and boycotted by the neighbouring world, to exercise a direct influence on national movements throughout the Middle East. But the barriers which now divide us from our neighbours will not forever endure. The power of a contiguous example should not be underestimated. If Israel succeeds in creating a synthesis between political freedom and social and economic progress, it will have established a pilot plant which all Middle Eastern nations might emulate. If all nations in our area will grant to each other the rights which they claim for themselves, there will be harmony. If national movements will address themselves to the crea-

60

tion of a fair society assuring individual and collective welfare, the region can even come to know a measure of prosperity.

If we are asked, as so often we are, to define our attitude toward this Middle Eastern nationalism in terms either of positive approval or of resistance, we refute both extremes. We do not identify ourselves with those who would discredit the very theme of national liberation by drawing attention to the excesses of national movements. Nor, on the other hand, do we regard this as a benevolent or irresistible flood. Somewhere in between there must develop a critical attitude toward national movements, based not only upon initial approval of their aspirations but also upon a steady scrutiny of their objects. Middle Eastern nationalism suffers from the lack of altruism and the absence of social and economic responsibility. It ignores, too, the wider interests of the international order and seeks to express itself by unilateral violence which is outmoded by the present age.

There was a time, during the French and the American Revolutions, when liberal opinion had no reservations about national liberation when it was sought by violent means. Historians have come to applaud these revolutions and to draw a veil of forgiveness over the fact that, initially, they were movements of violent secession. That is because until the present century there existed no other way of securing the triumph of a national cause. If you denied the right of forcible secession or of violent rebellion, you denied the very objective of national liberation. However, in the modern world, violence and unilateral secession are no longer the only avenues to national freedom; and by that very fact they lose their appeal to the liberal mind.

It is true that conflict between the Great Powers has prevented the United Nations from exercising its responsibilities for the maintenance of world peace and security as the founders of the organization envisaged and as its Charter prescribes. But no such failure has attended the work of the United Nations in another vital sphere of international relations—the liberation of subject peoples and the creation of new units of national independence. Around the international table there are a dozen peoples, mostly from Asia, which owe the impulse for their liberation to the pacific processes of international judgment. Syria, Lebanon, India, Pakistan, Israel, Indonesia, and Libya, shortly to be reinforced by Eritrea and Somaliland, are all instances in which new units of political independence have had their liberation either completely or partially smoothed by international

Nationalism and Internationalism in the Middle East

judgment. If anything, the world might be accused of liquidating the previous régimes of domination with disorderly speed. For that reason, there is a legitimate ground of criticism today, as there would not have been in the nineteenth century, when a national movement seeks its objectives by force without exhausting international deliberation.

It has become fashionable also to assert that Israel's aspiration is for integration into the Middle East; that if it is not now a Middle Eastern State by every circumstance of political and economic connection, then that lack of Middle Eastern citizenship derives from the imposition of the neighbouring world; and that sooner or later it is its duty to become a part of the Middle East, flesh of its flesh, and bone of its bone, to become organically embodied in the political, economic, and cultural life of our region.

If I doubt this assertion, not merely from the viewpoint of its impracticability, which all will acknowledge at this time, but from the viewpoint of considering it a desirable objective, my reservations do not stem from any lack of regard for the cultural potentiality of the Arab or the Moslem world. The tradition of the Arab peoples is so rich, so versatile, so lucid, that the contemplation of it can itself constitute a complete humanistic education. If the Arab peoples are culturally impoverished at the present time, it is not because they possess no spiritual riches, but because they have lost the access to riches bequeathed to them. They have the right of entry by virtue of the central fact that they have preserved intact the language which is the chief embodiment of that heritage. It is, therefore, not in any spirit of anti-Arabism that I can be suspected of questioning the validity of this orientation. Yet I suggest that if Israel is now separated from the Arab Middle East, we owe that separation not only to the hostility of our neighbours but also to the nature of our own national movement.

Let us examine this idea of integration in its individual components. Do we seek to be economically integrated into the Near East? Our very mission is to establish a society which will bear no resemblance to the forms of social exploitation characteristic of Arab and Moslem society. Do we aspire to the same forms of political organization as those which engage the sentiment of the Arab world? Surely we are attracted neither by the theocratic monarchies of the Arabian peninsula nor by the protectorates or sheikdoms of the Persian Gulf, nor

Nationalism and Internationalism in the Middle East

by those forms of republicanism in the Levant states in which assassination is the conventional method of changing prime ministers and in which the parliamentary procedure reflects no public interest or educated popular concern. Neither the monarchies nor the republics of the Middle East offer us a form of political organization in which we can seek integration.

In the sphere of culture, while paying all honour to the potentiality of the Arab tradition, we come to Israel with the purpose of reviving and maintaining the Hebrew tradition. Moreover, Israel possesses unique interests, the paramount one of which is the network of connections with the Jewish world in all the countries of the Dispersion. This is something exclusive to the State of Israel; something which is entirely alien to the rest of the Near East. We should not, therefore, look upon the separateness of Israel as a transient phenomenon imposed by Arab boycott; it is imposed by desire, and the aspiration of Israel itself.

The idea should not be one of integration. Quite the contrary; integration is rather something to be avoided. One of the great apprehensions which afflict us when we contemplate our cultural scene is the danger lest the predominance of immigrants of Oriental origin force Israel to equalize its cultural level with that of the neighbouring world. So far from regarding our immigrants from Oriental countries as a bridge toward our integration with the Arabic-speaking world, our object should be to infuse them with an Occidental spirit, rather than to allow them to draw us into an unnatural Orientalism. The slogan should not be integration, but good neighbourliness; not Israel as an organic part of the Middle East, but Israel as a separate and unique entity living at peace with the Middle East. What we aspire to is not the relationship which exists between Lebanon and Syria; it is far more akin to the relationship between the United States and the Latin-American continent: relations of good neighbourliness, of regional co-operation, of economic interaction, but across a frankly confessed gulf of historic, cultural, and linguistic differences. The things which divide Israel from the Arab world are very often the most positive things which Israel exemplifies in its region. Nor should this interpretation be understood as equivalent to a desire for Israel to be regarded as an alien bridgehead in the area. There is a form of co-operation which falls far short of organic integration.

If Israel wishes to seek the most congenial world for its political relations and its cultural links, I suggest that that orientation be found in the word 'Mediterranean'—Israel not as a Middle Eastern country, but as a Mediterranean country. The Mediterranean is the only channel of intercourse and 'contact between Israel and the rest of the world. All Israel's commerce, all its connections, pass across that sea. If this is true as a geographical fact, it is even more true as a historic and cultural fact. The history of Israel has been powerfully affected, not by the currents of thought and action in what is called the Orient—in the Arabian Peninsula, in India, or in China. Since the earliest days of Israel's history, its crucial relationships have been with the countries of the Mediterranean Sea. In cultural terms the three cities of the Mediterranean world, Jerusalem, Athens, and Rome, form the partnership out of which Western civilization has flowed. There is therefore a certain logic in regarding Israel out of its immediate geographical context. It is not only geography which counts and determines the character of peoples. History and culture count no less.

The recent controversy on the place of Turkey in global defence is relevant to this point. There was an effort on the part of Western countries to remind Turkey of its Eastern and Moslem affiliations, to request Turkey to play its part in the world as the leader of a Middle Eastern community of nations, and, by implication, to claim no place in the Occidental world. It is interesting to record the vehemence with which Turkey demanded to be severed from its geographical background and to live, not in the family of the Arabic-speaking states of Saudi Arabia, of Syria, of Lebanon, and of Egypt, but to be regarded as the Eastern extremity of the Western world and to live in the same strategic, political, and cultural universe as Greece, Italy, and France. If Turkey by reason of the Occidental emphasis of its culture and its institutions is able to express that attraction, I consider that Israel has an even greater right. If anything, Israel has no part of the Moslem inheritance which would have argued in favour of Turkey's being regarded as a Middle Eastern state.

There is, therefore, both an historic and a contemporary logic pulling toward the Mediterranean interpretation of Israel nationalism in the modern world. First we see a prospect of Israel's emergence from a political and cultural isolation; for if Israel is an isolated country in terms of the Middle East, in terms of the Mediterranean it is not. With all the states of the Mediterranean world, and certainly with those of the northern Mediterranean, Israel possesses contacts of diplomacy and trade. The Mediterranean orientation of Israel's nationalism offers our state a higher standard of cultural perform- ance and of social and economic organization on which to base itself.

Finally, I should like to present a few observations on the concepts of internationalism and nationalism as they affect Israel and the Jewish world. The theory of antithesis between the universal mission and the national mission in Judaism was once in vogue. And yet, I believe that at every stage those who argued this antithesis were mak- ing a virtue of necessity. Since the Jewish people lacked a national centre, since it was deprived of the dignity and pride of sovereign independence, there were those who argued that the absence of these things did not matter. There were others who went even further and who argued that Israel's lack of a national status was a positive asset. Here was a people abstract and disembodied, uncontaminated by the compromises of national and political responsibility, free to let its mind and spirit roam in the stratosphere of abstract ideals, to carry to all the nations a suffused and sublimated vision beyond the am- bition of mortal sovereign states. Everybody will recognize in this analysis some of the excesses of the Reform doctrine which made a pure necessity out of this allegedly impure virtue of national free- dom. The universal cause, it was said, can be served as well, nay, it may even be served better, without starting from the point of national identity.

Against this argument there arose Zionism as an interpretation of Jewish history. Zionism as a political movement is subsidiary to this wider concept of Zionism as a version of the destiny and mission of the Jewish people. It argued, with admirable foundation in Jewish tradition, and therefore with ultimate success, that the validity of a spiritual doctrine can only be tested in the arena of social performance and international relations; that it is easy but valueless to uphold ethical ideals in a vacuum; and that Judaism itself is a doctrine of practice. The important thing is the realization of spiritual and ethical precepts on the hard ground of human and international relations. It is this which proves the validity or the obsoleteness of an ethical system.

Strangely enough, and perhaps to our good fortune, the non-Jewish world agreed with this interpretation. Perhaps the greatest paradox of modern history is that the Zionist interpretation of Jewish identity, which was looked at with indignation and fear lest it should undermine the popularity of the Jewish people in the world, became the only movement in Jewish life to obtain the ratification of the universal conscience on two separate occasions within one generation, each time against the fierce challenge of powerful interests. In other words, Zionism has so far furnished the only serious bridge of Jewish-Gentile collaboration in the sphere of political or international interaction. The State of Israel has arisen in testimony to a doctrine which held that the Jewish tradition should not be disembodied, should not wander from place to place in search of a home, should not assert its values in the vacant air, but prove them in the realm of political and social action.

The question arises: Where do we go from here? Is the creation of the State of Israel the final vindication of this interpretation of history? Does the existence of Israel really settle anything?

Within the terms which interest us here, the mere existence of Israel answers nothing and settles nothing. What constitutes the final answer is not the existence of a state, but its nature and quality. What kind of political entity is this that we have created through the tenacity, sacrifice, and toil of two thousand years? Is Israel just the sixtieth unit in the international community? Is it a state like other states which have newly arisen, with no roots in past tradition and with no prospect of exemplifying any progressive ideal? The sound of the trumpets will die away, the glitter of liberation will wear off, and everything will depend both for the people of Israel and for the world upon the quality of the state.

We have reached a critical turning point to which some of the concern heretofore invested in Israel's physical existence must now be devoted. The scientific, educational, and cultural picture in Israel is cause for the gravest disquiet. Although we are saved from provincialism by the brilliance of our tradition, and the Hebrew language, our greatest single national asset, gives us the key to all the glories of the past, Israel has not yet proved itself in the ultimate category of quality. In this vital respect, everything remains to be done, and the establishment of the state is a beginning and in no sense a consummation or an end.

The answer to this question of quality lies along three lines. First, Israel must recapture its Hebrew roots. It must establish among all its people a sense of lineal descent from ancient Israel, the source and repository of the values which dominate Western civilization.

Nationalism and Internationalism in the Middle East

If we were to begin on a new slate as a new nation with no antecedents we would be doomed for many decades, if not for many centuries, to a life of novitiate sterility. If we can take our starting point in a spiritual and cultural system which is far in advance of the general level of modern performance, then Israel can indeed be a light to the world.

The greatest good fortune which attended the liberation movement out of which Israel grew was the Hebrew revival, the fact that the life of the new Jewish settlement from its very beginning was cast in the same mould as the spirit and culture of Israel of old. Of course, what we call Hebraism is a concept far wider than that of language, although language is the key to every compartment of our cultural experience—to history, literature, religion; and to a prospect of unification of the scattered tribes of Israel who now come into our gates, and who but for the Hebrew language would forever remain a generation of Babel; and, potentially, a key whereby the people of Israel can seek partnership and solidarity with Jewish thought beyond their borders. It was not an accident that in the first impulse of statehood we cast the emblems of sovereignty in a mould which recalled the previous eras of Israel's independence. The choice of the historic name Israel was an act of insight.

The second task before the State of Israel is the retention of its Jewish roots. One of our most disquieting cultural problems is a psychological gulf growing up between those educated and born within the atmosphere of Israel and the rest of the Jewish world, a complete incomprehension of the historic fact that the Jewish people underwent two thousand years of exile and in returning to its homeland brings back not merely the scars of that experience but also the accumulated riches of the Western world. Therefore, the attitude of being shamefaced in Israel about the fact of *galut*, of envisaging the new community of Israel as a separate tribe distinct from the general polity of the Jewish world, should be resisted not merely for its lack of political realism but also because it is a culturally negative concept. If we have suffered the whips and scorpions of exile, let us at least compensate ourselves with the retention of those Western concepts which we have acquired. Ancient Hebrew civilization, with all its depth and grandeur, was limited in scope. Hebrew Israel did not flourish in the plastic arts or in the applied sciences; its genius was exercised in a supreme but constricted avenue of cultural experience. And if through our contact with the West we are enabled to enlarge

67

the range of the original native Hebrew tradition, this is not an opportunity to be lightly cast away.

But Hebrew roots and Jewish roots are not enough, and Israel has every title and every right to enrich both its Hebrew and its Jewish traditions by the products of modern Western civilization. It is this civilization which the Hebrew spirit has profoundly affected. Western man throughout the two thousand years of Jewish exile has achieved standards of political organization and technical progress which deserve to be embodied in our tradition. In our concern with recapturing Hebrew and Jewish roots, we must somehow avoid the pitfalls of provincialism.

In a recent visit to the United States, Mr. Ben-Gurion attempted to interest some of us in a new movement of literary ingathering. His vision was to ensure that the Hebrew reader should have access not merely to the fruits of the Hebrew genius but also to the best products of the Western mind, to the basic documents of Western civilization —to Greek and Roman literature, to English literature, and to the literature of Persia, India, and Europe. He proposed that within the space of a few years we should undertake a movement to translate these works, a movement perhaps no less significant than that which the Ibn Tibbon family undertook for different reasons in another age, in order to ensure that the people of Israel should be able to look out over the widest windows into the most distant and inspiring horizons, into all the nooks and crannies of the Eastern and Western mind. To the degree that we succeed in interesting Jewish opinion in this project, we shall be able to judge whether or not there is a genuine perception by the Israel public into the real challenge and danger of our cultural destiny—the challenge of progress and the danger of limitation.

If we were asked to summarize the true compatibility in Jewish thinking between a national and a universal mission, we should only have to go back to the Prophet Isaiah, who brought his mind to bear upon this problem of maintaining an independent State of Israel amid the clash of powerful empires, and who had these words to say:

> *Yea, He saith: 'It is too light a thing that*
> *thou shouldest be My servant*
> *To raise up the tribes of Jacob,*
> *And to restore the offspring of Israel;*

68

I will also give thee for a light of the
    nations,
That my salvation may be unto the end of
    the earth.'

ISAIAH, 49 : 6

CHAPTER VII

Israel and America*

This is an exalted moment in the history of American-Israel relations. For the first time an Ambassador of Israel is able to bear public testimony, in the hearing of the President of the United States, to the deeds of high courage and sympathy whereby America illuminated the early records of our national liberation.

Israel is now four years old, but its annals are already part of universal history. Here is a people which defended its hearth and its home against the fury of a preponderant foe; established free institutions in a wilderness of absolutism and tyranny extending around it on every side; brought 750,000 of its kinsmen out of misery and anguish beneath the shelter of its protective roof; pushed the areas of verdant cultivation ever farther and deeper into the wilderness and the swamp; planted twenty-five million trees on the barren hills and roadsides of a country devastated by centuries of neglect; began to explore and lay bare the natural riches of its soil; embarked upon a great cultural adventure to create out of varied and divergent elements from all the four corners of the earth a new civilization in the image of Israel's past; established its flag in the family of nations and gave utterance to Israel's universal longing for peace. This is the record of Israel's performance in these four years of its national life. The history of every people fixes its eye upon a particular hour when its qualities shine forth with special radiance above the levels of normal achievement. We cannot doubt that posterity, looking back on these four years, with all their turbulence and adventure, will recognize them always as the formative years in the life of our nation. We, beyond our expectations and, perhaps, beyond our merits, belong to the generation of Israel's founding fathers.

No human purpose has ever been accomplished against heavier calculations of chance. All the circumstances of time and place argued against our success. The place was fixed by history on the shores of the eastern Mediterranean, where vigorous nationalisms

*At a dinner in honour of President Truman, Washington, D.C., 26 May 1952.

70

were arising, far more disposed to claim national freedom for themselves than to concede it to others. The time was the sequel of the Second World War, when the Jewish people rose battered and bleeding from the violent onslaughts of tyranny. Six million of our kinsmen had been slaughtered in the fields of Europe; men, women and children had been carted off to furnaces like unwanted rubbish. The institutions of Jewish life and learning lay about us in ruin. The pride and repute of the Jewish people had been dragged down in calumny and degradation. Out of the darkest depths of man's divided nature, there had sprung at the throat of the Jewish people the most violent hatred which ever convulsed or distorted the spirit of man. This was the lowest ebb of our fortunes, when many believed that we had marked the end of the Jewish people's journey across history's stage. Yet within a few years of this unexampled decline, behold, the Jewish Commonwealth had come into triumphant existence. Its flag flew bravely in the circle of banners which symbolized the freedom and equality of all nations on earth. Its life and culture entered upon a new birth of freedom. Warm waves of confidence and pride flowed into every Jewish home through the length and the breadth of the world, where the traditions of Israel were still cherished and revered. The history of the Jewish people in this generation is dominated by this violent contrast between the dark frustrations of 1945 and the high peaks of achievement and opportunity to which we suddenly rose. Never was this people stronger than in its moment of weakness, never more hopeful than in its moment of despair.

But what was the precise moment at which this transition began from paralysing weakness to a great eruption of initiative and strength? It came first in the spring of 1946 when thousands of displaced fugitives in the squalid camps of occupied Europe suddenly heard a strong and resolute voice lifted up in their behalf. President Truman had urged, in the name of the American people, that the remnants of Israel should be admitted in accordance with international law and policy into the country designated by the world conscience as the Jewish National Home.

It is a good test of friendship for men or nations to recall the moment of their greatest loneliness and ask themselves who then stood at their side. By this crucial test President Truman must be surely accounted Israel's most authentic friend. The political movements set up by this first intervention in favour of Jewish refugee immigration to Israel led directly to the discussion on Palestine's future in the

Israel and America

councils of the United Nations. Here the cause of Jewish statehood was fully vindicated in the spirit of national self-determination. World statesmen, with the United States at their head, looked upon the great new expanse of Arab freedom embodied in nine sovereign states, extending over a vast continent covering more than a million square miles. No balanced conscience could withhold from the Jewish people, so sorely beset, the opportunity to exercise its national freedom within an infinitely smaller domain, less than one hundredth of that in which the Arab peoples had achieved their freedom with the strong assistance and influence of the Western world. The nations said: Just as it is right for the Arab world to exercise its freedom in a vast continent, so it cannot be wrong for the people of Israel to renew its sovereignty in the tiny corner which had been immortalized in history through its connection with the Hebrew spirit and tradition. Thus, on 14th May 1948 the founders of our State declared their independence and showed cause for their secession from the union in which they had been previously held. The event, announced in due form to all governments which composed the international society, was a direct challenge to the imagination and statesmanship of the world. In five minutes President Truman announced that the State of Israel and its government were recognized by the United States. The government and people of Israel are deeply grateful to all the countries of the world which have since established friendly relations with them. We should, however, be less than human if we did not have a special place in our hearts for those who supported us in our days of solitude and adversity, when our prospect of survival was dim, and the forces arrayed against us appeared insurmountable. In the works of Hebrew prophecy, we recall those 'who went with us in the wilderness, in the land that was not sown'.

These first acts of friendship set up a momentum which has never run down. In the sequel to statehood and recognition there came the support of the United States for Israel's admission to the United Nations, bringing two thousand years of anonymity and inferiority to an end. In the second year of our independence powerful forces begrudged us the empty, parched wastes of the Negev which we regarded, with as much faith as reason, as our development area, to be fertilized by the sacrifices and toil of pioneers. Again President Truman stood in the breach. It must be a source of satisfaction to him to know that our most promising auguries of mineral wealth, of industrial productivity and even of agricultural bounty have since

72

been revealed precisely in that area which was coveted so arduously and so long, and which was so often written off as a sterile and useless wilderness. In later years the United States, in performance of its duty as member of the United Nations, came forward to initiate and to uphold the armistice which brought armed conflict with our neighbours to an end. When Israel's action in opening its gates to the hunted and dispossessed of Europe, Africa and Asia led to an inevitable gap between our needs and our production, the United States joined with us in our struggle for economic stability. The investments of the Export-Import Bank and the inclusion of Israel in the Mutual Security Programme have had a crucial effect upon our survival, and will help to decide the issue of our stability and prosperity as well.

Why is it that this community of purpose and sentiment has asserted itself so constantly between Israel and the United States? Is it a mere accident of diplomatic history, or do the causes lie buried more deeply in the soil of·our separate traditions? I am convinced that the rise of Israel would not have made so deep an impact upon the American nation and its elected leader, were it not for three links which unite our two countries across the oceans of space. First, there is a common body of historic experience; second, there is a common devotion to democracy; third, there is a common allegiance to the same system of moral values.

This community of historic experience could not fail to impress itself upon any American who understood the processes whereby his own republic came to birth. The convergence of destitute immigrants upon Israel, in search of dignity and freedom, recalled the epoch of American history when this continent rose to power and strength by opening its doors to those who sought liberty. Israel's task in creating a unified discipline of loyalty and culture from scores of varying tongues and backgrounds has only one parallel in modern history; it is the creation of American civilization by the synthesis and harmony of many races, creeds and tongues which have composed the symphony of American life today. Israel, like America, is a country built by pioneers, by men who set their strength and their spirit against the forces of nature and the allurements of immediate comfort—men who built for their posterity, rather than for themselves. Israel, like America, values its freedom the more because it was dearly purchased with the best of its blood. Israel, like America, did not emerge without struggle and strife from the system of government under which it was previously ruled. Is it not as though the

73

very processes which characterized America's struggle for freedom were played out anew within our own lifetime upon a smaller but no less significant stage?

But these mysterious links of common history would not have availed were it not for two other ideals which we hold in common. Israel proudly belongs to the family of democracies. It rejects the pretensions of political or social tyranny. A people which in antiquity first rebelled against idolatry, which rose up against the might of Assyria and Rome will never, never, in its modern life, yield to idolatrous concepts of dictatorship. The parliamentary democracy of Israel now emerges as a factor of deep significance in the destiny of the Near East. We do not live in a region where responsible and representative government has struck any roots. If you look upon our democracy with American eyes you may see little in it that is special or new. A parliament elected by free ballot; a government which changes on the behest of the electorate, and not by assassination or military *coup d'état*; long discussions between rival political parties which regard each other with something less than unlimited enthusiasm—all these things are part of the familiar scene of Western democratic life. The crucial point, however, is that they are not part of Middle Eastern life. There is scarcely an area in our immediate neighbourhood where at this moment the authority of the State is exercised in direct response to the will of the people. Surely the success of democracy in one country of the Middle East where it is fully practised can help to determine whether the whole of this crucial area will be won for freedom, or lost to tyranny. No wonder that the American people, concerned for the victory of democracy as a world cause, feel a profound solidarity with this new democracy which has arisen at the crossroads of the world.

Common historic experience, common devotion to democracy are reinforced in the relations between our two countries by strong links which are of the spirit. It is no ordinary people—this people of Israel —whom the American people have assisted to regain its freedom. In the great peril of war which now confronts the world and casts its shadow over every peaceful home, men have grown accustomed to fix their eyes upon the central purposes of their existence. A modern society is accounted good to the degree that it upholds three principles: individual morality, social justice and universal peace. But these very three concepts were first expressed and proclaimed by the people of Israel, in the Land of Israel, through the language of Israel,

Israel and America

in the previous phases of Israel's independent national life. We reflect, not with pride but with deep awe and humility, that there is nothing essential or original in the moral heritage of Western civilization which cannot be traced back to the hills and valleys of our country, to the rare spirits and immortal voices which issued forth from it. The founders of the American Republic, indeed of all free lands, fully recognized their debt to the Hebrew tradition for these truths of individual, social and international virtue, out of which democracy was born. I feel moved to conjecture that President Truman is among those who see modern Israel as the lineal descendant of Israel of old. To anyone who possesses that degree of historic insight, the destiny of Israel assumes a meaning far beyond the dimensions of its size or physical strength.

I am proud to be my Government's spokesman tonight in celebrating the great theme of American-Israel friendship. To the President of the United States we offer our gratitude for past and present sympathy. But the waters of this friendship run deep and strong; and we shall surely draw from them in future ordeals. We continue to have passionate need of that friendship as we move towards the unfulfilled objectives which we hold in common. We hold in common a vision of peace between Israel and its Arab neighbours. We hope that these two kindred peoples, which contributed so much to the thought and spirit of mankind, will again unite their strength for the defence and progress of the East Mediterranean, and revive upon its shores the full glories of ancient and medieval times. While we cherish our new-won independence we do not begrudge our neighbours the freedom which they have inherited in so lavish a measure. Peace will come to our area when all its nations recognize to other nations the same rights and freedoms which they claim for themselves. We hold in common not only the vision of political harmony but also the aspiration to economic and social progress without which no political institutions are securely founded. The rivers and valleys, the forests, the hills, even the deserts of the Middle East can, by patient and co-operative effort, be restored to their ancient fertility and productivity. A Near East at peace within itself and resting upon the contentments of prosperity and honourable reward, will constitute a strong bulwark of freedom 'amidst the conflicting elements of a troubled world'.

In gratitude and in appreciation; in memory of solitudes and sorrows in which we were heard and understood; in dedication to the common purposes which we pursue in the world, the people of Israel wish to confer upon President Truman the only honour which is in their gift. We do not have orders or decorations. Our material strength is small and greatly strained. We have no tradition of formality or chivalry. One thing, however, is within the power of the People of Israel to confer. It is the gift of immortality. Those whose names are bound up with Israel's history never become forgotten. The annals of this people have a way of entering the records of unlimited time. We are, therefore, now writing the name of President Truman upon the map of our country. It is the most illustrious living name to be thus recorded upon the contemporary map of the Holy Land. In this village of farmers, near the airport of Lydda, at the gateway to Israel, we establish a monument not of dead stone, but of living homes. Thus for all eternity when the eyes of men alight on Truman Village in Israel, they will pause in their successive generations to recall the strong chain which, at the middle of the twentieth century, drew the strongest and the smallest democracies together with imperishable links.

CHAPTER VIII

A Prince in Israel*

A Tribute to Chaim Weizmann

I rise to express deep gratitude for the action of the General Assembly in paying silent homage to President Chaim Weizmann, who is being laid to rest in Israel at this very hour.

He led Israel for forty years, through a wilderness of martyrdom and anguish, of savage oppression and frustrated hope, across the sharpest agony which has ever beset the life of any people; and at the end of his days he entered in triumph upon his due inheritance of honour as the first President of Israel—the embodiment in modern times of that kingly and prophetic tradition which once flourished in Israel and became an abiding source of light and redemption for succeeding generations of men. His presidency symbolized the swift journey of the Jewish people, in this its most awesome decade, from the horror and degradation of European slaughter-houses to the shelter and freedom of a sovereign State securely established in the international family.

During years of deep darkness and little hope we looked with pride and longing upon his erect and majestic bearing; his dignity of mind and spirit; his scientific intellect, refined and ordered as a cultivated garden; and his profound moral influence in every free country upon the best minds and spirits of his age.

I thank all representatives who have offered their condolences. We are sorely bereaved. But we may serve our tradition worthily if we establish the life of our first President as the standard to which Israel should aspire in all the expressions of its national spirit, in deed and thought and word. The waves of sympathy which have flowed in upon us in recent days will sustain our people in this solemn hour of remembrance and grief.

* To the General Assembly of the United Nations, 11 November 1952.
77

CHAPTER IX

A Blueprint for Peace*

The problem before the United Nations has now been considered by the General Assembly of the United Nations in eight consecutive sessions. Controversy between Israel and the Arab States is becoming a tradition of international life. By now we have developed fixed patterns of argument, familiar slogans and well-tried formulas. Each year, as the season of this debate approaches, conciliatory processes have been suspended so that private statesmanship may yield to public denunciation.

Looking back over these records in recent months, we have noticed how much they have been concerned with the past, how little with the future. Their central theme has been not the contemporary life and future destiny of the Middle East, but the wording of documents, their interpretation and the degree of binding force to be attributed to them. There is now a whole literature revolving around every paragraph and every phrase.

This year once again the theme of Arab speeches has been: 'Who is to blame for these difficulties?' not 'How can these problems be constructively and justly solved?' A preoccupation with grievances rather than with solutions is characteristic of many discussions now taking place in the United Nations, especially on Middle Eastern and Mediterranean affairs. The psychological implications of this attitude are interesting, but they do not help us to come face to face with the factors which govern the life of our region and determine the future of its peoples. For meanwhile, during these years in which the content and tone of this debate have remained unchanged, the people of the Middle East have lived the life of a region alive with movement and innovation; a region in which countries and peoples, régimes and political systems, economic processes, social structures and international relationships have undergone swift transformations from year to year.

Having followed the speeches of Arab representatives with deep

* To the General Assembly of the United Nations, 1 December 1952.

78

attention, I believe that it would be accurate to define their essential purport as follows: The only just and reasonable way in which the Arab States and Israel can adjust their relationships for 1953 and thereafter is to 'implement' the recommendations which the Arab governments themselves rejected by armed violence in 1947, and by obstruction and boycott since 1948. In other words, the only recommendations which can produce agreement in the future are precisely those which have been the subject of all the disagreements of the past.

I respectfully submit that if this is all that we have to say about the Near East in its hour of destiny; if we refuse to seek new solutions of old deadlocks, then we shall be living far below the level of our responsibilities and opportunities.

But I am confident that the General Assembly is not satisfied to perpetuate failure. In recent months the air of the Near East has been astir with a spirit of change. We have a feeling that the United Nations, too, in its relationship to this problem is ready for innovation and renewal, for the pursuit of simple courses related to the challenge of tomorrow, and not to the unsuccessful remedies of yesterday. I do not doubt that the international community strongly desires to see Israel and the Arab states engaged, earnestly and together, in an attempt to resolve their differences by their own judgment and responsibility through the normal processes of international intercourse. If there was ever a time when it could be assumed that an Arab-Israel settlement might be evolved, either in general principle or in detail, by external parties or international organs without the direct interplay of Arab and Israel minds, then that belief cannot be seriously held today. Nobody can help Israel and the Arab states solve problems which they will not discuss freely and directly between themselves.

Israel has faced many preoccupations in the first five years of her national independence. First, there was the struggle for physical survival. Then came the quest for international recognition. These accomplishments, which together established our statehood, were succeeded by an epic process of rescue, in which we gathered remnants of our people into the shelter and freedom of our State, thus inheriting awesome burdens as well as high exaltation. As a result of this swift growth of population, we were soon plunged into an intensive campaign for higher economic productivity. And all the time we

A Blueprint for Peace

were building the structure of our democracy, developing its constitutional forms and mapping out the great journey which faced us in the domain of cultural and scientific endeavour. Although these concerns have all pressed upon us simultaneously and together, we have never lost sight of our chief objective—the attainment of peace in our region.

Today Israel is prepared to make the attainment of peace in its region a primary theme of its national policy, and to bring all its resources to bear upon that task. There are special reasons which lead us to believe that an active quest for peace now holds more promise than ever before. In speeches and in resolutions we have seen evidence that the United Nations now regards peace as the direct responsibility of Israel and of the Arab States, to be pursued by them in perfect freedom, limited only by their obligations under the Charter. There are also signs that Arab statesmanship in its best expressions is awakening to a new constructive impulse. This is, therefore, a moment to embark upon the earnest contemplation of a peace settlement based on neighbourly relations between Israel and the Arab States.

We are discussing this morning an area which extends over a vast expanse of two million square miles. In the whole of this vast region, teeming with natural and mineral resources, full of latent and potential wealth, eight separate Arab sovereignties have arisen where not a single independent Arab state existed three decades ago. Any constructive imagination would be elevated by the national opportunity which the Arab people has inherited in so short a time. In a world where few peoples ever attain their total ambition, it must be admitted that none has ever been blessed with such political good fortune, or secured a greater measure of its national aspiration so rapidly. The blood and sacrifice of victorious coalitions in two world wars contributed much to this Arab liberation. International opinion through the United Nations has helped to free many of these countries from foreign occupation; while only recently the United Nations established a new and eighth sphere of Arab sovereignty, in an area twenty times the size of Israel, through the establishment of the United Kingdom of Libya—a decision to which Israel gave full and important support. From the Arab people, thus endowed with every prospect of greatness and of broad opportunity, the United Nations has the right to expect a modification of an unyielding attitude

80

towards a small neighbouring state. Indeed, it was this huge expanse of Arab sovereignty which stood before the eyes of the United Nations when the question of Israel's right to statehood first came before it. The nations of the world could not fail to perceive a simple truth. They said: 'If it is right for the Arab peoples to possess their vast continent, it cannot be wrong for the Jewish people to enjoy the tranquil and secure possession of its cherished home.' No balanced conscience could withhold from Israel, in its smaller domain, the rights and opportunities with which the Arab peoples were so abundantly endowed.

I have not alluded to the broad scope of Arab freedom in order to suggest that it should be begrudged, or regarded as beyond merit. We hope that the Arab people will consolidate its political freedom and move on towards social and economic advances commensurate with its success in the attainment of institutional liberty. It is important, however, to correct the atmosphere of these debates. The Arab people should not appear here as a party wronged or aggrieved, injured by a malevolent history, deprived of something which others possess in larger measure, and therefore entitled to heap bitter denunciation upon Israel and upon the United Nations. It is that denunciation which I should like to avoid as we go forward to examine the prospects of peace.

The problem before us is that Israel and four contiguous countries —Egypt, Syria, Jordan and Lebanon—have entered into armistice agreements. These treaties, concluded by direct negotiations, have for four years given us a minimal stability, which, however, falls short of the positive relations which should govern the intercourse of sovereign states, members of the United Nations. The task is to develop the present provisional relationship, resting upon signature and consent, into a new relationship, also to be achieved by signature and consent, conforming with the best examples of regional co-operation in the present age.

With each or any of the four governments bound to us by armistice treaties, Israel is prepared to negotiate a final settlement for the establishment of peaceful relations. We would neither impose nor accept any preconditions for such negotiations, in which each party should be free to make its proposals. The parties can, by mutual consent, use available United Nations machinery or other good offices, to help them in their negotiations, if they so desire.

A Blueprint for Peace

I should now like to present the views of my Government on three major questions which arise in connection with a negotiated peace settlement.

First: Who shall define and shape the peace settlement? Is this the task of the Arab States and Israel themselves, or does it fall within the competence of other states, individually or collectively?

Second: Shall any prior conditions be laid down for the peace settlement? More specifically, are the parties entitled to reach any agreements to which their own consent shall lead them? Does past experience and present evaluation persuade the United Nations that it has revealed a successful formula for agreement in its past resolutions? Or, should all parties admit that the truth may still have to be found, the formula for agreement still to be discovered?

Third: Does the Government of Israel have a clear view, even in general outline, of the nature of the peace settlement which it seeks in advocating direct and unfettered negotiations?

It should be unnecessary to offer proof that a peace settlement between Israel and the Arab States is the primary responsibility of their governments. Indeed, the right of states to conclude agreements with each other is the natural corollary of their sovereignty. If we deny a state that right, or qualify its free exercise, we encroach upon the very essence of statehood. Along with the acquisition of the right, there goes the acceptance of responsibility. For it is our conviction that all members of the United Nations have not merely a right, but a moral duty and responsibility to establish normal and peaceful relations with all other states. If it is not in their power to achieve agreements, it is surely their minimal duty to attempt to achieve them.

What is called 'the Palestine problem' bears no resemblance now to the nature of that problem when it first came before the United Nations. At that time, the issue was the attempt of the General Assembly, at the invitation of the mandatory power, to recommend a form of government for a territory in which the United Nations had greater responsibilities than it has in relation to sovereign states. The problem now is of a different character. It is the normal problem of relations between soveriegn states, and has thus become assimilated in its nature to the usual pattern of international relationships.

Thus, when we say that Israel and the Arab states are alone re-sponsible for reaching agreement on their relations, we are doing nothing more, but also nothing less, than affirming their statehood, both in the context of their rights and in the context of their duties.

When we assert that only the governments concerned, by direct negotiations, can settle their outstanding questions, we do more even than affirm the statehood of the parties, the experience of five intensive years, and the conclusions of expert authority. We also record an inescapable legal and political fact: all the relations now existing between the parties, affecting their provisional frontiers and their security relationships, are embodied in four armistice agreements which derive their validity from the consent of the parties and which, under their own terms and until they are revised, prevail over any other proposals not embodied in those agreements. Nothing in them can be changed in any degree except by a further act of agreement between the parties, who may, at their mutual discretion, amend those agreements, or develop them into peace treaties. This provisional relationship resting upon consent can never be changed except by a new settlement arising from a further process of consent. This means that no measures affecting such fundamental matters as frontier demarcations, passage and communication from one state to another, whether of civilians or goods, by land or sea or air, can have any status in law unless or until the armistice agreements are amended or replaced.

A call for a direct settlement by free and unconditional negotiation would be fully in accord with the purposes of the United Nations and with the development of international relations in our time. It was never the purpose of the United Nations to supersede direct diplomacy. It was never envisaged that member states would consider themselves entitled to refuse contact or negotiation with other states, and yet complain to an international organ because no agreement had been reached.

This absence of contact between Israel and the Arab states has become such a familiar part of the international scene that we sometimes fail to realize what an extraordinary and solitary fact it is. The period which has elapsed since the Second World War has not been one of triumph for international conciliation; yet there have been marked achievements. A peace treaty has been signed between Japan and the governments of its former enemies. Agreements liquidating a state of war and establishing relations have been arrived at between Germany and her former enemies. The United Nations is seized of other disputes, which all its members follow with deep sympathy and concern, such as the questions outstanding between India and Pakistan. But in all these cases full political and economic relations exist, and disputes which arise are periodically discussed within the framework of those normal diplomatic relations. Thus the failure of Arab governments to meet with Israel brings them into conflict with the whole tendency of international relations in our generation.

Having spoken of direct negotiations, I now come to discuss whether the agreement to be reached between Israel and the Arab States must necessarily conform with previous resolutions of the General Assembly.

I do not believe that we have ever thrashed this problem out with sufficient clarity. First, I am forced to join issue with one impression which my Arab colleagues may have left in some minds. If I could believe the evidence of my ears, the representative of Syria told this Committee that the Arab governments 'have always accepted United Nations resolutions'. Now, with all due allowance to the exigencies of debate, this goes beyond any conceivable definition of truth. What we call the 'Palestine problem' is, in essence, nothing but the result of the decision of Arab States to overthrow General Assembly resolutions, not by peaceful non-compliance which they may consider to be their right under the Charter, but by the aggressive use of armed force. I recall that the first resolution of the General Assembly was a recommendation to the mandatory power and to the peoples of Palestine to carry out certain provisions for the establishment of partition. The report of the United Nations Commission responsible for supervising the implementation of that resolution states:

'Arab opposition to the plan of the Assembly has taken the form of organized efforts by strong Arab elements, both inside and outside Palestine, to prevent its implementation and to thwart its objectives by threats and acts of violence, including repeated armed incursions into Palestine territory. The Commission has had to report to the Security Council that powerful Arab interests, both inside and outside Palestine, are defying the resolution of the General Assembly and are engaged in a deliberate effort to alter by force the settlement envisaged therein.'

The representative of Egypt elevated this resistance to a general creed and said:

'No one could say that compliance is imperative or that the countries which did not comply are acting against the Charter or undermining the structure of the United Nations. We, the Egyptian Government, do not choose to comply with the General Assembly's Resolution on Palestine. This is our privilege under the Charter.'

The issue, of course, was not the 'privilege' of peaceful non-compliance but the crime of armed invasion.

The next substantive resolution was that of 1948. The central theme of that resolution was Paragraph 5, calling upon the parties to settle their outstanding differences. On this the Conciliation Commission has recorded that the Arab governments, in their contacts with the Commission, 'have shown no readiness to discuss a peace settlement with Israel as envisaged in that resolution'.

I could, but will not, speak at length on the Security Council Resolutions of 22nd May and 5th July 1948, calling for a cease-fire which the Arab States rejected; of the Resolution of July 10th, calling for a renewal of the truce, which they rejected, leading the Security Council to invoke Chapter VII of the Charter for the first time; of the proposal for a ten-day breathing space for a cease-fire which they rejected; of the Security Council's Resolution of 1st September 1951, calling for a cessation of blockade practices which Egypt still disregards. But in the light of this record, the Arab insistence on the infallibility of resolutions rings strangely in our ears. I am not attempting here to reprove Arab governments for past actions; but do not their representatives owe us the honesty of not appearing as the virtuous exponents of the sanctity of resolutions? If we are to be as frank as the gravity of this problem requires, it can be shown that all governments concerned with the Palestine problem since the mandatory power submitted it to the United Nations have on some occasions found themselves unable to comply with resolutions of the General Assembly.

What is unique in the Arab record is that four of their acts of non-

A Blueprint for Peace

compliance have had a special attribute which does not mar the record of Israel or of any other state. On three occasions Arab opposition to resolutions has taken the form of armed attack; and on one occasion it has taken the form of a stubborn maintenance of a warlike blockade. Nobody has any record of non-compliance with resolutions in the slightest degree comparable to this. Their practice, I fear, has been to oppose resolutions at the time and in the conditions when their implementation was possible; and then to invoke their implementation when it has been quite safe to assume that they were no longer capable of being put into effect.

It reminds me of the practice in which some of us indulged in our early youth, of ringing doorbells and then running away when there was the least chance of the doors being opened. Like the Arab references to previous Resolutions in the present context, this practice caused amusement to some, annoyance to others and practical advantage to nobody at all. It is in the Jerusalem case that the Arab habit of ringing doorbells is most vividly illustrated. If you ring the Jerusalem bell, two doors open: one towards the United Nations statute for the Holy Places, which was advocated here two years ago; the other looking out on an international enclave around the main Holy Places. Each of these solutions, so violently opposed by the Arab States, would have offered honourable access to the objective of the United Nations. But by the time either of these doors was opened, our Arab colleagues had fled so far down the street that they were completely lost from sight.

The argument against trying a negotiated settlement to past resolutions is more substantial even than the reference to the record. It is because past resolutions, individually and together, have not produced an agreement or a settlement that we are discussing this question in the Committee today.

Let us think of the great transformations which have come upon our region since the original resolutions were adopted. The emergence of a sovereign state in place of an international territory; a vast influx of population into Israel from Europe and the Arab world adding nearly one million people to the population of Israel since the time when the first refugee resolution was proposed; the initiation of great works projects for the employment and integration of refugees in Arab countries; the conclusion of armistice treaties creating relationships completely unprovided for in the resolutions which preceded

86

their signature; the annexation of large parts of western Palestine by Jordan and Egypt, in place of the establishment of a separate Arab state economically federated with Israel; five years of boycott and blockade instead of the close economic co-operation originally envisaged; the rise and fall of régimes and political systems; the emergence, as we hope, of new dispositions and tendencies of thought in all countries of the area—how can all these vast and revolutionary changes have occurred and be deemed to have no effect upon the validity of recommendations which were regarded as effective in totally different circumstances prevailing years ago?

If we are to be faithful craftsmen in the greatest of all arts—the construction of world peace—we must continually perfect our instruments, and sometimes not hesitate to change them.

In the light of all these far-reaching changes of circumstance and outlook, for which the Arab governments are no less responsible than anybody else, the need for 'solutions, not for resolutions', as Secretary Acheson has expressed it, should be frankly affirmed. I could not think of anything more negative, more hostile to our prospect of success than to stultify the prospect at the very outset by requiring the new vision of the Middle Eastern future to conform with unfulfilled proposals of the past.

The relations between Israel and the Arab States have six major aspects, all of which should figure on the agenda of direct peace negotiations. In presenting this outline I am, of course, not suggesting that the General Assembly should burden itself with a direct discussion of these detailed provisions. My Government has merely deemed it fitting that this Committee, seized of a proposal for a directly negotiated settlement, should see for itself the broad vistas of common interest which the adoption of that Resolution would open out for the parties. I should like to summarize these questions under the following headings:

1. Security Questions.
2. Territorial Questions.
3. Refugee Questions.
4. Economic Questions.
5. Regional Co-operation.
   (*a*) Communications.
   (*b*) Social and Health Questions.
   (*c*) Scientific and Cultural Questions.

A Blueprint for Peace

(d) Technical Assistance Co-operation.
6. Questions of Diplomatic and Juridical Relations.

1. SECURITY QUESTIONS

The starting point of this discussion is the system of armistice agreements which were concluded between Israel and the Arab States in 1949, and which have governed our relations ever since.

The states of the Near East owe to these armistice agreements whatever peace and stability they have been able to enjoy in the past four years. The armistice agreements have proved their capacity to solve, within their own framework, all disputes, including some resulting in armed action, which have arisen from time to time. Where such solutions could not be secured in the first instance by the parties themselves, they have been reached by appeal to the Security Council, acting under its duty to deal with situations likely to cause a breach of international peace. In all cases except one, the directives of the Security Council have been successfully fulfilled. The one exception relates to the Security Council's injunction of 1st September 1951 for the cessation by Egypt of all acts of belligerency and blockade. Here, too, of course, my Government retains the right to redress the matter by further appeal to the Security Council, should it so decide, or by any other legitimate means.

Now, the armistice agreements, while preferable to whatever preceded them and irreplaceable except by a peace settlement, do not constitute a satisfactory basis for the relations between Israel and the Arab States in the realm of security. They leave the military forces of both states in close and vigilant scrutiny of the frontiers. They require security provisions of a sternness and caution which would not be necessary if frontier disputes could be settled at a diplomatic level, through the normal civil network of controls, with the frontier and customs officers of both parties working together every day. The unsatisfactory nature of the position is reflected in a series of incidents involving frequent loss of life, and many dangerous tensions, especially on the long and intricate frontier between Israel and territory of the Kingdom of Jordan.

There are other features of an armistice position which distinguish it from a normal, peaceful relationship. There is a necessity, after our experience of sudden invasion four years ago and in the light of continued infiltrations, to receive more binding guarantees against agression than those contained in the agreements. I would recall that the armistice agreements were meant to be succeeded after a short time by peace settlements. They are described in their own texts as transitions between armistice and permanent peace. Their maintenance for so long a period puts them under strain. It is therefore appropriate that the peace settlement which succeeds them should contain strong affirmations of non-aggression. Moreover, there is no doubt that the governments of the Near East in the present situation are maintaining heavier military budgets than they would in other circumstances. Thus, there is a permanent danger of an arms race, and excessive sums are being diverted to security in its narrower sense at the expense of economic and social progress.

Moreover, while each state tries to be strong in its relation to the other, the Middle East as a whole remains vulnerable in the contingency of wider international conflict; and no steps are possible which would enable the region to consult and concert all its action to strengthen peace in the Middle East as a whole, and to contribute to international security.

It is, therefore, my Government's belief that a peace negotiation should contain four elements under the security heading:

First, the peace settlement should include a non-aggression clause. I wish to emphasize that in our view a non-aggression undertaking should be an element of a total peace settlement and not a substitute for it. We have heard assertions that the Arab states on their part profess a fear of Israel expansion. Here I would give assurance that these fears are quite unfounded. Moreover, a country which has a genuine fear of its neighbour's expansion should welcome a peace treaty embodying non-aggression guarantees and treaty obligations recognizing the territorial integrity of each state. It is surely inadmissible to assert a fear of aggression and, at the same time, to refuse the exchange of non-aggression guarantees within a total peace settlement.

Second, such a settlement would enable a reasonable limitation of military budgets and the avoidance of competitive rearmament. At present we face both the dangers of an arms race and heavy financial burdens at the expense of economic progress and financial stability. If a peace settlement of the kind we are now discussing were achieved, the question of arms supplies to the area could be examined by both parties in relation to the defence needs of the region as a whole, and with a proper regard for a balance between its security on the one hand, and its economic and financial interests on the other.

Third, the transition from armistice to a peace settlement would eliminate local outbreaks and violence along the frontiers through armed incursions and infiltrations. The peace negotiators should consider practical measures to that end.

Fourth, the settlement here envisaged would enable the states of the Near East to survey methods of regional co-operation for strengthening peace in the area, within the terms of the United Nations Charter.

In summarizing the value of these four security provisions under the first item of the proposed peace negotiations, I should like to point out that the advantage accruing from a settlement of these matters would be mutual and would not benefit one side alone. Both parties would feel the advantage of a tranquillity arising from non-aggression pacts within the framework of a peace settlement. Both parties would benefit from the elimination of factors which draw their governments into arms purchases beyond their capacities, at the expense of their social, economic and financial progress. Both parties would benefit from a new framework of relations which would eliminate the tensions, outbreaks and periodic explosions which now take place at the armistice frontier. And a co-operative effort to plan the defence of our area would enable all its peoples to contribute more effectively to the strengthening of international peace in the Middle East. Also, the United Nations would benefit by being relieved of a difficult and expensive responsibility in maintaining a large and cumbersome machinery of armistice supervision.

2. TERRITORIAL QUESTIONS

I have already recalled that the armistice treaties established, by mutual consent of the parties, provisional frontiers within which they have crystallized their national life throughout the past four years. These frontiers can only be changed by negotiation and agreement. The peace negotiation would enable the parties to exchange proposals on the manner in which the armistice frontiers might be mutually adjusted for a peace settlement. One of the problems to be considered would be the elimination of demilitarized zones, where division or obscurity of authority has caused great tensions at critical times. It would also enable adjustments to be made, by suitable exchanges, for reuniting certain villages with their lands and fields in cases where the armistice frontiers now separate them.

A Blueprint for Peace

This position in favour of adjusting frontiers by mutual consent has been accepted by the parties in the armistice treaties themselves. I would point out that the tradition of the United Nations has always insisted that frontier adjustments, above all other matters, lie in the exclusive responsibility of the governments concerned, provided only that they are sanctioned by joint agreement and do not rest on unilateral force. Agreed territorial adjustments in development of the armistice treaties would give a sense of stability and contribute to the pacification of the region, and especially the border areas.

3. REFUGEE QUESTIONS

The views of my government on the refugee question were outlined fully by myself in the discussion of our first agenda item. I would state again that this tragic suffering is the legacy of the war against Israel and, therefore, the responsibility of those who initiated that war. This consideration in no way affects the anxiety and concern with which the Government and people of Israel have observed the languishing of these unhappy victims in refugee camps, without any integration into the lives of communities in which they would feel materially, spiritually and culturally at home.

My government supported the Resolution which was adopted by the General Assembly earlier this month with reference to the United Nations Works and Relief Projects. We do not doubt that if that programme is carried out with the sincere co-operation of all the governments concerned, a humane and just solution of the refugee problem will be facilitated. Israel, which has exceeded the efforts and sacrifices of any state in history on behalf of refugees coming to it from outside, regards this problem as of deep and urgent humanitarian concern. The peace negotiation should discuss the question of international co-operation for the solution of the refugee question. Nothing could be more inspiring than for the two negotiating parties to make joint proposals to the United Nations for international assistance in a solution of this problem, which both the Arab States and Israel have defined as international in its scope.

My government has seized every opportunity, even within the present political tension, of responding to requests made to it by international organs on behalf of refugees. We were approached last year for assistance in three matters affecting the welfare of refugees, two of them entailing, and the other portending, heavy burdens on

A Blueprint for Peace

our economy, which is already strained to the utmost degree. The Conciliation Commission invited our agreement to the release of blocked accounts held by Arab refugees in Israel banks. It is not usual for governments to arrange the flow of foreign currency into countries which are doing everything possible to strangle their economy by boycott, and which sometimes even claim the existence of a state of war with them. However, we did take this unusual step, because we saw the plight of the refugees first, and the political attitude of the Arab governments second. I renew my expression of appreciation for the words of gratitude which the Palestine Conciliation Commission has expressed in response to this illustration of Israel's goodwill.

Moreover, at the request of the United Nations Relief and Works Agency, my government agreed this year to take over full responsibility for the integration into Israel of 19,000 Arab refugees. The same humanitarian consideration guided my government in facilitating the uniting of families under an agreed programme, thus enabling the passage of thousands of refugees across the lines, notwithstanding the continued existence of a condition far short of peace.

The latest Progress Report of the Conciliation Commission describes my government's co-operation in making available the records on which a study of the compensation question may be pursued. One of the chief factors which affect Israel's capacity of payment is the boycott and blockade imposed by Arab States. Thus, the negotiation of this peace settlement, by removing those abnormal conditions, would have a direct bearing on the degree and rate of progress in payment of compensation. In the meantime, however, we shall co-operate with appropriate United Nations organs in making plans and detailed arrangements for that contingency.

In summarizing this question, I would observe that the refugee problem arose from war and has been perpetuated by the failure to institute relationships in which it could be solved by co-operative regional effort, with international aid. The peace negotiations which I am now outlining would enable representatives of Israel and of Arab States to exchange their views on this subject, in a spirit of sincere concern for the plight of these victims. The benefits which would flow from such a settlement would release the Arab states as well as Israel from the tensions and frustrations which this problem has brought to both.

A Blueprint for Peace

It is no less important for Israel and the Arab states to restore their economic relationships than it is for them to achieve political co-operation. The Middle East as a region suffers from the fact that its economic progress has not kept pace with its rate of political advance. This contrast between political progress and economic inertia is responsible for many of the dissatisfactions which afflict our area, and which have weakened democratic institutions within it almost to the point of disappearance outside Israel. It would be fruitful to have Arab and Israel representatives in the negotiation of a peace settlement allow their minds to range over economic problems relevant to all Near Eastern countries and related to the region as a whole; to its political stability as well as to its prosperity.

I should like to suggest five examples, to be considered by the negotiators, of the manner in which co-operation between peaceful states could enhance the economic welfare of the Middle East. *First,* of course, comes the replacement of the present boycott and blockade by normal economic relations. It is, perhaps, not sufficiently realized that the benefits of such a step would be felt no less by the Arab than by the Israel economies. Some Arab states, notably Jordan and Lebanon, suffer considerably from the boycott, as their own press is beginning eloquently to reveal. Israel, especially with its recent growth of population and its industrial development, offers a market for Arab products many of which do not find an easy outlet farther from home. I refer especially to the perishable agricultural products of Syria, Jordan and Lebanon, the meat of Iraq, the cotton of Egypt. So far I have referred to Israel as a market for exports from Arab countries. But in addition, there is no doubt that our own manufacture could yield a varied range of products to be available to Arab countries from close at hand. The end of the boycott and restoration of trade would thus be a mutual and not a unilateral benefit.

Second, the industrial revolution in Israel is accompanied by similar processes in Arab states. It is clear that Near Eastern countries, especially those with dense populations, can only achieve a reasonable level of prosperity by supplementing their agricultural production by industrial growth. Industrial progress in each country could be facilitated if there were processes of co-operation in the development of markets, in order to assure best results for the area as a whole.

A Blueprint for Peace

Third, there are projects for exploiting raw materials that could be greatly improved by inter-state co-operation. The Dead Sea, a great source of mineral wealth, extends over Israel and Jordan territory. The electrical power scheme in the north was originally envisaged as an inter-state project, and could again so become. Successful measures which have been taken by Israel to develop its phosphate and other mineral resources in the Central Negev have advantages to offer both as regards geological data and mining methods, which would be available for similar developments in neighbouring countries, into which those mineral resources extend. Such success as Israel has managed to achieve by its own efforts is merely an augury of the far wider benefits which all countries of the area could derive from co-operative efforts in the exploitation of raw materials.

Fourth, the water problem is the key to our region's economic destiny. In its totality the Middle East possesses enough water to enable a vast increase of population, of power and of industrial and agricultural activity. But the international frontiers do not correspond with any rational distribution of these water resources. In peace negotiations, serious consideration could be given to regional irrigation schemes, which are only possible by inter-state arrangements, and without which no rational utilization of rivers is possible. Israel, Syria, Jordan and Lebanon could all derive great benefits from such co-operation.

Fifth, an economic problem common to the whole region is the age-old encroachment of the desert upon the cultivated area. Modern science has taught us not to regard any desert as permanent. Not only can the advance of the desert be stopped; its present domination can be turned back and reduced—by afforestation, by conservation methods, and by irrigation. The necessity to create extensive economic opportunities in a small area has caused Israel to develop its research and activity in this field to a significant degree. There would be great advantage in the exchange of knowledge and co-operation between all governments in the area, facing as they do the problem of turning sandy wastes occupying great stretches of their national territory into flourishing gardens.

In the last months of his life, President Weizmann reached the conclusion that this was the most fruitful field in which the resources of science could be applied to the economic progress and, therefore, the political stability of our region. From his initiative there arose the plan for the Conquest of the Desert Exhibition, which will take place in Jerusalem in the summer of 1953. Many governments, especially those which have had the experience of conquering the desert in the American, European and Asian continents, and in North Africa, will be represented at an interchange of views and experiences, leading, we hope, to practical co-operation. 'As a prelude to this occasion, and also at Dr. Weizmann's initiative, there was held in Jerusalem in May 1952, under the auspices of the United Nations Educational, Scientific and Cultural Organization, a symposium of eminent scientists from all over the world to consider the problem of cultivating and settling arid zones. Owing to the present state of political relations, this discussion, so relevant to the central problem of improving living standards in the area, was not attended by a single Arab representative. Can anybody make sense out of a system of relationships which prevents us from freely exchanging our efforts and experiences in the battle against poverty and disease—these common enemies of our region as a whole?

5. REGIONAL CO-OPERATION

I should like to consider under four headings the manner in which regional co-operation could benefit all countries in the area, beyond the field of direct economic development, which I have just discussed.

(a) *Communications*

The absence of normal relations between the Arab states and Israel creates no greater anomaly than the complete non-existence of any direct communication by land, sea and air amongst the countries of the area. In the dawn of its history, at a time when communications were halting and primitive, the Middle East was a region of active inter-communication which accounted for much of its material and cultural primacy.

Today, the life of our region suffers in every sphere through a break ·in the chain of communication; and the peace negotiation should give urgent thought to ways of overcoming this unnatural heritage of the war. If you imagine railway communications running from Haifa to Beirut, Damascus and Istanbul in the north, to Amman and beyond in the east and traffic resumed on the Haifa-Cairo line, you can see at once that the trade and commerce of the area, as well as its cultural interchange, would be strengthened beyond measure. Similarly,

A Blueprint for Peace

esumption and expansion of road communications between Cairo, Jerusalem and Beirut, and between Haifa and Baghdad would stimulate the life and the commerce of the Middle East above any level so far attained.

In the context of a peace settlement there would be no justification for portraying the southern part of Israel as though it were some kind of a 'wedge' between various parts of the Arab world. Our very wedge-like position should compel the region to seek a more complete system of integration and to aspire to a permanent security in an all-round peace settlement. Indeed, within the context of the settlement which I am here presenting, Israel would regard itself as a bridge, and not as a wedge. There are many ways, without prejudice to the territorial sovereignty of any state, in which expression could be given to that concept in the sphere of inter-state communications.

It would also be fruitful for the peace negotiation to give thought to maritime communication, including the use of ports. The armistice system requires a suspension of blockade practices. But a peace settlement can carry maritime co-operation into more positive spheres than the mere agreement to leave each other's shipping alone. As a result of the present boycott policy, some Arab states inflict great damage upon themselves by their own exclusion from access to the coast. This is especially true of the Kingdom of Jordan which is completely land-locked as regards the Mediterranean, and is therefore dependent upon intricate and artificially long communications through other ports. In a peace negotiation my government would again give consideration to the provision of free port facilities at Haifa, thus creating a direct commercial link between the Mediterranean and the hinterland of the Fertile Crescent.

On the Red Sea coast, appropriate arrangements of inter-communication could take place between the Israel port development at Elath and those ports in the Gulf of Aqaba which lie in the territory of Egypt and Jordan.

The freedom of the region from the present blockade would have reassuring effects on the maritime world in general, and produce lower insurance rates for shipping proceeding to all Middle Eastern ports.

Air development could be a great source of wealth for the Middle East with its advantageous position astride three continents. The airlines of very many great aviation countries, of the United States, Great Britain and France, of the Netherlands, Switzerland,

96

Italy, the Scandinavian countries and the Philippines, as well as the
Israel National Airline, pass in and out of the airport of Lydda, as
they do to Cairo and Beirut by separate and parallel channels.
Egyptian and Israel airlines would have much advantage from normal facilities.

The discussion on communications could also deal with the institution of radio, telephone and postal connections in a continuous network throughout the countries of the Near East. At this time, the
artificial attempt to circumvent Israel imposes, we understand, upon
the Arab states long and circuitous routes to the increase of cost,
and the reduction of efficiency.

The tourist traffic between Israel, Egypt and Lebanon, which was
once a productive source of income for all countries, could again be
reopened, while the area as a whole with its historic monuments and
scenic beauty would attract greater numbers of tourists from outside
if the present dislocations and difficulties were eliminated in all the
spheres of inter-communication.

I would summarize this item by saying that the peace settlement
would, in the sphere of communications, re-establish the continuity
of our area, produce an atmosphere of integration and harmony, and
eliminate what is both a cause and an acute symptom of the present
regional conflict.

(b) *Social and Health Questions*

The Committee will be aware that one of the chief handicaps of
the Middle East in all its enterprises is its low standard of public
health and a lack of progress in social organization. In some of these
spheres, there is room for exchange of information and experience; in
others we envisage practical co-operation to be worked out in the
peace negotiations. Surely, the battle against malaria in the Huleh
area, the Jordan Valley and elsewhere, against agricultural pests and
traffic in narcotics are matters of mutual concern in which the absence
of regional co-operation is a prejudice to the general human welfare.
The medical centres in Israel and in the Arab countries have accumulated a great store of knowledge on those health problems which arise
from the special conditions of our region, its climate, its soil and its
endemic diseases. The medical traditions of each people are long and
distinguished. But the average health standards in Middle Eastern
populations are not yet sufficient to enable the area to succeed in the

G   97

A Blueprint for Peace

defence of its security, still less in its tasks of social, economic and intellectual revival.

But the health problem is only one of many which speak in favour of a regional approach to questions of social welfare. One of the acute problems in the Middle East is that of agrarian reform. We have observed with sympathy the recent efforts of the governments of Egypt and Syria to correct this long-standing disability. Israel, on her side, has experimented actively in this field, in the search of new forms of co-operative and smallholder settlements, and in the application of legislative and social restraints against the accumulation of large estates and against the creation of an agricultural proletariat without property or leasehold rights.

A new research project now being carried out under the United Nations Technical Assistance Programme for the provision of suitable rural housing out of a mechanical processing of soil is now in full progress. If successful, it will prove the possibility of providing rural housing without the import of expensive building materials at the cost of foreign currency.

Labour organization is another field in which the countries of the Middle East could, with benefit, beginning from the peace negotiation, exchange their experience and create procedures of co-operation. To sum up this item, I would say that the development of society in our countries, which are all at an early stage of their political growth, could profit by the institution of co-operative procedures in social organization.

(c) *Scientific and Cultural Questions*

There have been periods in history when the interaction of the Hebrew and Moslem minds has produced a flowering of cultural and scientific effort. Anyone who contemplates the common elements in the Hebrew and Arabic cultures will see their profound depth and high elevation, when they achieve their best expressions. Israel's culture nourished the great streams of Christianity and Islam, whilst keeping its own native stream perennially strong. Each culture is now faced by the problem of adapting its ancient language to the expanding needs of modern affairs.

The interchange by governmental agreement of students and of university personnel would have great effect in reminding both peoples of the common elements in their own traditions, thus removing, perhaps more than anything else, the unnatural estrangement

98

A Blueprint for Peace

which has come over our relationship in recent decades. There is no doubt that a reconciliation between Israel and the independent Arab states would be reflected in wider spiritual fraternity in Jewish-Moslem relations everywhere else in the world.

The problems which are the subject of research and investigation at the Weizmann Institute of Science and the Hebrew University of Jerusalem are of relevance to the area as a whole. The representatives of each party should exchange ideas on pooling and co-ordinating research.

(d) *Technical Assistance Co-operation*

The efforts of the United Nations and all friendly governments to assist our region in many aspects of its life have been frustrated by the character of our political relations. The peace negotiations should rapidly reach agreements releasing the area from this deprivation. It has been impossible to hold a regional Committee Meeting of the World Health Organization since 1950. The International Labour Office Employment Seminar to be held in Teheran had to be cancelled in November 1951. Where we do not have cancellation, we have expensive and wasteful duplication. Thus, such enterprises as the Seminars on Evaluation of Economic Development Programmes were held jointly by the Food and Agricultural Organization and the World Bank in Turkey in 1951 for non-Arabs, and in Beirut in 1952 for Arabs. The International Civil Aviation Organization has actually had to set up an Air Traffic Co-ordination Centre in Cyprus at a high cost, both for maintenance and installation, and with impaired efficiency because Beirut refuses to communicate weather reports or give flight information to aircraft bound to and from Israel airports. Are there no human solidarities which prevail over political rancours? Do not the unlimited expanses of sea and air appeal to anything common in our human personality?

Important technical assistance programmes are at work in the Near East, both under the auspices of the United Nations and of the United States. All the countries in the region suffer from the absence of technical assistance co-operation in the fields of regional water development, public health, social organization, agricultural experimentation and meteorological research. Israel would welcome full participation by the neighbouring states in the United Nations Technical Assistance projects now being carried out in Israel, such as the pilot plant for adobe housing, and the F.A.O. Soil Conservation

99

A Blueprint for Peace

School. We, on our part, would welcome participation in the United Nations Statistical Centre at Beirut, and the UNESCO Fundamental Education Centre in Cairo.

The considerations which I have outlined apply to similar regional problems, such as locust control. All of these measures could be carried forward with permanent advantage by the establishment, so far prevented by Arab reluctance, of the United Nations Regional Economic Commission, which could duplicate and, I hope, even exceed the successes of similar economic regional commissions which operate for Europe, Africa and Latin America. My Government is prepared to support the establishment of this Commission and to co-operate in its work.

These are merely illustrations of the wide variety of co-operative efforts on which the negotiators could build a strong foundation for regional prosperity.

6. DIPLOMATIC AND JURIDICAL RELATIONS

This final item in the proposed pattern of new relations is the framework for all the others. The establishment of normal relations, in all the fields which I have outlined, should be given formal effect in diplomatic instruments. There should be a declaration abandoning the unilateral theory of a state of war; for a people at war with another can make no claims on that state's consideration in any matter whatsoever. Treaties of peace should replace the armistice agreements. The boycott and blockade should be succeeded by trade treaties and transit agreements. Treaties of commerce, navigation, and friendship should replace the ostracism and silence which mark our relationship today. Air agreements, visa agreements and the conventions which normally exist between sovereign states at peace with each other should be negotiated. The peaceful relations to be thus established would have their reflection in the work of this Organization, upon which the boycotts and enmities of the Arab-Israel war have cast a persistent shadow. Liberated from the burden of this ceaseless and sterile controversy, freed from this contemplation of old resolutions and old conflicts, our delegations could make a much more purposeful and co-operative contribution to the common effort of the United Nations in defence of universal peace and progress.

Such is the general outline of a peace negotiation: security guaran-

tees and co-operation; agreed territorial adjustments; joint consideration of the refugee question with immediate preparatory work on
compensation; economic co-operation, including joint water projects and development schemes; regional co-operation, including the
opening of access to ports and renewal of direct inter-communication
between all parts of the Arab world; formulation of peace treaties and
trade pacts.

It should not be said that there is anything utopian or visionary in
the prospects which I have described here. This is the Israel view of
a possible agenda for a direct peace negotiation between Israel and
the neighbouring Arab states. We should wish to meet with each Arab
state, as we met with each Arab state to conclude armistice agreements, in order to discuss the application in each relationship of
the principles which I have described. It should be understood that
any negotiations between two states should not encroach upon
the interests of any third state, or upon those of the international
community in the Holy Land.

For those who consider that this is a prospect beyond realization,
I would point out that but a few years ago there existed, in simpler and
less ambitious forms, a process of interchange between the Jewish
people in Palestine and the neighbouring countries. The countries
around us derived full benefit from our work when it was on a much
smaller scale. Our immigrant population, which began to be fully
productive only after a time-lag, provided a steady and growing
market for their agricultural produce and industrial raw materials.
Palestine headed the list of export markets of all the neighbouring
countries. Interest was evinced all around in our scientific achievements and social innovations. Experts of the Hebrew University of
Jerusalem went to Iraq by invitation to draw up plans of afforestation
and combating locusts and to organize an entomological service.
Emissaries from Iraq were amongst us to investigate commercial
organization and rural education. Syria sent missions to study
workers' housing. Lebanon despatched agricultural officials to study
methods of botanic research.

Governmental missions from Egypt carried out comprehensive
studies of agricultural co-operation and experimentation in Jewish
Palestine. From all Middle Eastern countries patients flocked to
Jerusalem for medical treatment, and Jerusalem doctors were called
to neighbouring capitals for consultations and operations. On the

A Blueprint for Peace

other side of the picture, our own experts and emissaries travelled in the Arab countries to observe and to learn.

To-day, with the great dynamism of newly won independence and swift industrial progress, we could achieve together, each in co-operation with others, a development of the area, with its vast human and material resources, on a scale and spirit commensurate with the renaissance which came upon the American continent when its communications were opened up a century ago. This is the prospect which the United Nations would inaugurate if it would recommend to Israel and the Arab states that they enter into direct, free and un-fettered negotiations for the establishment of peaceful and neigh-bourly relations. The blueprint of peace which I have here outlined is different in many respects, sometimes fundamentally different, from that envisaged in past resolutions. If it does not conform with our past conception, it does, I think, accord with United Nations objectives and the requirements of our common future. The General Assembly and all governments, especially Arab governments, will, we hope, give their most mature, serious and deliberate consideration to this plan.

The governments of Canada, Cuba, Denmark, Ecuador, Nether-lands, Norway, Panama and Uruguay which have sponsored this resolution for a directly negotiated settlement have given us the most solemn moment in the development of our relations since Israel's statehood was established. If we seize it, we may assemble next year and be able to echo the words which the Pilgrim Fathers of the American continent observed with thankfulness, after enduring the rigours of their first arduous months. We shall say, as they said: 'We have made a clearing in the wilderness; and another year will see a larger clearing, a better garnering. We have made a beginning in a hostile world.'

When these proposals are translated into reality, the prestige of the United Nations will be forever enhanced by the fact that it sought the establishment of peace in the proud and venerable region where the arts of civilization were born, and whence the call for universal brotherhood came down across the ages to successive generations of mankind.

CHAPTER X

Atomic Challenge*

No one who takes part in this debate can fail to be awed by its potential influence on the destiny of mankind. When President Eisenhower brought his momentous message to the General Assembly on 8th December 1953, he engaged us in an issue far beyond the scope of the political disputes on which this Committee has deliberated throughout these past eight years. He challenged the false equation which has grown up in men's minds between nuclear physics and human disaster. Like all previous advances in natural discovery, but more than any of them, the liberation of atomic energy can be the herald of a more abundant age. For there is nothing inherently evil in atomic power. Whether this new energy becomes a source of destruction or of expanding welfare lies fully within the realm of human decision; and the direction in which the balance falls will depend on our success or failure in the adjustment of international relations. Never has diplomacy been able to influence such broad issues of opportunity or danger. Never have the alternatives of disaster and salvation confronted the human race in such acute and poignant contrast.

The representatives of small nations approach this issue from a special point of vantage. In discussions of atomic war, we possess no equality with more powerful countries, nor do we envy them their awesome preponderance with its consequent burdens of responsibility. At most we are among the passive objects of such debates, conscious that international discord and atomic power together make an equation full of menace for humanity.

But our position is transformed, our stature increased, when we come to discuss the application of this energy to peaceful ends. Here we stand on more equal ground. Wherever the human mind can actively probe the mysteries of this force, there is a chance of some new insight into its nature, some original contribution to its range of potential use. All nations which develop a sound scientific tradition

* To the General Assembly of the United Nations, 15 November 1954.

may have a constructive purpose to fulfil in an age of atomic peace. Similarly, all countries, small as well as great, can be the beneficiaries of the new inheritance which science has bequeathed to our universal opportunity.

The peaceful use of nuclear energy opens out especially exciting vistas for countries which are deficient in the conventional sources of power, such as coal, oil or falling water. Indeed, the discrimination which nature has established between the 'rich' and 'poor' countries by the unequal distribution of these resources may be eliminated, with far-reaching social and international results, by the general availability of this uncannily compact, transportable and potent fuel. It has been estimated that a cube of uranium, 1 in. by 1 in. by 1 in., contains as much latent energy as 2,600,000 pounds of coal. In such a world, well-trained scientific minds and disciplined hands may become the only indispensable condition for establishing the highest standards of welfare to which any society can reasonably aspire.

Previous speakers have done well to caution us against any impression of imminent change in the current realities of natural power. On the other hand, we should not be excessively restrictive in our expectations. Estimates of the period within which nuclear power may replace other fuels without exorbitant difficulty or cost have varied within a range of five to fifteen years. Even if the more conservative anticipation is accepted, it is clear that this prospect already belongs to any realistic planning of our economies and societies.

Thus, the initiative of the United States is timely, as well as being constructive and profoundly humane. One of its most valuable features is the decision to submit the problem to discussion and action through the United Nations. This shows a sensitive regard for the attributes of this Organization. Atomic power confronts mankind with opportunities and dangers of universal scope. The United Nations alone in the modern world holds the promise of controlling such forces for the universal interest. Out of successful co-operation in the peaceful use of atomic power there may well emerge processes of supranational thought and action which may assist the evolution of the United Nations towards a broader universalism in other questions, including the problem of atomic weapons. Nor does the United Nations enter this field without a previous background of specialized interest; the reports of the Atomic Energy Commission and the bibliographies compiled by the Secretariat are already a valuable part of the basic literature in this field.

104

Atomic Challenge

Before giving my delegation's views on the specific proposals embodied in the joint draft resolution, it may be useful if, like other representatives who have spoken before me, I were to outline the specific points of my country's concern with the problem. Israel is both a contributor to the universal sum of theoretical and applied nuclear knowledge, and also a prospective beneficiary of the new potentialities.

There has been a double incentive for Israel's special concern with nuclear studies. First, the number of physicists and chemists in our country engaged in theoretical and applied research is, in relative terms, probably as high as in any other country of the world. Secondly, sheer necessity, the greatest of all spurs to initiative, has impelled us to devote our deepest interest to the quest for new sources of power. We face heavy tasks of economic and social progress with a notable lack of any cheap source of fuel or electric power. For this very reason, the time when the use of atomic energy will be economically viable in comparison with existing sources of power may come sooner for Israel than for countries more lavishly endowed with electric power from conventional fuels. We have noted, as Mr. Lodge has pointed out, that atomic reactors point the way to an age when all countries can be sure of an abundance of electric power even when natural fuels are scarce. But we also know that these promising horizons will only be attained by communities well versed in nuclear studies and standing high in general scientific training.

These two factors, scientific interest and practical need, both existing in unusually intense degree, have determined Israel's preoccupation with this problem from the earliest days of the atomic decade. Our first President, Dr. Chaim Weizmann, was concerned both as a scientist and as the architect of a nation, with the problem of compensating for natural deficiencies by the results of advanced scientific research. This theme guided much of his chemical work in the field of synthetic processes, where he sought means of creating substitutes for deficient raw materials. It was equally natural that his interest should be aroused by the prospect of finding substitutes for natural power. Together, these two prospects—new materials and new power—appealed to his scientific imagination, as well as to his vision of a broader welfare for Israel and other small countries than their existing conventional resources seemed to promise. Thus, from the concluding days of the Second World War to the end of his life he was in contact with leading figures in the world of nuclear physics,

105

Atomic Challenge

many of whom shared both his scientific interests and his over-riding concern for the successful establishment of a Jewish homeland. With them, including the great Einstein, we have maintained the closest bonds of kinship which have exerted a formative influence on our scientific tradition. We could say of Israel, as Mr. Jules Moch so eloquently said of America, that we have been 'a sanctuary for scholars and scientists exiled by dictatorships because of their opinions or their faith'.

It thus happened and perhaps it is not surprising that within a year of Israel's establishment, with President Weizmann at the head of our State, the foundations of our nuclear programme were laid with the establishment of the Department of Isotope Research in the Weizmann Institute of Science at Rehovoth in the coastal plain. This department has worked assiduously and successfully for five years in the following fields, both theoretical and applied:

1. Radioactive isotopes of low activity;
2. The enrichment of heavy water by fractional distillation, and other related projects;
3. Cosmic rays;
4. The exploitation of low-grade uranium ores such as phosphates;
5. The study of the mechanism of chemical reactions by means of isotopic tracing;
6. Natural radioactivity. The determination of the sources and average age of underground water by measuring the tritium concentration;
7. The prospecting of possible underground deposits of radioactive solid materials. This work is conducted mainly in the Institute of Technology in Haifa.

This list covers a varied field. The second item which I have enumerated in the work of the Weizmann Institute has led to the construction of a pilot plant already producing heavy water. The method of production, originated by Dr. Israel Dostrovsky in Rehovoth, has been adopted and applied in Europe. The representative of France, whose brilliant address has illuminated this discussion, referred to a process which associates 'an Israeli invention with French technology'. This is a partnership between a young state barely seven years old and the great European country which became the pioneer in the field of radioactivity, through the discovery of polonium and radium fifty-six years ago. It illustrates the significant fact that co-operation in this highly specialized field should be conceived functionally rather than regionally. Geographical proximity is less important than community of scientific interest or qualification.

The fourth item, the exploitation of low-grade uranium ores such as phosphates, is significant for my country owing to the presence of large phosphate deposits in Israel.

I will confess that the progress achieved by the Weizmann Institute in this brief period is a source of stimulation to our scientific community. Indeed, the nuclear science is itself so young that this is one of the few fields in which Israel does not feel any disadvantage in the brevity of its years. Encouraged by the results of the work achieved in the Department of Isotopes, the Weizmann Institute is now about to cover a wider field through the establishment of the Department of Nuclear Research.

I now turn from Rehovoth to Jerusalem where research falling within the purview of this discussion is being carried on in the Hebrew University's Physics Department and in the Hadassah-Hebrew University Medical Centre.

The Physics Department of the Hebrew University has worked and is still working in four fields:

1. The structure of molecules (nuclear spectroscopy);
2. Micro-wave research;
3. Energy radiation;
4. Semi-conductors.

The first subject, now being investigated by Professor Racah, could be a far-reaching contribution in a fundamental field.

Meanwhile the results of tracer research have become used in some of Israel's leading medical institutions. In the Hadassah-Hebrew University Medical Centre isotopes have been applied for diagnosis and treatment in blood diseases, in cancer and in thyroid conditions.

In discussing our experience and aspiration in nuclear physics, I should mention the establishment of the Israel Atomic Energy Commission in 1953 with wide powers to supervise, co-ordinate and encourage the work which I have described in Jerusalem, Rehovoth and Haifa.

The record of achievement and of effort which I have outlined is,

Atomic Challenge

of course, modest in comparison with the impressive surveys which we have heard from the representatives of the United States, the United Kingdom, Canada, France and the Soviet Union. It is, however, interesting in relative terms and it is certainly sufficient to explain why my Government has a specific as well as a general interest in each of the four proposals which were outlined by Secretary Dulles in plenary session on September 23rd, and later analysed more fully in this Committee by Mr. Lodge and other representatives of the seven-power group. I now come to offer comments on each of the proposals in turn.

My delegation applauds the decision of the sponsoring Powers to establish an international organization for the peaceful use of atomic power without delay. This organization should be conceived in terms of universal membership. Indeed, it is unlikely that any country with a specific stake in this problem will wish to be excluded. We hope that the discussions now proceeding will result in the full association of the Soviet Union in every part of the project, an aim to which the United States has clearly devoted much effort in its diplomatic relations.

Great importance lies, of course, in the responsibility of the new organization or agency for fostering the interchange of information and diffusing the results of research. At the same time it appears to us that research is, after all, only the very first stage in the application of atomic power to peaceful uses. By far the most important objective is the actual generation of power through the establishment of reactors and the distribution of fissile material. My delegation therefore sympathizes with General Romulo's thoughtful address in which he urged a role for the United Nations itself, beyond the limits of research and scientific interchange.

As problems of cost become progressively easier, many countries, including my own, will soon approach a moment when power derived from an atomic reactor will not be less economic than that produced by expensive imported fuels or even by large-scale hydraulic projects. Accordingly, there is great value in the generous willingness of the United States Government to offer training in reactor engineering even before the establishment of an atomic organization.

In considering the time factor, we should again do well to take note of the cautionary words spoken by the sponsoring Powers against expecting the new organization or agency to fulfil all its potentialities from the first day of its creation. It should not be expected that atomic reactors will spring up all over the world irrespective of high costs, limited availability of trained operators, and the existence of unresolved safety problems. In some countries these obstacles will be overcome earlier than in others; but in any case an international agency would have an impressively varied programme from its earliest days.

In deliberating on the immediate practical tasks of the organization or agency, my delegation, in consultation with some of our scientists, has formulated certain special objectives which may be of interest to this Committee, or at a subsequent stage in the fulfilment of this project.

Another subject worthy of early investigation would be that mentioned by the representative of Sweden, who suggested, on the authority of an American expert, that it might be technically possible to 'denature' dangerous materials so that their military utilization would be rendered impossible, thus enabling an international agency to distribute fissile materials without risk of improper diversion.

Countries afflicted with deserts and plagued by centuries of erosion are deeply interested in processes for adapting brackish water and sea-water to irrigation purposes. The feasibility of this transformation has, I understand, been convincingly proved; but a prodigious burden of cost still makes the dream of conquering the world's deserts by these means remote from reality. This may well be one of the first practical problems which the international organization could try to solve, with incalculable benefits to countries in the Middle East and elsewhere in which a shortage of water for irrigation prevents the attainment of self-sufficiency in food production.

In discussing the use of nuclear energy as the power resource of countries where conventional power sources are scarce, Mr. Moch suggested that such areas might be assigned 'some sort of priority'. I should like to complete that thought by suggesting priority for such subjects of research and application as would solve some of the pressing problems of the under-developed areas.

I come now to the international scientific conference proposed for the summer of 1955. This conference will do much to expedite the

109

interchange of knowledge already acquired by research in many countries. We believe that this conference should be open to all states willing to take part, and hope that they will appoint those of their scientists who have the greatest experience in problems of nuclear energy.

Israel will certainly wish to enable its leading nuclear physicists to participate in this gathering. We have crystallized some detailed ideas for inclusion in the agenda, and we shall be glad to make them available when the matter is more specifically discussed.

It would be wise if the advisory committee established to assist the Secretary-General in convening the conference were to include not only the major atomic Powers, but also others more specifically aware of what smaller countries could hope to contribute and derive through their participation. The representative of Canada, on November 9th, indicated that the minds of himself and his colleagues were not closed on this matter, and I have a feeling that his suggested list could be usefully broadened by applying the criterion defined by our Swedish colleague at the same meeting.

The offer of the United States to give training courses at reactor schools is of the highest importance. Countries in which there is an intensified interest in atomic theory would certainly do well to have personnel trained in the operation and interpretation of the basic tools for the actual production of atomic power. Of great importance also are the facilities and forms of aid offered at this table by the representatives of the United Kingdom and Canada. In at least one field—the production of heavy water by the Israeli process already used in France—my country could already contribute to the training of selected specialists.

Similarly, the generous offer by the United States to share with foreign experts in the knowledge of atomic medicine, could have a great effect in making these processes more widely practised. Our own doctors have already been impressed by the versatile functions which tracers can fulfil in various fields of diagnosis and treatment, and there is much that we could all learn from the matchless facilities of American medical practice.

Accordingly, the Israel delegation approves the spirit and intent of the draft resolution, and will give careful and constructive consideration to its terms.

Atomic Challenge

This debate transports our minds into areas far removed from the morbid fears which have hovered over discussions held in this Committee in the context of atomic war. The deadlocks and suspicions which have prevented agreement on the control of atomic weapons should not be allowed to invade this domain of peaceful use. Here the primary theme is co-operation, not competition. Precisely because the discussions in the Disarmament Commission have so far produced such scanty agreement, my delegation hopes that our Soviet colleague will see the virtue of giving this new enterprise a separate chance of success, while work goes forward simultaneously in the Disarmament Commission looking towards an agreement for the control of atomic weapons. I fully agree with what the representative of Sweden has said in favour of such separation. May we not hope that in peaceful research and application, our governments and scientists will develop co-operative habits which will illuminate a path towards agreement in the control of atomic weapons, and thus lift a weight of anguish from the heart of suffering and apprehensive mankind.

No disputes of national interest, no conflicts or envies of political rivalry should stand between the United Nations and this opportunity to become the agent of a broader welfare for all peoples.

For good or ill, but in any case with complete irrevocability, atomic science has set us on a crossroads from which two paths branch forth—the one leading to immeasurable abundance, the other toward disaster beyond comprehension by heart or mind. May our deliberations be guided with wisdom and humanity, as we stand within the shadow of this fateful choice.

CHAPTER XI

An Adventure in the Human Spirit[*]

Four thousand years of history have extended their span between Israel's first nationhood and her restoration to freedom at the turning point of this century. The redemption from Egyptian bondage must be regarded in any serious view of history as one of the authentic points of climax in the progress of mankind. In the words of Henry George: 'From between the paws of the rock-hewn Sphinx rises the genius of human liberty; and the trumpets of the Exodus throb with the defiant proclamation of the rights of man.'

These forceful phrases do not overstate the case. The flight across the Red Sea and Sinai preserved a revolutionary idea, which could never have evolved in the idolatrous despotism of the Pharaohs. The idea was the sovereignty of God, the Ruler of the universe, omnipotent, one and indivisible, the embodiment of righteousness and the loving Father of all creation. From this idea there flowed acceptances and rejections which came to dominate life amongst the children of man. Recognizing this event as the beginning of our true destiny we, the descendants of those fleeing slaves, have, in all succeeding generations, commemorated the ancient saga. Our tradition, to this day, exhorts every Jew to recite the story of the Exodus from Egypt at the appointed season as though he personally had experienced this redemption from servitude to freedom.

The narrative of this rebellion against idolatry by men charged with the custody of an idea also occurs in the history of thought in a more secular aspect. The Exodus is the original and classic episode of national liberation. The memory of Israel's first struggle for freedom has inspired and consoled many subsequent movements for national independence. When Benjamin Franklin and Thomas Jefferson were consulted on the emblem of the future American Union they suggested that the Seal of the United States should represent the Children of Israel fleeing across the parted waters of the Red Sea on their way to freedom. This portrayal was to be surmounted by the

[*] At Notre Dame University, Indiana, 11 January 1955.

uncannily Hebraic slogan: 'Resistance to Tyrants is Obedience to God.'

It is not, I think, presumptuous to believe that future generations will keep the memories of Israel's modern revival with a similar reverence and tenacity. This will certainly come to pass in the particular domain of Jewish history. Nothing since the miraculous redemption four thousand years ago can compete in our history with this recent transition from martyrdom to sovereignty, this most sudden ascent from the depths of agony to new peaks of opportunity and pride. The attainment of Israel's independence seven years ago is already much more than a political or secular event in the Jewish consciousness. The date is bound to be numbered amidst the festivals of a people whose other temporal milestones have endured with rare constancy.

I have come to this abode of Christian faith and learning to suggest that Israel's resurgence is an event to be conceived in the highest dimensions of human history. It evokes from the past and may portend for the future a deep lesson on the nature of spiritual impulses. The attention which this event has already received in the thought and writing of our age is itself a proof of some special quality within it. It is evident, however, that if Israel's rebirth comes to have this eternal renown, it will not be because of any material dimensions which belong to it. There is nothing global, or even massive, about the State of Israel in political terms. The territory of our new independence is great in history, but pathetically meagre in geography. True, it is the bridge between the three continents of the ancient world. It looks out over the highway which has marked the migrations and invasions of history's pageant. But in the calculations of the atomic century this is a small and humble piece of earth. The bridge is fragile; the highway is narrow, and in the age of air transportation it no longer obtrudes itself inevitably athwart the paths of conquest and empire.

The population directly affected falls short of two million. Even when we portray this event in its real essence, as a collective climax in the history of the Jewish people, it still remains true that the conscious agents of Israel's revival are but a small fraction of the total human family. Clearly then, if modern Israel is to be regarded as an incident of universal scope, this is because of a stature to be ascribed to it in a completely different dimension. If modern Israel is to have any elements of greatness, then this quality must be vindicated in the spiritual realm.

To say this is not to deny that some of Israel's material achievements are impressive and sometimes deeply moving. The collective survival of the Jewish people is itself a rare event of history. Many other peoples have lost their independence under the heel of invading empires; but no people other than this, having been so engulfed, has shown such a capacity for recuperation as to preserve amidst martyrdom and dispersion all the elements of its union and identity—its language and tradition, its consciousness of attachment to the land of its origin, and the undying hope of eventual restoration. For long centuries this people, whithersoever it wandered, continued to regard its inner life as rooted in a distant land which few could ever hope to see with their own eyes. This connection, which for many generations was an act of mystic faith, became transformed, against all material calculations, into one of the political realities of our age. The banner of a free Israel now flies proudly again in the family of nations from which it had been absent for so many tragic generations.

There is surely something here to arrest the attention of those who study history in terms of national politics and international relations. Nor are these the only achievements which may be accounted remarkable in secular terms. There is the pioneering toil and sacrifice which have transformed the wilderness to a semblance of its ancient fertility. There is the epic of mass immigration which has brought hundreds of thousands of returning newcomers to our shores. There are great efforts, and at times serious results, in the increase of industrial and agricultural resources. There is the formation of a new culture, welding many varied immigrant traditions, tongues and experiences into the tapestry of a distinctive civilization, in the image of the ancient Hebrew past. There is the struggle against the ravages of pestilence and erosion which had debased the physical aspect of our land and degraded its historic reputation as 'the perfection of beauty, the joy of the entire earth'. There is the adventure of establishing within a region dominated by despotism and autocracy a sanctuary for the democratic way of life and the principles of free government. There are advances in literature, the sciences and arts which, without yet reaching the peaks of the ancient revelations, are yet significant and promising in relation to the circumstances of time and of space in which they have been accomplished. Nor can I omit from the positive

An Adventure in the Human Spirit

record of Israel's achievement the struggle for physical security by a small people besieged on all its embattled frontiers by an unyielding and comprehensive hostility. To have achieved so large a volume of international recognition within so brief a time and against such heavy challenge is also among the most notable of Israel's victories.

If despite all this, we concentrate our gaze upon the spiritual aspects of Israel's achievement and destiny, it is not because we renounce our claim to sympathetic appraisal in political, economic, social, and even military history. But when all is said and done there have been greater battles, more far-reaching economic upheavals, vaster irrigation projects, broader revelations of physical power than those which we have recorded, memorable as they are for us. Moreover, even these achievements by Israel, while being political, economic or social in their outward aspect, are primarily significant as illustrations of spiritual forces. They are testimony to the power of the human will. A few decades ago the prospect that an independent Jewish state could be established in its ancient homeland appeared so fantastic as to bring its advocates under suspicion of insanity. Statesmen and diplomats to whom the idea was broached in the early years of the First World War were startled at hearing so eccentric an idea even submitted to their official attention. A British ambassador in Paris to whom our first President, Dr. Chaim Weizmann, summarized this project in 1915 wrote in his diary that he had encountered a remarkable contradiction—a man of eminent scientific attainments with a keen power of rational analysis who, on this particular issue, appeared to have gone completely off his head. Back in London, Prime Minister Asquith expressed surprise that one of his cabinet colleagues of Jewish faith, normally a man of excessive rationalism, was afflicted with delirium on this special point.

Today, with the third Jewish commonwealth in tangible existence, it is the sceptics and the rationalists who appear incongruous to our eyes. Yet their scepticism seemed then to rest on strong foundations. After all, the Jewish people was dispersed and divided, split up into divergent fragments, lacking any element of political unity. The greater part of them dwelt thousands of miles away from the prospective scene of their national revival. The land itself appeared to have been sucked dry of all its vitality and to offer no prospect of resettlement. Moreover, it was neither empty nor available. It was controlled by strong nationalisms and imperialisms and coveted by others, all of which had a stronger chance of possession than had a

115

dispersed and politically anonymous people. The concept of a Jewish nationhood or indeed of any special link between the Jewish people and its original homeland was completely unrecognized in the jurisprudence of nations. It seemed unlikely that the Zionist programme could possibly overcome such hostilities and natural adversities.

Yet within a single lifetime we have passed from a world in which the existence of an independent Israel seemed inconceivable into a world which seems inconceivable without its existence.

I know of few more tangible testimonies in history to the power of the human will to assert itself against material odds. This is the primary value of Israel's rebirth to all those who are concerned with the vindication of faith against the fatalistic or deterministic theories of history, which see the human being not as the primary agent of historic processes but merely as their helpless subject matter. Thus, quite apart from its context in the annals of the Jewish people, the rebirth of modern Israel would earn its place in history as a crushing argument in the eternal discussion between the claims of faith, and the doctrines which deny the human will any central part in governing the world's destiny. Those materialistic doctrines would have an impossible task to perform to explain Israel's revival solely in material or economic terms.

Now this belief in the power of the human will is a recurrent theme in Israel's history. The most distinctive attribute of Israel's character, the source of some weakness but of greater strength, is this tenacious refusal to recognize the distinction between imagination and reality. In the grammar of classical Hebrew there is none of the sharp differentiation possessed by modern languages between that which is and that which shall be. This deliberate confusion between imagination and reality, between the will and the fact, has been illustrated at many stages of our history.

Now just as the establishment of Israel proves the power of the human spirit, so is this theme illustrated by many acts which have unfolded themselves within the general process. The most vivid example is to be found in our immigration movement. The dispersed Jewish communities from which this immigration came were divergent in all material things. Their social, economic, political and linguistic backgrounds had nothing in common. Unity existed only in the plane of spiritual allegiance. Here was a convincing experiment

116

for proving the relative strength of the material and spiritual forces. If material elements were really decisive then the influences of division and alienation would prevail. Spiritual unity here had not merely to exist but actually to overcome a great aggregate of divisive material forces. That it did so triumph and that hundreds of thousands responded by immigration to the call and the challenge of Israel's sovereignty proved that unity will prevail against divergence, provided that the unity is truly spiritual and the divergence is only material. The Ingathering of the Exiles in modern Israel also represents the most precise and tangible fulfilment of Prophecy available to all those in all Faiths who accept the literal truth of the biblical promises 'and I will bring them out from the peoples and gather them from the countries and will bring them again into their own land and I will feed them upon the mountains of Israel, by the streams and in all the inhabitable places of the country'.

Thus far I have spoken of Israel's establishment as a victory for spiritual forces. But we also owe attention to the particular lineage of Israel's spiritual history, which has now entered upon a new dispensation. This tradition, saved from extinction and endowed with a new birth of freedom, has played no ordinary role in the evolution of the human spirit. All that is authentic in modern theistic traditions can be traced back to the achievements and insights of Israel in the previous era of her independent national life. The consciousness that the Hebrew mind had had such a strong impact on human thought caused millions throughout the world to be exalted by the prospect that this tradition was now to be reinstated in the shelter of free political and social institutions. The union of this people with that land, through the medium of its incomparable language, had once given mankind its deepest revelation. Ancient Israel had taught individual morality, social justice and universal peace. That the conditions in which that florescence had been achieved should once again be restored was a prospect that could not fail to appeal to any sensitive imagination.

The community of nations is also a society of cultures and civilizations. I notice this variety very directly as I look around the table at the United Nations. Many modern states, whatever their formal relationship to established religion, exemplify and embody the Christian civilization in its various forms. Some fifteen modern states are dominated by the heritage of Islam. Three or more sovereignties in the

An Adventure in the Human Spirit

Far East are cast in the mould of the Buddhist tradition. There are many states, as we know only too well, which uphold the materialistic philosophies of our age. But until seven years ago there was one culture, and one alone, which had no distinctive representation in the family of nations; one civilization which nowhere on earth could test its ideals by their power of response to the challenge of statehood society and international relations. No single government anywhere spoke on the grave international issues in the voice of the Hebrew tradition. When we think of the influence which this tradition has exerted on the currents of historic progress, this was surely an intolerable paradox. In our age, for the first time since the legions of Titus subjugated Jerusalem, the Hebrew tradition has become embodied in free political institutions, on a level of equality with all other nations in the human family. By this act of remedy, the family circle of the world's free cultures has become complete. The community of nations is now a comprehensive symphony of the traditions and cultures of mankind.

It is true, of course, that even after the destruction of the Jewish Kingdoms, the Hebrew concept, working through Christianity and Islam and within the national traditions of countless peoples, continued its creative course. It would be unduly restrictive to limit the story of the Hebrew mind to those expressions of it which were realized in the period of separate national independence. Nevertheless, it is a fact that it was in conditions of nationhood in the Land of Israel that the Hebrew spirit rose to levels of inspiration which it never subsequently achieved in conditions of exile and dispersion. Now the Hebrew mind has escaped the great handicap and reproach of homelessness. No longer need we poignantly recite in the words of the Bible: 'They have appointed me to keep vineyards, but mine own vineyard have I not kept.'

The aspects of this revival which belong ostensibly to political history, cannot be denied their place in a spiritual appraisal. The homelessness and martyrdom of the Jewish people was not merely a source of Jewish grief and of international political tension; it was also a burden upon the Christian conscience. The weight of this burden became heavy beyond endurance in the aftermath of the Second World War, when the curtain went up on the burnt and mangled bodies of six million Jews, including a million children. The Jewish people had fallen victim to the most fearful agony which had ever

118

beset any family of the human race. A whole continent was saturated with its blood and haunted by its unexpiated sacrifice. As the world rose from the ravages of the Second World War, it came perilously near to creating an injustice more heinous than any which had been eliminated by the triumph of the Allied cause. It became horribly but seriously possible that every nation would be granted its freedom, amongst those which had suffered under the heel of tyranny, except the people which had suffered the most. All the victims of tyranny would be established in sovereignty, except the first and the most sorely ravaged amongst the targets of totalitarian persecution. If the world order had been established under Christian leadership upon this discrimination, it would surely have been conceived with an intolerable measure of original guilt.

From this spiritual peril the community of nations cleansed itself belatedly, perhaps a little too grudgingly, but nevertheless decisively, when it ordained and later recognized the establishment of Israel. An international society including a Jewish State, and an international society after the Second World War excluding any satisfaction of the Jewish claim to equality, would have been two totally antithetical concepts from the ethical point of view. Thus the renewal of Israel's sovereignty, though ostensibly a fact of political organization, was, in the deeper sense, an act of universal equity. It is a stage of preferment in the history of the Christian conscience.

The same consideration applies with particular force when we examine the problem of equity in its regional aspect. No people benefited more lavishly than the Arabs from the new inheritance of freedom bequeathed by the victories of the Allied powers in two world wars and the establishment of the United Nations. In an area where not a single free Arab or Moslem had lived in political independence four decades ago, there were now to be created seven, eight and then nine separate Arab sovereignties extending over a vast subcontinent from Pakistan to the Central Mediterranean, from the Taurus mountains to the Persian Gulf. This region of Arab independence was immeasurably rich in physical power. Great fertile valleys spread out within it. Abundant rivers flowed across its lands. Unlimited resources of mineral and natural wealth lay beneath its soil. Never since the great era of the Moslem Caliphate, a full millennium ago, had the Arab world commanded such elements of strength and opportunity as those which now came within its reach.

119

An Adventure in the Human Spirit

Here again the international conscience was faced with a burning problem of equity. Would it be considered right for the Arab people to hold sway over a vast continent, and wrong for the Jewish people to establish its independence in a mere fragment of this huge domain? Would it be the decree of history that the Arabs must be independent everywhere and the Jewish people nowhere—not even in the land which owed all its renown in history to its connection with the Hebrew tradition? This was the problem of conscience which underlay those political discussions in international forums and in the chancelleries of the powers. Here again there was the peril of an award so one-sided and discriminatory as to weigh down the international conscience for generations to come. After many hesitations the world community purged itself of any such reproach. It rightly established and encouraged the emancipation of the Arab people on an almost imperial scale. But the benefit, nay the elementary right, which it conferred upon the Arabs in such abundance was also bestowed upon the Jewish people, albeit within more meagre and austere limits. This picture of an Arab freedom beyond the wildest dreams of recent generations, side by side with an immeasurably more modest satisfaction of the principle of Jewish independence should stand before us whenever we consider the spiritual implications of the controversy between Arab and Israel nationalism. It would have been an indelible disgrace to universal justice if a world which had rightly bequeathed this vast liberation to the Arab nations had begrudged the Jewish people its small share of freedom. The morality expressed in the parable of Naboth's vineyard would have come as a cloud over the life of the Middle East.

As we survey the origins of Israel's independence in spiritual terms, we cannot fail to let our minds linger on the question of Israel's cultural destiny. In the final resort, modern Israel will vindicate the efforts, sacrifices, longings invested in its rebirth to the degree that it strives towards high levels of intellectual and cultural progress. As a military power, as a political force or as an economic unit, Israel faces horizons restricted by deficiencies of material power. Much, of course, remains to be achieved in political organization, in the strengthening of security and in economic consolidation. But in these realms Israel will never compete with the might and influence of the great continental and imperial powers. The only domain in which we are free to soar to the highest peaks available to any nation

120

An Adventure in the Human Spirit

are those of spiritual, scientific, and cultural progress. However pressing are Israel's preoccupations with physical security and economic welfare, the challenge of cultural achievement cannot be set aside. Would we not be an extraordinary people if we were to devote all our efforts to those material fields in which, after all, our limitations are inexorable, and stand aside from the only areas in which, at least, the potentialities of greatness lie open before us.

These considerations invite our attention to Israel's aspirations in religion, literature, science and art. Our intensive efforts in these fields is not something marginal or secondary to our concern: it touches the very core and essence of our destiny.

Three elements are available to us in the formation of Israel's new culture. First, there is the Hebrew biblical tradition expressed in our glorious language and evoked by the physical associations of the country itself. This is no new Esperanto nation writing its history upon a clean slate. Modern Israel is, in its own consciousness and in that of the world, the descendant of the ancient Hebrew civilization which exercised such a potent influence on the thought and spirit of mankind. It is no small thing, I assure you, for the citizen of modern Israel to speak the same Hebrew language as that in which Amos wrote the prophecies of social justice, in which Isaiah proclaimed the vision of universal peace, and Ezekiel contemplated the mysteries of regeneration and resurrected hope. In our educational process in modern Israel a great source of enrichment is to be found in the historic memories evoked by the very hills and valleys in which our people has resumed its national story. The sentiment of belonging, in the most intimate way, to the great sweep of Israel's history in this immortal land has a greater influence than is commonly realized in the formation of our national character. The emblems of our modern Israel statehood carry the modern citizen of Israel back to its roots in the early Jewish Kingdom. Our literary movement and recent discoveries in archaeology are also constant reminders to our people of this primary element in their spiritual formation.

The second element in Israel's culture is the experience accumulated by the Jewish people in its wanderings after the period of national independence. The years of dispersion and persecution were also a period of constant interplay between the Hebrew mind and the cultures of Europe and the New World. The Rabinnical and Tal-

121

An Adventure in the Human Spirit

mudical literature, the post-biblical Hebrew poetry and philosophy, the attachments of the Jewish people to the arts and sciences of the Western world, are all part of the reservoir from which modern Israel draws its sustenance.

The third element available for our cultural development is Western civilization, with special reference to its political institutions and its scientific and technological progress. It is Israel's fortune to be the sole representative in its immediate region of political democracy and scientific advance which are the two most distinctive sources of strength in the European and American civilization. This Western civilization is strongly expressed amongst us by the Anglo-Saxon tradition with which Israel has two links of special intimacy. First, the great bulk of the free and extant Jewish people is a part of the English-speaking world; and second, the tradition of the English-speaking people is not something alien or external to Israel's life and experience. It is itself morally derived from the original Hebrew tradition of which Israel is the modern embodiment.

From the effervescence of these three elements—the Hebrew biblical tradition, the broader Jewish experience, Western science and political organization—from these the culture of modern Israel will emerge. There is, of course, no way of ensuring that the result will be of universal significance. We cannot promise a new period of revelation. It is not for us to command the inscrutable sources of inspiration. All that we can do is to create opportunities whereby to express whatever potentialities lie within our soul, as it seeks communion with the great mysteries of intellectual and spiritual creation. We have at least restored to our people the conditions of a creative culture—pride of soil; a sense of historic continuity; deep roots in a superbly aristocratic cultural tradition; and the special exaltation which attends a people in the great hours of its national revival. Who can really be certain that these conditions will not bring a message at least in the spirit and quality of our original inheritance?

I am certain that your invitation to me to discuss these high themes within this Catholic sanctuary reflects your conviction that the unfolding of Israel's career as a modern nation is a matter of moment and concern to the Christian world. The great issue in this generation is drawn, not between Christianity and Judaism, or between Israel and the Christian nations. The frontier lies rather between those who assert and those who deny the supremacy of faith and of freedom.

122

An Adventure in the Human Spirit

You and we occupy different areas of tradition, experience and outlook, but we occupy them on the same side of that fateful demarcation. Our differences as Jews and as Christians are not insignificant, and we should not be disposed to obscure them. It may well be that those elements of our personality which are separate and distinctive are precisely the most creative parts of our contribution to the common cause. But if the rise of Israel is a victory for the human spirit, a triumph of international integrity, a burden removed from the international conscience, the addition of a new voice to the symphony of human freedom, then this is a victory for the Christian cause as well as a direct salvation for the Jewish people.

It is, therefore, memorable and significant that the Christian world lent its sympathy to Israel's revival. The Catholic countries of Europe and Latin America were amongst those who most ardently sustained Israel's struggle for independence and recognition. Our devotion to a kindred heritage, our common respect for human values, our unremitting resistance to tyranny, are unifying forces which transcend all secondary divergences of judgment or interest. The people of Israel who first in history rebelled against barbarism and pagan empires, this people which raised the first voice against idolatry—this people in its new life of independence will never bow the knee to totalitarian dictatorship.

These common ideals of Judaism and Christianity, of Israel and of other free nations command us to assert our underlying fraternity. A distinguished prelate of the Catholic Church, Msgr. Gustave Franceschi, wrote of his visit to Israel last year in these terms:

'We understand that the Hebrew people has a spiritual connection with us, that their strange survival goes beyond the customary norms by which the life of an ordinary nation evolves; and we Christians, if we have not lost the sense of Christianity, cannot but perceive to what a profound extent modern Israel is linked to our own salvation. One merely has to read St. Paul's Epistle to the Romans to see this.'

These solidarities can serve as a bridge across controversies which sometimes disturb our essential kinship. An understanding of the Christian world ranks very high among Israel's chief aspirations. We are fully aware that many causes and assets sacred to Christianity lie within our control, and demand our most vigilant reverence. We have, therefore, never ceased in recent years to proclaim our readiness

123

An Adventure in the Human Spirit

to place under international influence the Holy Places in Jerusalem which are the cradle and inspiration of the Christian faith. By such a solution, reconciling the full political independence of the people of the Holy City with international interest in whatever is truly universal in Jerusalem, we could achieve a double purpose. We should prevent an encroachment on the political liberties of Jerusalem's population, while at the same time acknowledging the moral authority of the world communities over the sanctuaries of the Christian faith. Need I remind you that political freedom and national self-expression are themselves spiritual objectives of the highest value; that Jerusalem, the cradle of democratic thought, is the last place on earth in which citizens should be deprived of freedom and the satisfaction that national loyalties foster; and that no religious purpose could triumph in a discontented political community alienated from its national allegiance. These are the considerations which have caused the governments of Israel and of the United States to co-operate so constantly within the United Nations on behalf of solutions which would respect both the sovereignty and secular independence of Jerusalem's population, and the acknowledged rights of the Christian world to see its Holy Places kept immune from turbulence and desecration. I believe that this attitude is now shared by a majority of the members of the United Nations.

In the same spirit, you will understand how deeply we have welcomed the warm praise expressed by Msgr. Antonio Vergani, representative of the Latin Patriarch in Israel, by the Very Rev. Father Brunet and by visiting Cardinals and Prelates, to the efforts of my government to ease the journeys of pilgrims, to effect a road link to Mount Tabor and to repair the ravages inflicted by war on some of the buildings and properties of the Catholic churches in Israel. In paying this warm tribute to the Government of Israel for its 'substantial subventions, enabling the rehabilitation of the Hospice of Notre Dame de France in Jerusalem', Father Brunet eloquently and devoutly concludes: 'May God vouchsafe us to see this edifice arisen from its ruins, and pilgrims coming once again to recite their prayers on the soil of this Holy Land, where spiritual interests should bring all hearts together in peace.'

This is indeed the very goal of Israel's spiritual adventure in the freedom of its ancient home—to live a national life consecrated to a vision of fraternity and peace. We have not accomplished every stage

An Adventure in the Human Spirit

of that journey. The road stretches out before us, long and hard. But if at least we labour to serve this ideal within the limits of our human imperfection, the new era of Israel's freedom will be not unworthy of the inheritance from which she derives the glory of her name.

CHAPTER XII

The Toynbee Heresy*

I come before you tonight not in any diplomatic capacity but rather as a student of history and letters, seeking a brief respite from contemporary affairs. The subject before us is not unrelated to the urgent issues of Israel's destiny; and I do not feel that I am deserting the arena in favour of an ivory tower of academic detachment. The place which Israel occupies in the pride and love of our generation has not been won solely by the achievements of this decade. It is an eminence earned largely by historic repute. The emergence of modern Israel is an event conceived in the highest dimensions of history. It is the result of one of the most tenacious passions in the records of human action. It marks a triumph of faith and will over rational chance. It symbolizes the survival, and perhaps the renewed florescence, of mankind's oldest culture. More than any other national revival in modern times, it has been sharply contested, agitated, and discussed as a theme of conscience, as well as of international politics.

Thus if the bright image of Israel's resurgence is distorted, if this historic process is held up to ridicule, if the stature of this event is degraded—if our new birth of freedom is portrayed as a squalid and bloodthirsty conspiracy, then Israel loses a priceless asset of her security and honour. There is no state in the modern world whose progress has been more dependent on idealistic and moral postulates. A response to an assault upon Israel's historic repute is not a mere exercise in academic controversy. It affects the very essence of Israel's destiny in life and thought.

It is against this background that I come to discuss a view of Israel's history which has recently been proclaimed with the authority of an impressive name in contemporary scholarship.

In order to define and rebut the heresy, it is necessary to recall the orthodox historiography from which the heresy deviates.

* At Yeshiva University, New York, 18 January 1955.

The Toynbee Heresy

The writers of Jewish history portray the national experience of a people in a continuous narrative of four thousand years. The experience in antiquity is well-documented and preserved, clad in the raiment of superb literary artistry, articulate and coherent in all its parts, and drawing substantive confirmation from the recent discoveries of archaeology. At the centre of this experience stands the revelation to Israel of a concept of history in terms of progress. This people of shepherds and farmers, in a small country on the shores of the eastern Mediterranean, evolved ideas of startling originality which have remained an unattainable standard for mankind across the generations. First came the doctrine of the moral choice. The pre-Jewish civilizations were gripped by religions of fatalism, determinism and resignation. They saw human life in relentless cycles coming back to a starting point in darkness and chaos. They denied the concept that the will and conscience of man governed the world's future. Mysterious and inscrutable forces of nature or of supernature disposed of human destiny by arbitrary superstitious laws. Man was the passive object, not the conscious agent of historic processes.

Against this determinism and resignation there arose the revolutionary concept of Judaism in the realm of the individual conscience. The capacity of choice between good and evil could determine the destiny of human life, in accordance with a coherent system of moral thought. This concept of the power of moral choice was the authentic contribution of Judaism to the question of purposes in individual life.

The societies which preceded the Jewish kingdoms were dominated by concepts of permissible exploitation. Man was helpless against the adverse forces of nature and against the cruelties of his innate avarice. Against the doctrine of social resignation, there arose the Hebrew idea of social justice. The primary theme was, Thou shalt love thy neighbour as thyself. From this notion of solidarity in human relations came the concept of moral law applicable to societies, as well as to individuals.

Spreading out into its third circle of influence, the Hebrew ideal attacked the prevailing concept of war as a natural state of the universe, a part of mankind's very nature. Three thousand years ago the Prophets proclaimed the doctrine of universal peace. 'Nation shall not lift up the sword against nation, neither shall they learn war any more.'

These were the triple foundations of the Hebrew ideal: individual

127

The Toynbee Heresy

morality, social justice, universal peace. Historians have portrayed their development in the experience of a people who, believing themselves to be the responsible custodians of these ideals, conserved their integrity and union even against the disparate forces of dispersion and exile. They conserved this union and identity not for their own sake, but in order to maintain trusteeship over these revolutionary ideals. The narrative goes on to describe the break-up of the Jewish kingdoms, the dispersion of its citizens, and the subsequent struggle to preserve a sense of nationality and spiritual mission without the political and territorial attributes of statehood.

In every appraisal of Jewish history particular attention has been devoted to the doctrine of Restoration. With unique tenacity this people maintained the theory of its exile as a temporary state to be succeeded by a reunion between the people, the land and the language out of whose original coalescence the Hebrew revelation was born. True, the Jewish people continued its creative course in many scenes after the loss of national independence. But the fact remains that it was in conditions of separate national independence in Israel that the Hebrew mind rose to levels of creativeness which it never subsequently attained.

The restoration is described by Jewish historians both as a Divine will and as a human duty. The Divine promise decreed that this people should be restored; it was, therefore, its own duty not only to dream but also labour for that redemption. As Jewish history enters the eighteenth and nineteenth centuries, the doctrine of the Restoration assumes concrete form as a response to homelessness. The absence of an independent physical centre for the Jewish people results in the danger both of physical extinction and of spiritual assimilation. The problem of survival is seen as a function of Israel's capacity to emerge from the handicap and reproach of homelessness. This theme dominates Jewish history at the turn of the century, when Zionism becomes the central collective purpose of the Jewish people. Finally there comes the great crescendo, a symphonic climax with overtones of tragedy and grandeur, of horror and salvation. The deepest agony is succeeded by the sudden illumination of hope. The massacre of Jewish communities in Europe is followed, within a single decade, by an act of salvation through the restoration of Israel's sovereignty, the salvage of its authentic personality and the assurance of its national and cultural survival. This last climax, a fantastic transition from the depths of paralysing weakness to new peaks of sovereign opportunity, is played out on a broad universal canvas with the international conscience actively engaged. Twice within a single decade the world tribunal recognizes the right of the Jewish people to the restoration of its homeland. The recognition itself creates new incentives for the renaissance.

The themes which I have described in very broad and, therefore, approximate strokes, do not vary considerably between one historian and another. Jewish historians stress the undying validity of the original Jewish heritage, while Christian scholars see their own civilization evolving in progress from the Judaic ideal. But even the writings of most Christian historians pay tribute to the affirmative qualities of the Hebrew spirit and to the achievement of Jewish survival. They, too, revere the Hebrew tradition as the parent source of their own Christian civilization. As apostles of faith and opponents of determinism, they rely upon Israel's resurgence as a lesson in the potency of the human will. A dream which had no ostensible prospect of realization was carried to fulfilment against all calculation of material chance. There had seemed to be no historical prospect a few decades ago that this people could establish its sovereignty in a land coveted by more powerful nationalisms and imperialisms; that it could overcome the diversive factors of its exile in a measure sufficient to restore national unity; that it could revive the original medium of its culture; or that it could secure international recognition of the link between the Jewish people and its ancient homeland— a concept which a short time ago had no place in the jurisprudence of nations. In these circumstances, any historian of unprejudiced insight would see Israel's rise as a vindication of the spiritual impulse in human history, a crushing argument in the eternal discussion between the advocates of faith and the adherents of materialistic or deterministic doctrines of history which deny the human will any status as a governing factor in human destiny.

I have stated some of the orthodox attitudes in Jewish historiography. They are not free from challenge or controversy. It is not difficult to find moments, or even whole generations, in which this people fell short of its elevated standards. There are those who argue that other currents of human thought overtook and broadened the original insights of the Hebrew mind. It is possible to advocate but not possible to prove this theory of improvement. But a generally affirmative approach to the history of the Jewish people can be dis-

The Toynbee Heresy

cerned in all but the most eccentric historical writing until Toynbee. Indeed, the attempts to discredit the Jewish historic process have, until this year, been confined to those who have sought an academic rationalization for religious or political hostility.

We cannot, therefore, fail to regard Professor Toynbee's analysis as a significant event in contemporary scholarship. Here we have no partial or selective criticism of the Jewish historic performance. We have an almost total negation of anything affirmative in the entire record. The attack is not alone upon the credit of contemporary Israel. There is a vehement assault on the antecedents of modern Israel reaching back into antiquity. Rising up in revolt against orthodox history, Professor Toynbee, in a grandiose framework of a study of the rise and fall of civilizations, presents the story of Israel over thousands of years as a grotesque aberration leading to a tragedy of historic injustice.

The Toynbee thesis begins with the picture of a 'Syriac community' which recognizes the supremacy of 'a provincial and jealous god' marked by fanatical vengefulness and exclusiveness. There is something in this provincial and jealous god, perhaps the very ferocity of his exclusiveness and fanaticism, which gives him supremacy in his contemporary world of ideas. But soon, everything which is of value in the Hebrew concept of divinity is inherited by the higher religion of Christianity, thus leaving the Jewish mission fulfilled and exhausted.

In this part of Professor Toynbee's writing there is a reluctance to recognize any ideas as authentically Jewish, except the quality of fanaticism. This is singled out as the most typical of all the Hebrew qualities. Indeed, the Jewish people is awarded the original copyright. Whenever there is a description of extreme brutality, it is described as being 'Judaic' in character. The persecutions of the Visigoths are portrayed as being of typically 'Judaic' fanaticism, and Professor Toynbee finds no records of religious persecution before the Maccabees, who thus became the historical parents of forcible proselytism.

There is a refusal to recognize divine and human love as indispensable and central themes of the Hebrew tradition. The domination of love is represented as a deviation achieved by Christianity from the original concept of the provincial and jealous god. The three circles of Hebrew morality—individual conscience, social justice and uni-

The Toynbee Heresy

versal peace—would not present themselves at all to any reader dependent on Toynbee for his insight into the Hebrew ideal.

From this provincialism and tribalism the Jewish people, having outlived its mission almost in its infancy, lingers on in Toynbee's world of history as 'a fossil remnant'. The word 'fossil' fascinates this writer. He rolls it lovingly over his tongue with the complacent air of one who has coined an immortal aphorism. Statisticians will be delighted to count the number of occasions on which the Jewish people is described as a 'fossil' remnant in the eight volumes. Dr. Toynbee will not tell us what he means. The concept is never defined. It is indeed a basic weakness of his work that it evades the definition of its fundamental terms. But the word 'fossil' has a scientific definition. It denotes something petrified, which retains its original shape and semblance without the breath of life. The mollusc or shell lingers on eternally, while the spirit which once gave it the glory of animation has long since departed.

Now, the doctrine of the fossil is the very core of the Toynbee heresy. If Israel was a fossil centuries ago, then its survival is certainly an archaism and its restoration a grotesque paradox. On the other hand, if the concept of Judaism as something petrified and embalmed cannot be sustained, then it is difficult to challenge the right of a sentient living spirit to seek survival and restoration. Prof. Toynbee fails, indeed declines, to substantiate the fossil theory, despite the fact that it is the absolute starting point of all his subsequent judgments.

But the fossil, not having read Toynbee's eight volumes, is unaware of its own petrifaction. It clings to its sense of mission, and even strives for national restoration. For Toynbee, this is a rebellion against the orthodox Jewish tradition which decrees that the restoration, if it comes at all, must proceed exclusively from the Divine initiative. Toynbee portrays the movement for the restoration of Jewish nationhood as a usurpation by human beings of a destiny which can only be righteously envisaged as the work of the Creator. The fossil remnant, instead of accepting what is called the doctrine of 'political quietism' and waiting in resignation for the Divine purpose to unfold itself, has presumed impiously to take the law into its own hands and to conceive Jewish restoration as a process of human activity. In attributing political quietism and resignation to orthodox Judaism, Professor Toynbee becomes an unexpected and explicit adherent of *Agudath Israel*. This movement is mentioned with a

131

straight face several times as the embodiment of the authentic tradition; Orthodox Judaism, decrees Prof. Toynbee, in a mood of Rabbinical dogmatism, requires acceptance of Disapora until, in God's good time, if at all, a Divine initiative, unsupported by human revolt, will bring about the restoration together with Messianic redemption. The natural Jewishness is the condition of Diaspora. The return is an archaism, a paradox, an impiety, and an injustice.

Direct quotation will prove that the principles of this heresy have been stated by Professor Toynbee in terms not less drastic than those which I have ascribed to him. Moreover, the story is told with a vehemence, a moral passion, a subjective indignation, rare in historical writing and indeed without parallel elsewhere in Toynbee's work. The adjectives are those of journalism, of political polemics. The writer is not content to describe. He insists also on the capacity to judge and condemn. It seems vitally important to him that the reader should despise many of the processes and the most striking recent results of the immemorial Jewish story. In the end, Professor Toynbee, too, takes his story to a climax—but not to a climax of chivalrous triumph, of recuperation of will power vanquishing material obstacles and impediments. His is a climax full of tragedy, pathos and paradox. The torment of Jewry under Nazism is described in violent indignation. But this indignation forms the bridge to the blasphemous conclusion that the torment of Jewry under Nazism is 'less tragic' than the circumstances in which 750,000 Arabs are homeless, though alive, upon the soil and the territory of the independent Arab States. Finally, the State of Israel is portrayed as a caricature of all the imperfections of society, a squalid little Ghetto without grace or meaning, the abode of 'a Janus figure, part American farmer technician, part Nazi sicarius'. With this chivalrous pat on our shoulder we are sent on our way down the road to damnation on Judgment Day.

Let me vindicate the accuracy of my summary in Professor Toynbee's own words. Here is how he begins with a description of the Jewish concept of Divinity:

'It is not, of course, surprising to find these two traits of provincialism and exclusiveness displayed by Yahveh simultaneously. A God who keeps to his own domain may be expected to warn other Gods off it. What is surprising, and even repellent, at any rate at first sight, is to see Yahveh continuing to exhibit an unabated intolerance towards the rivals with whom he courts a conflict when, after

132

the overthrow of the Kingdoms of Israel and Judah, and the establishment of the Syriac universal state, this God of two highland principalities steps out into the wider world and aspires like his neighbours to win for himself the worship of all mankind.'

Provincialism and exclusiveness, then, rather than Oneness, love and justice are the dominant characteristics of the Hebrew God. Provincialism is diagnosed by Professor Toynbee in his attack on the doctrine of the chosen people. This concept is described as the arrogation of a privilege, not as the acceptance of responsibility and obligation. It is, in fact, defined by Professor Toynbee in terms of a narcissistic self-idealization. He writes:

'The most notorious historical example of this idealization of an ephemeral self is the error of the Jews which is exposed in the New Testament. In the period of their history, which began in the infancy of the Syriac civilization and which culminated in the age of the Prophets, the people of Israel and Judah raised themselves head and shoulders above the Syriac peoples by rising to a monotheistic conception of religion. Keenly conscious of their spiritual treasure, they allowed themselves to be betrayed into an idealization of this notable but transitory stage in their spiritual growth. They had indeed been gifted with unparalleled spiritual insight but after having divined a truth which was absolute and eternal they allowed themselves to be captivated by a relative and temporary half-truth. They persuaded themselves that Israel's discovery of the one true God had revealed Israel itself to be God's chosen people; and this half-truth inveigled them into a fatal error of looking upon a momentary spiritual eminence as a privilege conferred upon them by God in an everlasting covenant. Brooding on a talent which they had perversely sterilized by hiding it in the earth, they rejected the still greater treasure which God offered them in the coming of Jesus of Nazareth.'

My criticism of this passage is directed not, of course, against Toynbee's reverence for the Christian revelation, but against his invidious definition of a Jewish doctrine for the sake of its debasement. He states without proof that the doctrine of Israel's selection is the assertion of exclusive membership in a restricted club. He ignores the true essence of this idea, which is the acceptance of a burden of obligation heavier than that carried by other peoples who were not the original custodians of the inspired revelation. The concept of Israel's choice is one of humility, not of arrogance. The selection is a burden, not a grace. There is a vast exegesis on this theme in Rabbinical

133

The Toynbee Heresy

literature. But Professor Toynbee need not have gone beyond the first documents which expound the theme of Israel's selection:

'You only have I known of all the families of the earth; *therefore* I will visit upon you all your iniquities.'

From this description of a provincial self-idealization and the assertion of a privileged status, Professor Toynbee goes on to grapple with the mystery of Jewish survival. He has no device except the metaphor of the fossil:

'The Jews and the Pharisees are fossils of the Syriac society as it was before the Hellenic intrusion upon the Syriac world.'

And again:

'A number of fossils in Diaspora have preserved their identity through a devotion to religious rites and a proficiency in commerce and finance.'

This doctrine of Jewish survival as a result of an excessive ritualism and of financial astuteness is disturbingly akin to the diagnosis of anti-Semitic historians, from whom Toynbee would justly claim dissociation. The economic history of the Jewish people is in fact a poignant record, with a ghastly volume of starvation and poverty. The legendary proficiency in commerce and finance is a characteristic which modern Israel has still failed to discover. But for Dr. Toynbee it is sufficient to assert these time-worn platitudes. It is not necessary to prove them. He rules by negative implication against any idea that Jewish survival is the result of an affirmative spiritual dedication. It is by commercial shrewdness and rigid ceremonial orthodoxy that the fossil survives. There is more of Shylock than of Isaiah or Maimonides in this prototype.

'At the present moment they survive as a mere Diaspora; and the petrified religion, which still so potently holds the scattered members of these communities together, has lost its message to mankind and has hardened into a fossil of the extinct Syriac society.'

A fossil cannot create or even interpret original ideas. Thus by his very definition Professor Toynbee disposes negatively of the entire post-biblical Jewish culture, through medieval Hebrew philosophy and poetry, right up to the achievements and insights of Hebrew literature and scholarship in the present day. It is doubtful whether Professor Toynbee is equipped, linguistically or otherwise, to deny the breath of life or the spark of inspiration to this vast literature. But the beloved slogan of the fossil is, in fact, judgment on the ideas and writings of these many generations.

The Toynbee Heresy

That the natural state of the fossil is the Diaspora is another central theme in Professor Toynbee's heresy. Hear it in his own words:

'The historic Jewry was the Diaspora and the distinctively Jewish ethos and institutions. . . . *A meticulous devotion to the Mosaic Law and a consummate virtuosity in commerce and finance* were those which the Diaspora in the course of ages had wrought into social talismans endowing this geographically scattered community with a magic capacity for survival.'

All would have been well, then, if this people had patiently accepted its petrified status. Unfortunately, however, the fossil revolted against its petrified nature, and this is the source of the paradox and the tragedy.

'So long as the Jewish Diaspora was content, *bona fide*, to leave the future of Palestine in the hands of God, the existing Christian and Moslem inhabitants of the promised land could afford to do likewise. And when the orthodox Jewish doctrine of an eventual repatriation of Jewry to Palestine through an act of God was thus accompanied by a traditional Jewish practice of political quietism, the doctrine, like a derivative Christian doctrine of the second coming of Christ, could be interpreted in crude Machiavellian or Marxian terms as a psychological device, not for bringing to pass a far-off Divine event to which the whole creation moves, but for maintaining *en attendant* and *ad infinitum* the social confusion of a mundane community in Diaspora.'

If you will allow me to translate that last passage into simple English, Prof. Toynbee says this: So long as the doctrine of the Restoration was held as a pious abstraction, with nothing done to fulfil it, the idea could exist harmlessly. But any attempt to put it into practice was bound to reveal its inherent contradictions and to lead to a climax of tragedy.

It is a far cry from a fossil in diaspora to a robust modern nation in its original home. Professor Toynbee feels that the transition needs much explanation. He finds the explanation in a catchword. It is 'archaism'.

'Archaism, as we have seen in another context, is always a perilous pursuit. But it is most perilous of all when it is taken up by members of a community that is a fossil relic of a dead civilization, since the past to which the archaists have it in their power to cast back in such

135

The Toynbee Heresy

a case may be more sharply at variance with present realities than even the remotest past state of the society belonging to the living generations of the species.'

Now, it is amply clear at this stage that Professor Toynbee harbours a fierce resentment against Jewish survival and still more against Jewish Restoration. The fossil whose lack of animation he has so authoritatively diagnosed keeps getting up and biting him in the ankle. All he can say is that the entire phenomenon is against the proper theory. His answer is not that the theory is wrong, but that the phenomenon is reprehensible. Thus, the tenacity with which the Jewish people worked for the Restoration invites Professor Toynbee's greatest indignation. It is here that he attacks the Restoration as a usurpation of the Divine Will. For a truly Divine objective must be carried out by the Almighty alone; and any effort to advance it by human effort is an impious rebellion against the Divine prerogative. Man may not busy himself in the reform of the world into the Kingdom of God.

To establish this analogy in another sphere, we might say that if social justice is a God-given ideal, then any human being who strives for social justice through political or economic organization is guilty of impious revolt against God's purpose, for he is denying the capacity of the Almighty, unaided by human agencies, especially fossilized ones, to bring about the realization of the ideal. Lest you think that this is an exaggeration, this very *reductio ad absurdum* actually occurs in Professor Toynbee's thesis:

'A Western-inspired archaism carried the twentieth-century Zionist faction of a Jewish Diaspora back to the aims and ethos of the generation of Joshua. The consequent replacement of the traditional Jewish hope of an eventual Restoration of Israel to Palestine on God's initiative through the agency of a divinely inspired Messiah, by a Zionist movement working to establish a Jewish national state in Palestine on Jewry's initiative by mundane political and military means, had the same explosive effect as the contemporary replacement of the Christian hope of social justice to be inaugurated at the second coming of Christ, by a communist movement working to establish a mundane new dispensation by means of a world revolution.'

This is too wonderful to be true. But it is there in black and white. Just as the human efforts to achieve Jewish Restoration lead to the 'impiety' of Zionism, so any attempt to achieve a social millenium by

The Toynbee Heresy

human struggle is a distortion of Christianity and may lead to such aberrations as Communism. It is faith to cherish a Divine vision; it is 'impiety' to stumble forward towards its fulfilment.

We can see how the love of slick analogy, the most perilous occupational hazard of an historian, has gripped Prof. Toynbee. Having related the dream of Jewish Restoration to a usurpation akin to Communism, he goes on to prove that traditional attachment of Israel to its original soil is a form of Fascism. Observe how this record *tour de force* is accomplished. First, it is stated that the Jewish people's title to the soil of Eretz Israel is based 'on the physical grounds that they are a master race in virtue of having Abraham for their father'. This definition of the theory of the link between land and people in terms of 'master race' is stated as a fact. The attachment is not a cultural tradition, it is not a spiritual link, it is not a mystic unity of the mind between the people of Israel and the physical conditions in which it underwent the immortal biblical experience. It is the concept of blood and soil and herrenvolk. This is the basis of our claim, and by this 'the Zionist is unwittingly testifying that he has been ensnared by the lure of a post-modern Western gentile racialism in which a late modern Western gentile nationalism had denounced itself through the self-exposure of a self-caricature as being the naked neo-paganism that it was'.

In simpler language (for Toynbee's turgidity of language is one of the most unprepossessing features of his study), Zionists claim Eretz Israel on the grounds that they are a master race descended from Abraham: this shows that they are ensnared by the Nazi theory of the herrenvolk: therefore Zionism is kindred to Nazism. There is a little difficulty about anachronism here, since the Jewish teaching on the relationship of Israel to Eretz Israel has been fully and sublimely developed for twenty centuries before Nazism existed to ensnare anybody. But if it is convenient to portray this link as the derivative of the Blood and Soil concept of the Nazi ideologists, let convenience prevail.

The passion for analogies between events and ideas separated by centuries and continents marks Toynbee's greatest weakness as an historian. Dr. Talmon has pointed out that there is nothing in his work of that particular intimacy which marks the authentic historians, who select a small sector of the scene, a single period or a single land, and immerse themselves in that special realm until they become a part of its very breath. Here the canvas is vast and broad.

137

The Toynbee Heresy

The aim is to say something about everything but not to know everything about anything. The effect is secured by grandiose dimensions. It is as though a painter in search of fame and repute were to seek it not by the intrinsic quality of his work, but by painting upon a canvas physically vaster than any work of art before. The absence of specialization, and the insistence upon generalized slogans is a primary weakness of Toynbee's scholarship. Nowhere does the superficiality become as unattractive as in these glib and invidious analogies which relate the Jewish dream of restoration to Communism and Nazism in turn.

· Against this background it is easy to predict how Dr. Toynbee will proceed from his historical premises to his contemporary appraisals of modern Israel. There is no purpose in discussing his modern picture, except by reference to his definitions of pre-Israel Jewish history. Never has the Hebrew tradition been described by any historian in terms of such profound disrespect. The rejection of Israel's rebirth is an organic consequence of his theories concerning the 'fossilized relic', the 'exhausted mission' and the impiety of any revolt against the 'natural state of Diaspora' or the duty of 'political quietism'.

If Zionism is a usurpation of the Divine province, then there is nothing more that need be said against it.

'The mystical feeling convicted the Zionists of an importunity which verged upon impiety in their attempt to take out of God's hands the fulfilment of God's promise to restore Israel to Palestine upon God's own initiative.'

Note that here again, the basic premise is stated without proof. It is affirmed *ex cathedra* to be the Jewish orthodox doctrine that the Restoration must proceed from the Divine initiative without human aid. There are, of course, countless refutations of that premise in orthodox Hebrew literature. It is true that the Hebrew doctrine of history describes the Restoration as a Divine purpose. But it also describes it as a purpose which human effort should strive to accelerate. Indeed, Judaism rejects Dr. Toynbee's persistent division between the Divine Will and human action. He constantly sees these two concepts in terms of antithesis. In Judaism, except for the mystical heresies, it is deemed that if something is willed by God, then it is the duty of man in his material life to strive for its fulfilment.

Toynbee's theory of 'importunity' brings him smoothly to the events of 1948 and the description of the processes which gave birth

138

to the State of Israel. The Zionists had jogged the Divine elbow to the brink of great events.

Three causes are cited by Prof. Toynbee for this event which he admits to be unusual.

First, the strength of American Jewry. You may be fossils but you are very formidable fossils and despite your petrified character, you have the rights of franchise and political influence. Second, the genocide committed by Nazism of which he writes with deep qualified indignation. Third, the cold war.

These are the three components of Israel's rebirth. By them, and by them alone, does Dr. Toynbee seek to explain the inopportune revival of the fossil, its emergence from its 'natural state of diaspora', its advance through 'archaism' and 'usurpation' to its present tragic lease of nationhood.

Instead of discussing what Toynbee says about modern Israel, it would be instructive to recount what he omits. He omits any treatment of the theme in terms of international equity. The rise of Jewish independence, side by side with a far broader Arab emancipation, is the essence of this problem from the viewpoint of comparative international equity. This is ignored. The historical material is dealt with in terms of British and American Realpolitik; and in the British and American pro-Zionist traditions he allows for no ethical or moral consideration at all. The British promise of 1917 was the product of a mistaken expediency; a bid for Jewish support in America and in the countries of the Central Powers. Similarly, domestic pressures, the reluctance of American Jews to allow Jews to immigrate to the United States for fear of anti-Semitism, and plain ignorance are the impulses behind American support. The Zionist theme in the idealistic literature of both Anglo-Saxon countries is not mentioned. There is no indication that there ever took place in the United Nations a discussion of Palestine from the viewpoint of self-determination. This judgment ruled that even as it is right for the Arabs to possess their empire, so it cannot be wrong for the Jewish people to enjoy the tranquil possession of its modest home. To all of us who took any part in that turbulent international controversy, it was clear that this contrast between the continental opportunities of Arab nationalism and the Jewish people's lack of any free domain determined the character of the discussion and its eventual outcome. Statesmen were simple-minded enough to believe that it would not be a cosmic tragedy if the Arab world made do with nine sovereign states, covering two million

The Toynbee Heresy

square miles; and that it would be a more authentic tragedy if every people were to be established in national freedom amongst those which had suffered the Nazi onslaught—except the people which had suffered the most. In ascribing to the United States and to Britain the responsibility for a blind tragedy of error, Toynbee entirely ignores these high themes, just as he ignores the part which small nations played in the judgments which helped Israel's rebirth. The fact that the first serious proposal for Jewish statehood came from a group of eight small countries against Great Power scepticism is not considered at all.

I do not dispute Professor Toynbee's right to argue with these international judgments, to deplore or regret them; but I cannot understand what concept of scholarship allows their complete suppression, the absence of any allusion to the chief milestones which led up to the results which he describes. But there is an even greater sensation in store. There is no war. Neither the Arab declaration of unofficial war on 30th November 1947, nor the historic document whereby, on 15th May 1948, the Arab States informed the United Nations of their intention to embark upon military intervention, is even mentioned. Since every residual problem affecting Arab-Israel relations is a function of the military clash of 1948, it is startling to find no record of the fact that the Arab rejection of Israel was put to the test of the sword. I could respect an historian who published these actions and then exonerated them; who said that the Arab States were justified morally or emotionally or historically in attempting by force to prevent Israel's emergence. But you would really have to look to George Orwell in his morbid vision of totalitarianism to find such a successful suppression of extant historical evidence. It is as though an historian of the First World War were not even to mention the assassination at Sarajevo and the invasion of Belgium, or if the chronicler of the Second World War were to mention neither the assault on Danzig and Poland in 1939, nor the bombing of Pearl Harbour in 1941. Even the Nazi apologists do not attempt to deny these military facts. They may ascribe to them a legitimacy or a righteousness of motive, but they operate with the same material as the rest of us. Here the most explosive dramatic fact in recent Arab-Israel relations, the convergence of Arab armies on Israel and their repulse, is not even accorded the courtesy of record.

From this massive suppression, we are bound to reach strange

The Toynbee Heresy

results. All of a sudden the Jews, a petrified fossil, without any international authority, usurping Divine purpose and rebelling against their own orthodoxy, launched themselves like a barbarian invasion upon a Holy Land with which they had nothing to do, wilfully drove out all the inhabitants and thereby committed an act of cruelty in the image of those of which they had been victims. The reason for this is that the Great Powers did not know of the existence of the Arab world. For example:

'President Truman's personal susceptibility to this popular American confusion of mind and mixture of motives might go far to explain presidential interventions in the Palestinian imbroglio which would have been utterly cynical if they had not been partially innocent-minded. The Missourian politician philanthropist's eagerness to combine expediency with charity by assisting the wronged and suffering Jews would have appeared to have been untempered by any awareness of the existence of wrongs and sufferings inflicted upon the Arabs.'

The picture, then, is that in 1947, the United States was unaware of the existence of an Arab world, and therefore made a unilateral award of self-determination, never attempting to balance the Jewish claims against those of a sated Arab nationalism. The fact is that the State Department was almost as aware as Professor Toynbee of the existence of Arab interests. Nevertheless the determination was made: the eight or nine sovereignties for the Arabs, the single little home for the Jews. I do not quarrel with Professor Toynbee for not accepting this award, but I am puzzled by his disdainful refusal to discuss it.

Apart from its origins in Great Power politics, Israel, according to Toynbee, derived its statehood from the incentives, the compassion, the yearnings evoked by the Hitler persecution. The Nazi extermination of six million Jews was an evil thing, and Professor Toynbee uses some of his most violent adjectives in describing this tragedy. But it is not the greatest tragedy. The Nazi gentile's fall was less tragic than the Zionist Jew's.

'On the Day of Judgment the gravest crime standing to the German National Socialist's account might be not that they had exterminated a majority of Western Jews, but that they had caused the surviving remnant of Jewry to stumble.'

Now, this is the most extraordinary sentence. First, let us note the reference to the Day of Judgment. This occurs more than once. Professor Toynbee is not merely the historian of the twentieth cen-

141

The Toynbee Heresy

tury; he is the Attorney-General of the Almighty upon the Day of Judgment. He knows already how the matter will appear in the eternal perspectives of history. And what is the 'lesser tragedy'? The lesser tragedy is that six and a half million Jews, including one million children, were exterminated and obliterated with all their life and institutions. They were butchered as cattle, cut off from their inheritance of life. A ghastly silence broods over these obscene ditches and incinerators. The shrieks of agony have died away; they are no problem for the United Nations. The potentialities within those millions, whatever they were, are lost to human destiny. This is, for Toynbee, a 'lesser tragedy' than the fact that Arab governments have not yet been persuaded to give their kinsmen, on their own soil, the opportunities of liberty and progress which lie within their gift.

Ponder first upon the arithmetical equity. Assume that Arab refugees had undergone the fate of extermination and massacre of our own brethren in Europe. Why even then would the 750,000 killed have been a greater tragedy than the six million? But the true comparison is not of arithmetic. It is between death and life. The six million are dead. The 750,000, with all their suffering, are alive. But their aliveness is for Toynbee a greater tragedy than those irrevocable deaths. Moreover, they are alive on the soil of their kinsmen, on Arab lands, not in captivity; in countries which are free, emancipated, entitled—even exhorted—to give them homes, Arabic environment, Arabic national loyalty and sentiment. A broad future stretches before them if their own people will open the door of its heart. That is 'more tragic' than the burning of our children in incinerators and the extermination of their parents in gas chambers!

The passion for analogy can never have run riot with more irreverent results. A writer of Christian faith stands before the most unfathomable agony of all generations and compares it with what is an admittedly grave hardship in a different and infinitely less tragic dimension. The one disaster is irrevocable, the other entirely within human alleviation; yet the former is 'less tragic' than the latter. The death of the many is 'less tragic' than the hardship, in survival, of the relatively few. The Nazi sum of deliberate massacre is not more heinous than the injury inflicted by Israel in a war for the defence of hearth and home. I am no authority, as Toynbee is, on the verdicts of Judgment Day but I cannot see how his cruel observations on the 'lesser tragedy' can ever win forgiveness in a compassion less than Divine.

The Toynbee Heresy

But when all is said and written, the State of Israel stands firm, and the pride of exaltation has come into the tents of Jacob everywhere. All that Professor Toynbee can do is to wish us ill. He genially sees American Jews and Israel becoming 'progressively alienated' from each other. Your nourishment of Israel, the most remarkable outpouring of a voluntary public spirit, is written off in a niggardly spirit with a suggestion that you are being duped into submission 'to taxation without representation' and will soon wake up to a more prudent and egocentric parsimony. After two thousand years the only people whose continuous historic memory comprehends all the cycles of civilization which Toynbee records, is reunited with its original inheritance. And Dr. Toynbee can only celebrate this wondrous consummation with the following invective:

'In its diminutiveness, its fanaticism, and its Ishmaelitish enmity with its neighbours, the new Zionist Israel in Palestine was a reproduction of the Modern Western national State that, in its faithfulness, verged on being a parody.'

If there is any consolation, it is in the knowledge that we are being castigated in the name of all nation states. For Professor Toynbee regards national sovereignty as obsolete, and hankers after the more perfect system in which national identities were suppressed under the *millet* system of the Ottoman Empire.

'The species of community (i.e. the nation State) of which this (namely Israel) was the youngest member was at last approaching its eclipse.'

This is a typical confusion between historical fact and a Toynbeesque wish. The eclipse of nationalism by some supranational federalism has been predicted so often that it is one of the platitudes of twentieth-century writing. But, in fact, this century is the triumphant epoch of the nation state, and the burial ground of broader associations and groupings. At least twenty separate nationhoods have been founded in the past few decades, mostly in Asia, while simultaneously the monocentric groupings have either been destroyed, like the Ottoman Empire and the Austro-Hungarian Empire, or have exchanged their dependence on a single centre for the looser liberty of separate orbits, as with the British Commonwealth, in which the nation state has claimed the institutional future. It is all very well to fulminate against 'the antiquated patchwork of ghetto-like nation states', and to talk of an irresistible tide sweeping us back towards the Syriac institution of the *millet*, which is Toynbee's institutional ideal.

143

The Toynbee Heresy

But has the tide been so irresistible after all, in a generation in which 'the species of community of which [Israel] was the youngest member' has been fruitful and multiplied to a degree which seemed inconceivable a few decades ago?.

Perhaps it is because we disprove the great sweeping thesis about the 'institutional future' not belonging 'to the western institution of the national state' that we are called upon to bear these unfaithful wounds, inflicted without love. I doubt whether an analysis in which a hostile passion smothers any spark of human sympathy will supersede the traditional appraisal of Israel's history, including its modern resurgence, as one of the greatest testimonies to the unconquered human spirit.

CHAPTER XIII

The Lofty Peak*

This assembly brings pride and consolation to Israel in an hour of tense ordeals. From every corner of this continent the leaders of the American Jewish community have come together to surround the State of Israel with the warmth and shelter of their devotion.

Israel has no greater strength than that which flows from these abundant sources of Jewish fraternity. The union of spirit between Israel and the Jewish people everywhere is a fact of Middle Eastern, indeed, of universal history, no less pertinent than the more familiar calculations of oil and military strategy. There could be no narrower statesmanship than that which would plan the relations of the Western world with the Middle East in terms of geography or mineral geology, rather than in the invisible but more enduring terms of history. To these terms of history belong these mighty links between Israel and American Jewry; and in this room today, these links shine forth, strong and gleaming bright.

This conference reminds us of all that we have celebrated together, in this the most fearful and most glorious decade of all the Jewish epochs. We forged this partnership a few years ago in an hour of fearful sorrow when we were dazed and haunted by a massacre beyond comprehension. Now, within seven years, we have together steered our people through its darkest night towards its most resplendent dawn.

Is it not natural that men who have shared such an experience should protect an inheritance restored at such ghastly cost? Within a single lifetime we have passed from a world in which the existence of an independent Israel seemed inconceivable into a world which seems inconceivable without its existence. As we take counsel together on our common responsibility, let us first reaffirm our faith that Israel's resurgence is an event to be conceived in the highest dimensions of history. In the symphony of Jewish life, this past

*At the Assembly of Jewish Organizations, Washington, 6 March 1955.

The Lofty Peak

decade appears in a sudden crescendo of transition, with overtones both of tragedy and of grandeur.

It is natural that your minds have been concentrated primarily upon those matters which cause us concern today. But I am glad that you found the time to turn aside from our dangers to study the affirmative elements in Israel's contemporary life. For Israel is not merely a problem; it should not be described as a function of regional and international rivalry. It is an asset in itself, meriting contemplation on the basis of its own achievements and its own ideals.

In recent months we have recorded a steady consolidation in every aspect of the national life. We have seen our society grow in cohesion as its divergent elements have strengthened their common mould. We have seen one vast wave of immigration triumphantly received; and a new beneficent trickle has begun to flow which might again this very year bring as many as 50,000 to our shores. We have seen progress both in agricultural and industrial production. Those of you who have visited the country in recent years have borne witness that Israel does not live all its life in the shadow of unresolved political problems. You have seen the enlargement of the rural landscape; you have seen the swift increase of our agricultural production; you have seen an industrial development which reflects the patient investment and sacrifices of previous years. You have seen Israeli merchandise meeting an ever growing proportion of our domestic needs, and winning an honoured place in the export markets. You have seen the beginning of our economic recovery which is already reflected in statistical terms. Whereas four years ago Israel's foreign currency earnings covered less than one-eighth of its minimal consumer requirements, we now pay our way to the extent of 33 per cent of our imported consumer needs.

This does not mark the end of the road towards consolidation. The manner in which we describe the economic picture depends largely upon our varying temperaments. The difference between an optimist and a pessimist was once described in terms of two men who look upon a half-full glass of whisky. One says that the glass is half full, the other says that it is half empty. Each is a correct definition of the same situation. One might therefore say that Israel's position is still alarming, since two-thirds of its minimal consumer needs have to be furnished by external aid. But no one can fail to see the great momentum of progress, which has carried us forward towards solvency. The people of Israel, I assure you, are no less preoccupied with the positive elements in their consolidation than with their unresolved problems. All this activity takes place together with dynamic and courageous effort in the realms of mind and spirit. Here is a heartening picture of Israel in forward march. We are becoming slowly but inexorably reinforced.

Israel and the Jewish world together could not have achieved, still less consolidated, this newly won freedom alone. There have been moments of apparent solitude, and there may be such moments again. But the significant fact about Israel's international relations has surely been the impressive help and recognition which have come to us from outside, beyond the limits of our own strength and capacity.

There is no greater fallacy than that which speaks of Israel's alleged 'isolation'. We stand in relations of friendship with the majority of states in the inhabited globe, and in special intercourse of mutual responsibility with our kindred communities in the free world. As is natural with a young state, our external relations bring greater help from others than we have yet been privileged to requite. The reinforcement—political, moral and material—which we have thus received in the framework of our international friendships is beyond the usual measure enjoyed by new states in the early revolutionary period of their emergence. While we move rapidly toward a greater measure of equilibrium in our international relations, that goal is still remote. For many years, especially while Arab hostility persists, the strength of our international friendships will do much to determine the pace and spirit of our consolidation.

In this process of establishing relations of mutual recognition and aid with other peoples, our strongest reliance has been upon friendship with the United States. This friendship rests on deep affinities of ideals and historic experience. These include common memories and aspirations—of immigration, pioneering, democracy, the harmony and synthesis of divergent cultures, and, above all, the dedication to a moral system to which the land and people of Israel once gave splendid birth. In every part of your Republic, including its most remote regions, in its public forums and its state legislatures, in its literature and journalism, in its cities and its villages, amongst its representatives and elected leaders, and in the council rooms of its government departments, I have received on Israel's behalf, and

The Lofty Peak

sought to transmit to Israel, a deep impression of this abundant goodwill. The practical expression of this friendship has found varied form: in swift recognition of our statehood; in assistance to build the armistice system from the havoc of an active war; in a basic respect for our sovereignty; in opposition to the more eccentric and extreme proposals for Israel's dismemberment; in repudiation of belligerency and blockade; in technical and cultural co-operation; in moral encouragement; and through a vast infusion of economic and financial strength which has been a decisive element in our growing stability. In all these avenues a gracious light has fallen and still rests upon American-Israel relations.

This friendship is far broader than any single clash of interest or judgment which may arise from time to time. It is important, though not always easy, that any specific divergence between our countries should not be generalized into a false assumption of sundered friendship. We have nothing to gain from such a rash generalization. But, on the other hand, it is equally important that any such divergence, when it touches a really vital issue, should be frankly tackled and swiftly reconciled before it can develop into an organic threat to our mutual understanding. These two considerations should guide the character and pace of our diplomacy as it comes face to face with the problem of Israel's security in a hostile region where the balance is being dangerously disturbed by the exclusive offer of reinforcement and guarantees to Arab states. This is the main divergence of judgment between our two countries today. Within the framework of our abiding friendship, we must seek an urgent reconciliation of this serious difference.

Let no one doubt the urgency of the problem for us. The fierce hostility of the Arab states is a constant threat to Israel's security. The fact that they aspire to Israel's extinction or dismemberment is frankly stated by Arab leaders themselves. These verbal threats are reinforced by constant hostility on land and sea, in international politics and in the arenas of world opinion. Above all, the traces of this enmity reflect themselves across our embattled frontiers. In such circumstances, assurances from Western sources that Israel's security is not threatened are neither thoughtful nor prudent.

Moreover, Israel's territorial, demographic and strategic postures are entirely to her disadvantage. Our neighbours and adversaries are thirty times our population. They are three hundred times our area.

148

They are infinitely more rich in natural and mineral resources. It is true that the Arab advantage in demographic and geopolitical terms is not reflected today in a corresponding disparity between our respective military capacity. But in terms of security planning, it is the potential that must determine the problem and its solution. Nor should we forget that the whole of Israel and her population are, by harsh facts of geography, closely accessible to the effect of Arab hostility, while the bulk of this vast Arab continent is immune from any alleged threat from Israel. If our encirclement (sometimes called 'the advantage of interior lines') is really a strategic advantage, then we would readily exchange the position of the encircled for the encircler.

You will, therefore, understand our concern and apprehension, when we see these factors of vulnerability, which cannot be changed, unnecessarily increased by the extension to Arab states of security guarantees and arms agreements which are withheld from Israel. A great network of security guarantees and aid agreements now arises in the Middle East. Look at this pattern of mutual security evolving within our region: treaty between Great Britain and Egypt; treaty between Great Britain and Jordan; treaty between Great Britain and Iraq; treaty between Great Britain and Libya; arms agreement between the United States and Iraq; arms agreement between the United States and Pakistan; agreements between the United States and Libya and Saudi Arabia; treaty between Turkey and Pakistan; treaty between Turkey and Iraq. Nor is this process yet at an end.

Thus a great structure linking the states of the Middle East and of the Western world together in mutual assistance is based upon the purposeful exclusion of one state and of one state alone—precisely the most vulnerable state in the region. To make the paradox more startling, the excluded country is one of the few centres of democratic life within the area. This is surely a disquieting picture of imbalance and discrimination. A man would have to be lost to reason to expect the people of Israel not to be alarmed by this sudden increase of their isolation within a hostile region.

We do not assert that there is any evil design in this discrimination, or that the Powers concerned deliberately wish to see our neighbours intimidate us from a new position of strength. But whatever is their tactical logic, and irrespective of friendly intention, it is the results which count: and these are very grave indeed. A political, psychological, and eventually a physical imbalance are in the making,

The Lofty Peak

unless measures are now taken to correct them by a policy of scrupulous equality. It is no simple matter, I assure you, for us to dwell amongst the fierce and active hostility of our neighbours, to see their status and their military posture reinforced month by month by their relationships with the Western Powers, while we ourselves are ostracized and left to rely on our current military strength as the sole barrier between life and destruction. I do not know of many other small countries in the world which are exhorted to see their own unaided military strength as the sole shield of their independence and their very life. I know of no other country which has been placed in this nerve-racking position. I do not know of any other part of the world where the powers have ever sought to organize security by excluding a single state from guarantees and arms aid which are made available to its hostile neighbours.

This is the motive for our concern. Anybody who envisages his country in our position of siege and regional solitude must judge for himself whether it is an illusory fear, or an apprehension soundly based. This is why, in recent months, I have been discussing the problem of Israel's security with your Secretary of State and his colleagues. I cannot, of course, comment today on the course of these continuing discussions to which Assistant Secretary Allen referred last night. I will repeat that Prime Minister Sharett has publicly stated that we feel entitled to request binding, formal guarantees for the integrity of our frontiers as well as direct assistance to maintain the balance of arms which is now being disturbed to our disadvantage. What is there difficult, immoderate or inequitable in such a case? Surely those who, however inadvertently, increase our dangers are responsible for offering available remedy, both as a matter of moral decency and for the sake of our region's peace?

The treaty recently concluded between Turkey and Iraq has made this situation more acute. I cannot discuss this problem without a word of introduction about the abiding character of the friendship which unites Turkey and Israel. Our regional isolation would have been formidable and disquieting indeed but for the beneficent role which Turkey played in illustrating to the Middle East the virtues of recognizing our integrity, in concluding firm and friendly relations of diplomacy, commerce and culture; thus demonstrating to the rest of the Middle Eastern and the Moslem world that a Middle Eastern country which establishes peaceful relationships with Israel has no

The Lofty Peak

reason to regret that constructive choice, but rather derives benefits from friendship with us no less than those which we derive in our turn.

Within that friendship, I must state quite frankly that we do not share the view that this new treaty is a favourable development in the reinforcement of Israel's security or of Middle Eastern stability.

The treaty in itself, quite apart from its contents, is another link in the network of relationships arising exclusively between the Arab States and the Western Powers. We were born into a world of imbalance, in the sense that Israel came into existence at a time when the chief Arab states—Egypt, Jordan and Iraq—were already integrated into a British treaty system. We make no complaint about this fact of our pre-natal history, but I stress the fact itself—as the starting point for what happened later. When American policy, concerned with certain objectives of world strategy, began to express itself in contractual arrangements in the Middle East, we observed that all American agreements dealing with security were made exclusively with Arab states.

Now comes the third partner in the growing imbalance: Turkey enters the field of Middle Eastern security organization and she too enters it with guarantees and arms agreements for the Arab states alone. Thus, even if this treaty had been perfect and impeccable in its contents, its very existence would have been an added argument in our cause.

Moreover, the contents of the treaty, to our regret, are not perfect or impeccable. There are specific provisions and omissions which are prejudicial to Israel's vital interests. Our deep friendship for one of the signatories compels us frankly to draw attention to the serious defects of this treaty.

First, we note the absence of the undertaking, which occurs in other treaties, to abstain from aggression against the territorial integrity and political independence of any other state. You can read all the mutual defence treaties in the Western world and everywhere you will find this undertaking to respect the integrity and immunity from aggression of all other states. It occurs with almost ceremonial regularity. That undertaking is omitted here. Why? Can anyone doubt whose integrity and independence it is that the Government of Iraq refuses to acknowledge? Must we not have some twinge of apprehension on observing the Turkish signature of a contract omitting this universal provision, and thus appearing to condone this reservation of Iraq?

151

The Lofty Peak

Second, there is a reference in an exchange of letters between Turkey and Iraq to what is called 'the Palestine problem'. These letters are introduced into the treaty as one of its supplements. In this Turkey implies agreement with an Iraqi letter on this 'Palestine problem'. I do not propose to weary you with a description of this stale fallacy which contends that there is some obligation to revive all the recommendations of the General Assembly and particularly those which Arab violence irrevocably once destroyed and which have been succeeded by new situations of fact and law. But, this concept with its implication of Israel's dismemberment does appear irrelevantly in this treaty. Whatever is its true significance, the fact is that Turkey has made an accord with Iraq on a matter adversely affecting Israel's interest without Israel's agreement. This in itself is an unusual practice in a bilateral treaty and nothing but harm and confusion can come from an impression, even a wrong impression, that Turkey is formally committed to the policies advocated by the Arab states in the United Nations.

Third, and perhaps most serious in its general significance, comes Article V of the treaty which states that adherence to it is open—and observe carefully to whom adherence is open—to all the members of the Arab League, or to other states fully recognized both by Turkey and Iraq. Now, surely, this is nothing but a euphemism for closing the door in Israel's face! A definition is formulated which excludes Israel and nobody else. The label, 'For all except Israel,' is becoming too common in the terminology of security agreements in the Middle East. There is a similar reference in the Anglo-Egyptian Treaty of 1954 which states that the various strategic advantages of that treaty shall accrue to Turkey and to all signatories of the Arab League's Collective Security Pact. There are so many ways of saying 'Everybody except Israel'. The diplomatic vocabulary is rich and fertile. How can we fail to be concerned, when under the pressure of Arab hostility, friendly powers are induced to establish our exclusion as one of the foundations of Middle Eastern security organization? You will fully understand why we cannot see advantage to Israel or even ordinary international justice, in a document which pays such disquieting deference and regard to the special Arab hostility to Israel.

The hostility evinced towards us by our southern neighbour illustrates the reality and urgency of our concern. In recent months Egypt

152

The Lofty Peak

has been the source of the most vehement enmity. Every circumstance of mutual advantage and of regional peace argues in favour of harmonious relations between Israel and Egypt whose encounters in history have been so memorable for the enrichment of civilization. Here are two countries which form the south-eastern basin of the Mediterranean between whom there exist no objective causes of antagonism or strife. Yet hostility to Israel has become the primary theme of Egyptian policy, thus disappointing the hopes of many who expected that the first break in the wall of tension would come from the present Egyptian régime. In recent months, especially since September last, Egypt has bombarded us with every form of belligerency. Between September 1954 and February 1955, Egypt was responsible for thirty-four armed clashes in Israel territory and for nine cases of sabotage. On twenty-seven occasions in these months, Egypt has been condemned by the Armistice Commission for these assaults. On January 24th, the Armistice Commission noted 'once again with extremely grave concern that despite Egypt's obligations, the penetrations and killings of Israel citizens have not been terminated'. The Commission 'called upon the Egyptian authorities to put an immediate end to such aggressive acts'. On another occasion the Commission denounced this aggression in similar terms calling upon Egypt 'immediately and finally to put an end to these acts of aggression'.

Turning to the acts of sabotage directed against our water system in the parched Negev, the Mixed Armistice Commission in October last expressed 'great concern over the repeated acts of planned demolition of main water pipe lines in Israel by well-trained, organized and armed troops, coming from Egyptian-controlled territory'. The Commission again 'called upon the Egyptian authorities to put an immediate end to such aggressive acts'.

Following this grave warning the assaults increased. Powers concerned with Middle Eastern security made vigorous representations in Cairo. While these assaults went on across the border, Egypt carried its warfare against Israel to the seas by blockade and seizure in defiance of international decisions. You are familiar with the case of the *Bat Galim*, confiscated in the Suez Canal—a case in which Egypt continues to violate the will of the international community and of the maritime world. The state of war which Egypt has frankly proclaimed as a juridical theory is being translated into the actual operation of its policy. The ideology of this policy was stated in November last by the official newspaper of the Egyptian régime in

153

these terms: 'Egypt and the Arabs must turn in the name of humanity and its culture to all nations of the world to ask their aid in wiping Israel off the map. . . .'

Would it not be eccentric if United Nations organs or interested governments were to examine specific clashes in any context other than this background of Egyptian belligerency? Anybody reading the press would receive a fantastic picture of tranquillity, serene calm on our frontiers with Egypt and upon the maritime approaches, into which there has suddenly erupted this unexpected armed clash. Is it not a falsification of historic judgment to fail to take account of these twenty-seven condemnations of Egypt in six months, of the unavailing attempts by the world community to put an end to the maritime blockade? Please consider that the area most deeply affected by Egypt's frontier assaults is the region facing the Gaza strip in which there goes forward Israel's most purposeful and dynamic attempt at pioneering, in which farmers and settlers are remote from the centres of physical security, in which the explosion of a pipe line can frustrate the great dream of fertilizing the Negev and restoring its ancient pride. These are observations on the background of current events. Some people have not been satisfied with a discussion of the background and have publicly given strong advance hints to the Mixed Armistice Commission as to what its findings shall be. I shall not follow them into such judicial prejudice. The basic issue is whether Egypt may declare a state of war, pursue acts of war and herself be immune from any defensive response even in a clash which she herself begins. The Egyptian position, as it has been enunciated almost in these words at our United Nations meetings, is simply this: Egypt is at war with Israel. Accordingly, Egypt claims the right to perform acts of war of her choice against Israel. But Egypt seeks protection from the United Nations from any warlike act which may be elicited in response. There is a situation of belligerency, but it is not reciprocal. Egypt may behave towards Israel as though there is war. Israel must behave towards Egypt as though there is peace.

Now this is no foundation for peaceful adjustment. I will only say that my government's policy, irrespective of any current clashes, has not changed. It is a policy of non-belligerency, by Israel and by Egypt, by land and on sea; tranquillity on the frontier, for Egypt and Israel; abstention by Israel and by Egypt from hostile threats; a purposeful attempt, by Egypt and by Israel, to make a transition toward permanent peace as our Armistice agreement requires. Surely

The Lofty Peak

it is not too much to hope that these simple ideas become the basis for adjustment between two neighbouring states upon whom the stability of our region so largely depends.

I cannot speak to you of these turbulent events without acute sorrow for our Middle East whose horizons are darkened by such heavy clouds. The grief is the more acute when we reflect what we would achieve if this hostility were renounced, so that our kindred peoples could unite their efforts for the renascence of their common region.

This sense of a high purpose obstructed by immediate preoccupation came to me with special force when I read of two events in Israel, ostensibly small events in the perspectives of journalism, which engaged our people's interest in recent weeks. The first was the extension, through new equipment, of a Department of Nuclear Physics at Rehovoth, which has already brought our country a modest but cherished international renown. The second was the acquisition by the nation of ancient scrolls inscribed with the literature from the golden age of revelation—the age when the Hebrew mind achieved its deepest insights into the nature of man and his universe. In these two disconnected items of news I saw reflected, in a sudden flash, the whole essence of Israel's destiny—the attribute of potential greatness which belongs to this small people in this land. Nuclear physics and biblical scrolls—the inscrutable mysteries of the future and the imperishable memories of the past! And now the one people, the only people whose continuous national memory has comprehended the full cycle from ancient prophecy to modern science, is restored to the land, the language and the freedom of its original inheritance. We have wandered too long in deep and lonely valleys, with narrow objectives before us, of mere physical survival, and defence against the fierce assaults of hostile worlds. And now the hand of history has restored us to our small but lofty elevation from which we look down on vast perspectives extending at our feet on either side—backward 4,000 years towards antiquity, and forward to the awesome challenge of atomic generations.

Let us resolve that we shall stand firm upon that small but lofty peak; that we shall never be dislodged or shaken from it; that we shall embody the concept of Eternal Israel at its highest level; that we shall carry this sublime story to the ears of free men everywhere, and proclaim it proudly amongst the nations.

155

CHAPTER XIV

The Titan Passes*

A TRIBUTE TO ALBERT EINSTEIN

It is not easy to speak of Albert Einstein in the conventional terms of obituary. He lived in solitude and grandeur in a realm of transcendent thought; and he looked upon his world from a vantage point which nobody else could fully share.

It is difficult to think of any single man since antiquity who so sharply transformed the thought of mankind by the influence and impression of his life.

Physics and philosophy, science and technology are all newly reflected in our lives through the dynamism and audacity of his perceptions. We live in a world in which the smallest mass holds the secret of the most violent energy; in which forces previously considered disconnected and arbitrary fit into a single potent equation; in which vast abundance and unlimited destruction confront mankind in sharp and awful contrast. It is a world quite different from that which preceded the Einstein epoch; and the change is the direct conclusion of his pursuit of new and uncharted truths.

His humility was profound and sincere, but it was also misleading. Because of the modesty of his bearing, we were not always aware that we had in our midst a giant of history, the chief pride and ornament of his generation. By his rebellion against scientific dogma, in a flash of insight beyond the realm of Newtonian physics, he forced men everywhere to think differently about their universe than had all previous generations across centuries of time.

Is it not moving for us to recall, in deep pride and solemnity, that this was a faithful son of the Jewish people, a mirror of its attributes in their purest quality, both a victim and a hero of its history? He was a Jew by the simplest definition of the term. He was a Jew because whatever happened to the Jewish people happened to him. In all the biographies and tributes which he has inspired, I have missed the

* At Town Hall, New York, 14 May 1955.

The Titan Passes

connecting link between Einstein the man of science and Einstein the Jew. One would think, in reading this rich and varied literature of appraisal, that his Jewishness was an incidental circumstance, a sort of biological accident, a mere nostalgic loyalty, or at best a kind of spiritual hobby, but at any rate a diversion from the main course and purpose of his work. But is this really a true judgment? Is the fact of his Jewishness really so separate from his scientific revelation, and so subsidiary to it, as conventional biography would have us believe? I am convinced, both by instinct and by personal association, that Einstein the Jew and Einstein the explorer of new scientific truth represent a perfect harmony.

Throughout the journey of our people across history for four thousand years from ancient prophecy to relativity, the Jewish mind has been dominated by one single theme. It is that the universe is not a chaos of wild, uncontrollable, arbitrary, mysterious forces, but that it is a pattern of order and progress guided by an articulate intelligence and law. This is the essence of the Hebrew revolution. This, in substance, is the whole difference between Judaism and paganism— even paganisms as aesthetically refined as those of Greece and Rome. If, says the Hebrew mind, the reason and progress in the universe are not always visible, then this is not because they do not exist, but only because the human mind, in its imperfection, has not yet completed its exploration. This was the essence of the Hebrew revolt, an assault against determinism and apathy, an attack upon superstition, resignation and irrationality, whether in the governance of nature or of man.

Is there not a direct link between this rebellion of his ancient forefathers and that of Albert Einstein? For what has he sought to teach us in his realm except that there are laws hitherto unknown which govern cosmic forces; that nothing in nature is totally disconnected from anything else; that there is nothing which does not possess a relative harmony with everything else; and that especially a calculable relationship exists between matter and energy. It was at this point that Einstein's scientific genius made union with the revelation of his Hebrew forebears. For the doctrine of order and progress in the universal design is the most essential of Israel's contributions to the history of human thought.

I believe that he was conscious of this harmony. The tragedy and exaltation of Jewish history moved him deeply and awakened all his compassion and indignation. He was a part of the tragedy which he saw in Europe very close at hand; and he was a part of the exaltation which he shared with us at Israel's rebirth. Of these events, he spoke always in the first person—'our Jewish people, our Israel cause'. 'My connection with the Jewish people,' he wrote to me in December 1952, 'is the deepest human emotion of my life.' The cause of 'our State of Israel', he wrote ten days before his death, 'moves me to lend my full influence and support'.

He saw the rebirth of Israel as one of the few political acts in his lifetime which was of an essentially moral quality. He believed that the conscience of the world should therefore be engaged in Israel's preservation. The reason for this sentiment was that he saw modern Israel as the embodiment in this generation of ancient Israel. Might it not happen that the ideals of liberty, of social justice and of universal peace would again find a sanctuary amidst that people in which they had then found first expression? When he felt the cold wind of Israel's insecurity, he apprehended that something very precious was being endangered; and at that moment he fell into a deep, responsible, and active preoccupation with Israel's future, which brought me to him in the final days of his life, in encounters which I shall everlastingly cherish, recalling the warm and proud Jewish solidarity which enriched his discourse and endowed it with undying grace.

Is not this the answer to those who sometimes wonder whether there is not something small about Israel; whether the attention, the turmoil and the reverberations which we set up are not out of proportion to the real stature of our statehood? Here was a man who should be regarded as an authority on greatness and smallness. Here was a mind which ranged over universal mysteries, which thought in planetary terms, which had unlocked the most fearful, and perhaps the most beneficent forces which matter could generate. Yet for his mind, small Israel loomed very large indeed.

Our impact upon human thinking has always had this quality. The broader a man's perspective, the higher the peak of his responsibility, the loftier the elevation from which he looks down upon the world, the more significant does Israel appear. To the true historians, to the great scientists such as Einstein, to statesmen of Churchillian grandeur, the rise of Israel shines forth as an event conceived in the highest dimensions of human history, and not to be described in relationship to the mere physical attributes of our population or our territory. If we have difficulties in securing comprehension, we meet

The Titan Passes

with them chiefly with men of a lesser understanding who see but a limited sector of the universal field. Israel, as an idea in history, can be comprehended only by a universal vision, one which sees us in the broadest context of space and time, as the culmination of four thousand years of continuous history as the memory and conscience of all the generations.

This, at any rate, is how Albert Einstein looked upon us. And in these terms he spoke of Israel in the concluding days and hours of his life. His modesty, his liberalism, his passion for freedom, his hatred of tyranny, his assertion of self-expression as the sovereign right of individuals and of nations—all these kindled in Albert Einstein the brotherly pride and love for Israel which occupied his final hours.

I cannot conceal my deep emotion at the reflection that this, the most illustrious man of his generation, whose mind had lit up the darkness of human knowledge, spent his last days in loving concern for Israel's future. His life, of course, belongs to all generations. His legacy comes down to all peoples; but the people of Israel, and the Jewish people everywhere, may within the framework of humanity's grief, feel a special intimacy in pride and bereavement as they attend this faithful son of the Jewish people on his journey to immortality.

CHAPTER XV

Ten Years Ago We Were Not Here*

The hour which we celebrate today is rich with enduring memories. It marked a crossroad in the journey of a generation which had passed through much affliction on its road to liberty and survival. The world had just seen the most destructive tyranny of all the ages crumble before its eyes in ruin and disgrace. The cruelty and malice of Nazism had been crushed by righteous force. The peoples who had joined hands in sacrifice and resistance now came together, amidst the grace and freedom of San Francisco, to renew their partnership in the cause of universal peace. Sharp grief for the past and soaring hope for the future were mingled in the universal emotion of that hour.

Israel approaches this anniversary in a special mood of exaltation. Ten years ago we were not here. Our absence revealed the deep chasm of weakness and disaster into which we had fallen. Here was the people that had sustained the full brunt of the tyrant's fury, from the first day of his ascendancy to the hour of his fall. Six million of our kinsmen had been slaughtered in savage hatred on the barbarous altars of the Nazi empire. Their survivors stalked in emaciation and despair amidst the obscene place of death and torture which the liberating armies of the United Nations had exposed to the horrified gaze of mankind.

Never in all recorded history had any family of the human race been overwhelmed by such a tidal wave of grief and havoc as that which engulfed the Jewish people during the Nazi decade. Every impulse of compassion had been violated by this assault. Against this background, the absence of any promise of Jewish independence in the new world order arising at San Francisco appeared as an agonizing paradox. It seemed seriously possible that every people would be established in sovereignty except the first and most sorely ravaged amongst the victims of persecution. Every culture and civilization

* To the United Nations Commemorative Assembly, San Francisco, 26 June 1955.

would be embodied in free political and social institutions except that culture and civilization which had conceived the revolutionary message of individual morality, social justice and universal peace.

The presence of Israel in San Francisco today, therefore, marks an act of historic remedy. It illustrates the sudden recuperation of the Jewish people from the lowest point in its fortunes to the dignity and opportunity which it had tenaciously pursued for two thousand years. A shelter of the body and a sanctuary of the spirit are now restored to a people which had previously lacked these attributes of a free creative life.

The active participation of the United Nations in this transition reflects the significance of Israel's rebirth in universal history and in international equity. Multitudes of people in every land owe the central purposes of their moral lives to the insights and conclusions expressed by the people of Israel in the land of Israel in the previous era of Israel's independence. How can they fail to be uplifted by the prospect that the people, the land and the language from which this revelation had sprung would now be restored to their original union? Seen in this light the smallness of our state in area and population became enlarged in the consciousness of men by the broad vistas of historic memory. This was also an act of unassailable justice. For Israel's accession to statehood within her meagre limits of territory was accompanied in this very century by the liberation of our neighbouring people in nine separate sovereignties, extending over a vast expanse, replete with all the potentialities of political and economic strength. Never since the golden age of the Caliphates had the Arab world commanded such elements of power as those which had now come within its grasp. There is nothing exceptional in Israel's modest opportunity, nothing which should be envied or begrudged by those more lavishly endowed.

Yet the Middle East which, by every circumstance of tradition, should help to lead the world towards universal peace, is itself still plunged in the turmoil of regional strife.

In confronting all its unfulfilled objectives, the United Nations would do well to define the extent of its limitations and its potentialities. These are not the same limitations and potentialities as those which our predecessors confronted here ten years ago. The founders of our Organization sought to establish an international system on the basis of certain political, juridical and military assumptions which had seemed valid in the years of the war and the Grand Alliance. In swift succession all these assumptions have fallen to the ground.

The political assumption was that the Great Powers which had united against aggression would maintain their union for the enterprises of world peace. Scarcely was the ink dry on the United Nations Charter before members of the Alliance split into rival camps, glowering at each other across a widening gulf of suspicion and mistrust.

The juridical assumption was that the United Nations would be able to enforce peace largely through the exercise of coercive powers and restraints similar to those which prevail within our national societies. But in the test of action the enforcement powers of the Security Council proved illusory. The Articles of the Charter providing for the establishment of international security forces under the authority of the Security Council have remained unfulfilled. While this fact is commonly known, it is less widely realized that the alternative machinery and procedures envisaged for the General Assembly in the 'Uniting for Peace' Resolution have similarly remained unimplemented. The detailed recommendations contained in that Resolution have, for the most part, not been carried out. Thus, while collective security has made its main advances outside the United Nations in the form of regional, bilateral and collective alliances for self-defence, the emphasis of United Nations action has shifted from enforcement to conciliation and pacific settlement. This is not necessarily a negative development. A solution of an international dispute by voluntary conciliation is intrinsically preferable to any solution by forcible restraint. Indeed, a disservice may have been rendered to the United Nations by an unrealistic emphasis originally placed upon its coercive powers. In the testing ground of action we have become a forum for conciliation and not as originally conceived an instrument for the enforcement of security by collective action.

The military assumptions of our founders have been submerged even more drastically by the course of events. The readiness with which the Charter envisages military action as a routine method of preserving peace can only be explained in terms of the concepts which dominated the pre-atomic world. But modern weapons have now led the military science into a remarkable deadlock. The power of modern weapons makes their possessors unable in all conscience to regard them as a response to any but the ultimate and desperate issues of security. The grotesque potency of military force is reducing the military argument to impotence, even in the domain of collective enforcement. This paradox is, indeed, one of the crucial threads upon which the security of our world is dangerously suspended. One might have wished that humanity, with its rich spiritual heritage and its long experience in the political arts, could have found a more affirmative stimulus to peaceful co-existence than the mere desire to avoid annihilation. But if this mutual dread is the only barrier between the world and its ultimate tragedy of error, it is better that we should cherish it than that we should possess no such barrier at all.

The collapse of the three principal assumptions which commanded the scene in San Francisco ten years ago has made sudden demands upon the adaptability of the United Nations to new limits of capacity and opportunity. Instead of Great Power unity we have had to operate in an atmosphere of Great Power conflict with no weapon but the moral force of majority recommendation. Instead of maintaining a structure of collective force, we have developed institutions with the main emphasis on conciliation and pacific settlement. Instead of relying on the use of military force in the common interest, we have come to regard the use of military power on an international scale as lying beyond any contingency that the human mind may willingly entertain. We have become a collective diplomat instead of a collective policeman.

The United Nations has thus become something entirely different from the organization envisaged in this place ten years ago. Its purpose is now to promote peace by conciliation, rather than to enforce it by coercive restraint. Unless we reconcile ourselves to these changes, in the essence and character of this Organization, we shall fail both in the accurate judgment of its record and in the correct application of its resources to the problems of our age. We have no semblance of supra-national authority. We have, instead, a framework within which attitudes of co-operation are arising between sovereign states in slow and painful stages, just as these attitudes arose slowly and painfully in the relations between citizens and groups within our national societies. We have the bare foundation and not the complete structure, the early promise but not the final consummation, of a world society governed by the rule of law.

The achievement of the United Nations in these ten years can be accurately appraised only in terms of its actual limitations and potentialities. By reference to these standards, the record is neither negligible nor unimpressive. Active hostilities in many parts of the

163

world have been localized in scope and limited in duration, instead of developing their full momentum and spreading out into an ever-widening circle of active conflict. In Kashmir and Indonesia, in Iran, in the Middle East, in the Balkans and Berlin and, above all, in Korea, the action of the international forum at an early stage of crisis has served as a barrier against the illegitimate encroachments of armed force. In the Korean dispute the United Nations went beyond political action to establish its first precedent for collective resistance to aggression. It is not fortuitous that since that episode no sustained effort has been made anywhere in the world to alter an existing situation by armed force.

It may seriously be doubted whether in any other generation a conflict as comprehensive, profound and widespread as that which has divided the East and West could have existed for so long without eruption into major war. We cannot lawfully deny the United Nations its due share of merit for this achievement. For years it maintained its solitude as the only bridge on which the rival worlds encountered each other in free and open discussion. The very exercise of seeking the support of world opinion imposes restraints of reason in the development of national policies, and operates against the formulation of national policies on the sole basis of egocentric emotion. Governments are inevitably induced to seek the kind of policies which can, at least, be internationally explained.

There are fields of international action in which the United Nations may claim to have exceeded the expectations of its founders. Under its influence many nations have made a swift and peaceful transition from colonial tutelage to statehood and sovereign equality. The twentieth century has been a golden age of national emancipation. Multitudes of people, especially in Asia, have emerged from various forms of dependency into a new era of national freedom and international responsibility. A large proportion of our present membership is composed of communities which but a short time ago lacked the opportunities and responsibilities of sovereign government. International opinion has expressed itself with force and constancy in favour of the orderly evolution of subject peoples towards self-determination. This process is still in full spate. The United Nations continues to promote the development of trust territories towards self-government and, in the meantime, to keep vigilant watch over their vital interests.

Ten Years Ago We Were Not Here

The active vigilance of the United Nations, its prudent concern for the interests of non-self-governing peoples, have created a situation distinctive to our generation. Until recent years the only path available to subject communities in their quest for freedom lay through the traditional processes of forcible secession, revolution or armed rebellion. Today a new alternative presents itself. The transition to sovereignty has time and again in this century been achieved by consent, often with the stimulus of international judgment. This new attribute of the world community lays special responsibilities both on administering Powers and on dependent communities—on the former to accept the impulses which drive all peoples to pursue their emancipation; on the latter, to advance their cause by the evolutionary process which international judgment has now made available, rather than by precipitate and, perhaps, superfluous recourse to violent revolt.

But nations do not live exclusively in a world of political relationships. It may be true that there is a lesser volume of starvation, poverty and disease in the world today than in any other period of human history. But the progress of science, the swift development of communications and the spread of education have made the peoples of the world more righteously intolerant of their disabilities, more exigent in their claim to partake of an economic inheritance which amply lies within the resources of the world community. The United Nations may take pride in its efforts to vindicate the solidarity of mankind in its battle against the ravages of want and disease. Studies in the economic development of under-developed countries; the expanded programme of technical assistance; the work of regional economic commissions; the impending establishment of the International Finance Corporation; varied social work in under-developed countries; the inspiring accomplishments of UNICEF; the activities of the High Commissioner for Refugees, the Korean relief funds, and the United Nations Works and Relief Agency in the Middle East— all these have helped to make the name of the United Nations in many lands a byword for fruitful and disinterested humanitarianism. There is perhaps a deeper drama, a more decisive significance in these activities than the media of world publicity have yet managed to convey. A sense of community is more likely to emerge amongst the world's peoples through these processes of institutional altruism than through any spectacular development in political relations.

165

Ten Years Ago We Were Not Here

The achievements of the United Nations in its first decade fall far short of humanity's total aspiration. They may even lead to disappointment if they are compared with the visions which illuminated these halls ten years ago. Anyone who expected a system of international peace to spring in full perfection from the havoc of the battlefield may well feel a pang of disillusionment. But if we regard our objective as one to be achieved by patient evolution; if we aim at the gradual but constant growth of community attitudes in international life; if we understand that this, the most cherished purpose to which human society can aspire, is not to be attained in a sudden flash of fortune—then our judgment of this decade will be less disheartened. We need not feel that the brave ambitions of our first summer have played us false.

Certain it is that there are impulses alive in the world which merit a deeper confidence. The past two years have been a fruitful period for diplomacy. The momentum of agreement has extended beyond points of marginal crisis, and begun to reach into the central issues of world conflict. In swift succession we have witnessed the Iranian oil settlement; the Trieste solution; the Korean armistice; the Indo-China settlement; the unanimous Resolution on the peaceful use of atomic energy; the Austrian State Treaty; and the decision of the Four Great Powers to confer, at the highest level of their responsibility, on the sources of world tension. Does not this prove that persistent negotiation, under the impulse of mankind's desperate need for peace, has not exhausted its potentiality of healing and that the absence of enforcement machinery, far from barring the road to fruitful conciliation, makes conciliation more indispensable, and, therefore, perhaps more feasible?

The United Nations need not regret that many of these achievements have been gained outside its immediate orbit. Our purpose here is to supplement and extend the domain of traditional diplomacy, not to replace it. Indeed, it is a legitimate interpretation of our Charter that member states have an obligation to attempt a solution of their differences by direct settlement before they have recourse to the international forum. The facile slogan which criticizes 'by-passing' of the United Nations deserves a sceptical response in the light of Article 33 of our Charter which implores us to by-pass our Organization and to regard it as a court of ultimate appeal, not of first instance. If parties to a dispute lack sufficient goodwill to attempt a settlement

Ten Years Ago We Were Not Here

by direct negotiation, then a demonstration of their disagreement by public debate is not likely to do more than aggravate their conflict. The experience of the past two years proves that the readiness of disputant states to bring their differences under direct review is likely to be the first step in the resolution of their conflict. For any state or group of states to refuse even to attempt a settlement by direct contact and free negotiation is to violate the essence of the Charter and to swim against the whole current of contemporary international experience.

The quest for international security is the dominating purpose of our age. If we succeed we shall have recorded one of mankind's decisive victories. If we fail, our imperfection may be beyond remedy or consolation. Never have the alternatives of salvation and disaster confronted mankind in such acute and fateful contrast. Israel can only raise its banner in an avowal of perfect confidence that the triumph of the United Nations lies within the power of our choice. Our authority for that faith is that three thousand years ago, in the very homeland to which we are now restored, we proclaimed rebellion against the prevailing fatalism of all preceding civilizations which saw human life as a relentless cycle coming back to a starting point in darkness and chaos. In the conception revealed to us, the cosmic pattern is not a wild anarchy of arbitrary mysterious forces, but is rather an articulate system guided by a merciful intelligence and a coherent law. Alone amongst the nations, our continuous historic memory covers the full cycle of human thought from ancient prophecy to relativity, from the old inheritance to the new potentiality. The doctrine of order and progress in the universal design is Israel's most authentic contribution to human thought.

If this vision of cosmic order and progress were not true then we would have nothing to say and nothing to vindicate. The Charter of the United Nations is a contemporary expression of that prophetic faith. It calls for order and progress in international relations to be inherited by an act of choice. No people can do better than commit its destiny to the triumph of that ideal. Let us see the labours of this first decade as a prelude to the decisive struggle which will only have reached its destination when all peoples shall dwell 'each beneath its vine and fig-tree with none to make them afraid'.

167

CHAPTER XVI

The Arab Refugees—A Record in Obstruction*

Five years have elapsed since the General Assembly established an Agency charged with the task of 'reintegrating the Arab refugees into the economic life of the Near East'. During that period the governments of our region have been enjoined to secure 'the permanent re-establishment of the refugees and their removal from relief'; to help convert them into productive members of Near Eastern societies; and to prepare them for a new life of dignity and freedom.

Today we confront a picture of misery and deadlock. The number of those receiving relief has increased, and not diminished. Arab governments hold all the major rehabilitation projects at a standstill, or in suspense. The Arab governments, which created this refugee problem by their brutal invasion of Israel seven years ago, now perpetuate its existence and deny the effective and merciful solution which lies within their power.

This Committee would be fortunate if it could fix its eyes on the challenge of the future, rather than on the rancours of the past. The fierce denunciations of Israel by Arab representatives deny us any such prospect. Nor would it be just to contemplate so deep a tragedy without frankly facing the question of responsibility. Unless we understand how this problem was caused, we cannot wisely judge how it should be resolved.

The problem of the Arab refugees was caused by a war of aggression launched by the Arab States against Israel in 1948. The purpose of that aggression was first to prevent Israel from coming into existence, and then to crush its newly established independence by armed force.

More than seven years have passed since that assault, but its

* To the General Assembly of the United Nations, 18 November 1955.

The Arab Refugees—A Record in Obstruction

memories are still vivid, its impression still profound. From the last day of November 1947 Arab forces had launched violent attacks upon our community with the avowed purpose of overthrowing the General Assembly's recommendation of 29th November 1947 by force. On the day of Israel's Declaration of Independence, which included a sincere appeal for friendship with the Arab world, the armies of Egypt, Jordan, Syria, Lebanon and Iraq, supported by contingents from Saudi Arabia and Yemen, crossed their frontiers and marched against Israel. Syrian tanks crashed into Upper Jordan. Lebanese and Syrian troops converged upon Galilee. Iraqui and Jordanian battalions pushed towards the coastal plain, and pressed us with our backs against the sea. Egyptian columns plunged into the Negev and crept northwards up the coastal plain to within twelve miles of Tel Aviv. Aircraft bombed our undefended cities. A ring of fire encircled us at Jerusalem and held its population in the grip of siege. Villages were destroyed, farm settlements devastated. In all the areas of Palestine which came under Arab occupation not one single Jew survived.

Arab governments understood well that their decision would take a fearful toll of life. The Secretary-General of the Arab League had grimly warned: 'This will be a war of extermination and a momentous massacre that will be spoken of like the Mongolian massacre and the Crusades.' But the people of Israel, fighting for life and freedom against overwhelming odds, were not the only victims. Caught up in the havoc and terror of war, hundreds of thousands of their Arab neighbours sought the shelter of Arab lands. Their departure was powerfully incited by the Arab leaders who sought to clear the battlefield for the slaughter, after which their Arab kinsmen would return in triumph. In an interview given to a Lebanese newspaper, *Sada al Janub*, Msgr. George Hakim, the Greek Catholic Archbishop of Galilee, has recalled:

'The refugees had been confident that their absence from Palestine would not last long; that they would return within a few days—within a week or two. Their leaders had promised them that the Arab armies would crush the "Zionist gangs" very quickly and that there would be no need for panic or fear of a long exile.'

An Arab political leader, Mr. Emile Ghoury, Secretary of the Arab Higher Committee, said with full candour on 15th September 1948:

The Arab Refugees—A Record in Obstruction

'I do not want to impugn anyone but only to help the refugees. The fact that there are these refugees is the direct consequence of the action of the Arab States in opposing partition and the Jewish State. The Arab States agreed upon this policy unanimously and they must share in the solution of the problem.'

It is an atonishing experience to sit here year by year and to hear the governments which created this problem disclaim all responsibility for its solution. We suggest to Arab representatives that they should rightly face this Committee, not in tones of violent grievance but in an attitude of humility and repentance. Their governments assumed a grave responsibility by their decision to launch a war for Israel's destruction. The international conscience was profoundly shocked by that decision.

The dominant sentiment of the United Nations found expression in the words of the delegate of the United States who said in the Security Council on 22nd May 1948, referring to the statements made by the Arab States:

'Their statements are the best evidence we have of the international character of this aggression. There is nothing in the resolution about aggression; it is a word which is not included in the text, but which has been mentioned in the statements of these aggressors. . . . Of course, the statement that they are there to make peace is rather remarkable in view of the fact that they are waging war.'

On 15th July 1948 the Security Council determined that the action of seven Arab governments had created a threat to international peace and security.

In December 1948 the United Nations—through its own representative, Dr. Bunche—recorded its grave verdict of responsibility:

'The Arab States had forcefully opposed the existence of a Jewish State in Palestine in direct opposition to the wishes of two-thirds of the members of the Assembly. Nevertheless their armed intervention had proved useless. The [Mediator's] report was based solely on the fact that the Arab States had no right to resort to force and that the United Nations should exert its authority to prevent such a use of force.'

These are amongst the documentary monuments of the Arab invasion. It has also left behind it the testimony of Israel's youthful graveyards; and the misery of Arab refugees is its living memorial. How monstrously do representatives of Arab States pervert the truth when they seek to lay responsibility for this tragedy at other doors!

170

The Arab Refugees—A Record in Obstruction

Those who launched the war are responsible, before history's bar, for all the suffering, misery, bloodshed and anguish which resulted from their fatal decision.

Nor is there any justice in ascribing the guilt to the United Nations, as some delegates have sought to do. The refugee problem was created, not by the establishment of the State of Israel, but by the attempt of Arab governments to overthrow that state by force. The crisis arose, not as Mr. Shukairy says, because the United Nations adopted a resolution in 1947; but because Arab governments attempted to overthrow that resolution and to frustrate its provision by illegitimate force. The United Nations should indignantly reject the charge of Arab governments that the United Nations is responsible for the creation of this tragedy. If the judgments of the United Nations had been peacefully accepted or even if opposition to them had simply been kept short of armed force, there would be no refugee problem hanging as a cloud upon the tense horizons of the Middle East.

The question of original responsibility is of more than historic importance. Once it is established that Arab governments have, by acts of policy, created this problem, it follows that the world community has an unimpeachable claim to invoke their full assistance in its settlement. This claim is all the more compelling when we reflect that Arab governments, in their own lands, command all the resources and conditions which would enable the refugees to be emancipated in full dignity and freedom.

After denouncing Israel for the crime of not having been defeated by the Arab assault, Arab delegates have occupied the Committee at great length with the idea that a solution may be found by the invocation of a single paragraph of a resolution adopted by the General Assembly seven years ago. The Arab governments find no difficulty in disregarding the main provision of the 1948 resolution requesting them to negotiate a final settlement with Israel, and to co-operate with her in the economic sphere, while they loudly invoke another provision which they interpret as an unconditional warrant for repatriation, at the unfettered choice of the refugees.

There is no such absolute warrant for repatriation in the 1948 resolution. Under its terms, repatriation is specifically limited by two conditions. The first is practicability. The second is the existence of a situation in which Arabs and Israelis are likely to live peacefully

171

as neighbours. It is clear from this very language that the General Assembly did not consider repatriation immediately practicable on 11th December 1948; and that a serious question arose in its mind with respect to the likelihood of peaceful co-existence between the refugees and the citizens of the country which they had left behind in the hour of crisis. These two conditions are far more remote to-day than they were in the more hopeful atmosphere of 1948. There is less practicability and less peace than there has ever been. All the available evidence has shown international opinion since 1948 moving away from the idea of repatriation, which was regarded as problematical even in 1948.

But, in any case, we find it difficult to take Arab representatives seriously as the righteous advocates of the General Assembly recommendations. Were they not the first governments in the history of the United Nations to take up arms for the forcible overthrow of a General Assembly resolution? A United Nations Commission reported on this question in the summer of 1948, in terms which have few precedents in the international literature of our time:

'Arab opposition to the plan of the Assembly of 1947 has taken the form of organized efforts by strong Arab elements, both inside and outside Palestine, to prevent its implementation and to thwart its objectives by threats and acts of violence, including repeated armed incursion into Palestine territory. The Commission has had to report to the Security Council that powerful Arab interests, both inside and outside Palestine, are defying the resolution of the General Assembly and are engaged in a deliberate effort to alter by force the settlement envisaged therein.'

This assault by violence on the General Assembly's resolution led to its abandonment, and to new attempts to reach a settlement by direct agreements, first under the General Armistice system, which was to be followed, in the expectation of the General Assembly and the Security Council, by peace negotiations. Throughout this period Arab governments developed their doctrine on the nature of General Assembly resolutions. Here are a few quotations from statements by Syrian representatives:

'In the first place the recommendations of the General Assembly are not imperative on those to whom they are addressed.'

'I fail to find in this Charter any text which implies directly or indirectly that the General Assembly has the authority to enforce its own recommendations by military force . . . the General Assembly only gives advice and the parties to whom advice is addressed accept it when it is rightful and just and when it does not impair their fundamental rights.'

The views of the present Foreign Minister of Egypt are on record as follows:

'No one can say that compliance is imperative or that states which do not comply with Assembly recommendations are acting against the Charter or undermining the structure of the United Nations. No one can speak of the General Assembly's resolutions as if they were obligatory decisions . . . the Charter and the United Nations will not crumble, will not fall apart if one or more of the General Assembly's resolutions is not put into effect.'

'We do not propose to comply with the General Assembly's resolutions on Palestine. This is our privilege under the Charter.'

In defence of this Egyptian jurisprudence, Dr. Fawzi invoked eminent authority:

'We have seen that the United Kingdom Government does not intend to comply with the General Assembly recommendation (1947) for the progressive turning over of the Administration of Palestine to the United Nations Partition Commission.'

Another Arab statesman, now the President of Lebanon, recorded similar views:

'The General Assembly's resolution of 1947 is a mere recommendation . . . it should be examined in the light of other recommendations of the General Assembly which have not been accepted by the country or groups of countries concerned and which have not been implemented.'

I do not propose to go deeply into the merits of these contributions by Arab delegates to our United Nations jurisprudence. I seek only to explain why we cannot possibly regard them as the sincere and consistent advocates of General Assembly resolutions. Those who denied those resolutions any validity at the time of their adoption are surely incongruous when they now suggest the resurrection of these resolutions without any allowance for the transformations of the passing years. Our Arab colleagues show no disposition to respect the decisions of the Security Council on belligerency and blockade; or the resolutions of the General Assembly on the need for peace negotiations and for close economic relations; or the resolution of the General Assembly defining Israel's recognized sovereignty within the United Nations system. We shall not advance towards a solution of

173

The Arab Refugees—A Record in Obstruction

this intricate refugee problem by engaging in juridical debates with governments whose armed rebellion against United Nations policies is the original cause of the crisis which we confront today.

It would be more fruitful and constructive to summarize the reports of the Director of UNRWA and of his predecessors who have dealt with this problem since the establishment of the Agency five years ago.

Let us first understand clearly what the objectives of the Agency have been. The General Assembly, in its Resolution 393 (V) of 1950, called for the 'reintegration of the refugees into the economic life of the Near East'. It advocated this reintegration on the grounds that it was essential 'in preparation for the time when international assistance is no longer available, and for the realization of conditions of peace and stability in the area'.

Each year since 1950 the General Assembly has repeated its exhortations to the host governments to facilitate the reintegration into their economies of the refugees living on their soil; to offer them the opportunities of labour, education and free movement; to allow them to realize the opportunities existing in Arab economies for the beneficial absorption of refugees; and to co-operate in new development projects to be financed with generous international aid. If the recommendations of 1950 and of subsequent years had been sincerely carried out, the refugees would now be the productive members of the Arab societies to which they are bound by every link of sentiment, language, culture and national loyalty. It is therefore grievous to record that the Arab governments have denied this salvation to their own kinsmen—preferring to maintain their refugee status undiluted and uncompromised for the sake of a sterile political controversy.

Thus, in January 1952 the General Assembly requested the host governments to assume the administration of the relief programme. In the report to the Eighth Session (1953) the Director stated bluntly and accurately that the Arab governments had 'been reluctant to assume the administration of the relief programme in accordance with the wish expressed by the General Assembly in its Resolution 513 (VI)'.

Were the refugees granted the right to work in the Arab states, great numbers of them could have thus become self-supporting. In its report to the Sixth Session the Agency complained that 'no

174

The Arab Refugees—A Record in Obstruction

Government except Jordan had proclaimed their right [of the refugees] to stay', neither did subsequent reports register any progress in this respect.

Over a number of years, the Agency has striven to eliminate the barriers which prevent the refugees from moving freely and seeking their own fortunes in the kindred Arab world. This problem of freedom of movement for refugees is of crucial importance. Recent years have witnessed a great expansion of economic potentialities in the Middle East. Last year the revenues of Iraq, Saudi Arabia and Kuwait from oil royalties alone amounted to 700 million dollars. This huge influx of wealth has opened up great opportunities of work and development into which the refugees, by virtue of their linguistic and national background, could fit without any sense of dislocation. There cannot be any doubt that if free movement had been granted, there would have been a spontaneous absorption of thousands of refugees into these expanded Arab economies. It is precisely this that Arab governments have obstructed. Thus in the report to the Eighth Session, the Director describes their policies in a highly significant passage:

'The full benefit of the spread of this large capital investment [in Arab countries] will be felt only if restrictions on the movement of refugees are withdrawn. This is a measure which was proposed in the original three-year plan, but little has been done so far to give effect to it. Such freedom of movement would enable refugees to take full advantage of opportunities for work arising in countries such as Iraq, Saudi Arabia and the Persian Gulf Sheikdoms where economic development has already taken place.'

In other words, there are vast opportunities in the Arab world for the Arab refugees to build new lives, but Arab governments have so far debarred refugees from these opportunities.

In Paragraph 11 of Resolution 302 (IV) the General Assembly requested:

'. . . to continue to endeavour to reduce the number of refugees by progressive stages.'

Only one country co-operated with this crucial recommendation. In his interim report to the Eighth Session the Director, speaking of the failure to reduce the total number of refugees, found only one ray of light:

'Had it not been for the assumption by the Israel Government of

175

responsibility for some 19,000 Arab refugees in Israel at the end of the previous year the number would have been still greater.'

This integration of 19,000 refugees in Israel has saved the Agency an expenditure of $600,000 for each year that has elapsed since then. By pursuing this same programme in the ensuing year Israel brought the total number of Arab refugees which it fully integrated into its economy and citizenry up to the figure of 48,500. By all other means only 8,000 had been taken off the records up to last year.

If, in proportion to their own population and area, or by any other criterion or capacity, the Arab host countries had adopted a similar attitude towards refugees on their own soil, this whole problem would have begun to melt away. In view of the close cultural and spiritual bonds of the refugees with the Arab states, and the superior economic resources of these nations as compared with Israel, it was surely not unreasonable to hope that Arab governments would have made it a point of honour to reduce the number of registered refugees each year, by integrating as many as possible into their economic and social life. Instead, the number has grown, and we are now faced with a suggestion for the further increase of the number of relief recipients by adding to them new and numerous categories.

The same record of obstruction has attended the rehabilitation schemes which the Agency tried to implement in co-operation with Arab governments. The thinking behind these programmes is simple, but imaginative. The international community is ready to help Arab governments create opportunities of livelihood by irrigating new areas of land, establishing new farms, or in some cases, new village communities with industrial as well as agricultural activity. Refugees are to be placed into these newly created labour opportunities. The result would be a reduction of the number of refugees accepting relief, and progress towards lightening the international burden. The by-product would be the promotion of economic progress in Arab countries with international aid. It is hard to think of a more enlightened or progressive approach than this.

What has happened to these programmes? They have been smothered by purposeful obstruction and delay. In his report to the Eighth Session the Director complains:

'Signs of progress on major schemes are lacking. The time taken to negotiate programme agreements with governments has been far longer than what was expected when the three-year plan was origin-

The Arab Refugees—A Record in Obstruction

ally conceived; it took, 7, 9, 14 and 17 months respectively to conclude the four now in existence.'

Today none of these schemes seem to be any nearer to implementation than they were two years ago. In October 1952 the Syrian Government had expressed readiness to co-operate with the Agency in the development of rehabilitation projects for the 85,000 refugees residing in Syria. Under the terms of the Agreement the Agency earmarked 30 million dollars for that purpose. Consecutive reports tell what has happened since the conclusion of the Agreement. The Agreement itself lapsed after 31st December 1954 'as the Agency did not consider themselves justified in continuing to earmark such a substantial sum of money for projects in Syria in the absence of some indication from the Government of potential projects'.

Great hopes were attached to the Sinai project under which refugees would have been settled on new land created by irrigation in the Sinai Peninsula. It now appears from Table 2, page 23 of the Director's report, that the agreement with the Egyptian authorities on the implementation of this scheme terminated on 31st March 1955 and has not since been renewed. We are left with a statement, welcome in itself, that the renewal of the agreement is 'being contemplated'.

For two years the governments of our region have discussed with Ambassador Eric Johnston a project for the co-ordinated use of the waters of the Jordan and the Yarmuk rivers. If agreement is reached, many thousands of refugees will find an opportunity for bringing new land under cultivation, while the national product of certain Arab states would swiftly expand. Under this agreement the greater part of the Rivers Jordan and Yarmuk—the only two major rivers of which Israel is a riparian state—would be made available for Arab use. My government has co-operated to the utmost with Ambassador Johnston in this project. Most of the technical problems involved in an agreed division of the waters have been solved. Now, after the investment of great effort during two full years, we learn that certain Arab governments are still not prepared to say whether they are willing in principle, and as a matter of policy, to co-operate in any co-ordinated use of these rivers. The Director's report leaves us in suspense with the statement that 'little further work can be undertaken pending decisions, mostly of a political nature, that have now to be taken regarding the division and storage of the Yarmuk and Jordan rivers'.

M 177

The Arab Refugees—A Record in Obstruction

Not content with obstructing the main purposes of the reintegration effort, Arab governments have also impeded its organizational functioning. Successive reports over the past five years show these governments imposing illegitimate taxes and customs charges on the Agency; placing obstacles in the way of its transport; attaching its funds; and withholding its proper judicial immunity in civil and criminal cases. The current report shows 70,000 names improperly inscribed on the rolls in Jordan alone.

No wonder that Mr. Galloway, a former representative of UNRWA in Jordan, said to an American study group in Amman last year:

'It is perfectly clear that the Arab nations do not want to solve the Arab refugee problem. They want to keep it as an open sore, as an affront against the United Nations, and a weapon against Israel. Arab leaders don't give a damn whether the refugees live or die.'

Can anyone doubt that the Arab governments have been determined that the refugees shall remain refugees; and that the aim of wrecking any alternative to 'repatriation' has been pursued by these governments with a skill and ingenuity worthy of a better cause? With an international Agency working for the integration of refugees, with tens of millions of dollars expended every year to move them away from a life of dependence, the Arab governments have brought us to a point where there are more refugees on United Nations rolls than ever before; and where their only new idea is to take thousands of indigent people who are not refugees at all—and put them on the international charge, thus swelling this problem beyond its already inflated proportions.

But despite the record of these past five years, the resettlement of Arab refugees in Arab countries still shines forth as a solution of merit. Its logic and morality cannot be denied. It is not only that the Arab governments bear the responsibility inherent in their creation of this problem. Far more important is the fact that they are endowed with all the conditions for its solution. With its two and a half million square miles of territory, its vast resources of mineral wealth, its great unharnessed rivers and its uncultivated but fertile lands, the Arab countries are easily capable of absorbing what would be for them a relatively small population. Moreover, resettlement in an Arab society would, for the refugee himself, be 'repatriation' in its truest sense. He would be united with peoples who share all his attributes of personality, his language, his spiritual heritage, and his system of national and cultural loyalties. 'Patria' is not a mere geographical term. The resettlement of an Arab refugee in Israel would, paradoxically, be not 'repatriation', but alienation from Arab society and transference to the only statehood in the area in which non-Arab loyalties and attachments predominate. For an Arab state, the refugee would be a reinforcement of its security; for Israel, he would be an inherent source of danger, since for seven years hostility to Israel has been the primary theme of his environment, his thought, his deepest sentiment.

The capacity of the Arab world to absorb this refugee population has been increased by the emigration to Israel of 350,000 Jews from Iraq, Syria, Egypt, Yemen and other Arab lands, who left behind them their homes, their property and their labour opportunities, and who have been proudly received in Israel, without any plaintive outcry or rush for international help. What could be more natural than that Arab countries such as Iraq and the Persian Gulf Principalities, with their vast oil royalties and their chronic shortage of manpower, should absorb a like number of Arab kinsmen in the homes and labour opportunities thus vacated? The national revolutions of the Middle East have produced a two-way movement of population of Jews from Arab lands into Israel and of Arabs from Israel into Arab territories. The crucial difference is that Israel has made the effort and sacrifice to integrate its newcomers, while the Arab governments have deliberately obstructed integration in their territories.

If Israel, with its small area of 8,000 square miles and its pitifully limited resources could build houses, create work and provide citizenship for 800,000 destitute immigrants, nearly half of them from Arab countries, how much more easily could the vast Arab sub-continent with its 45 million people in eight separate sovereignties find homes for an equivalent number of its kinsmen?

The problem before us, acute as it is, should not be distorted beyond its true limits. It is not a vast or unprecedented problem. The political changes which have taken place in the post-war period, including no less than five partitions, have produced a number of refugee movements. Thirteen million refugees in West and East Germany; 15 million in India and Pakistan; 400,000 Karelians in Finland; 350,000 Volksdeutsche in Austria; 2½ million who moved from North to South Korea. In none of these cases was repatriation the answer to the problem. In each case the problem was solved because there was a co-national or co-religious host country which was willing to solve it. At an earlier date the Turko-Greek exchange stood as a triumph of enlightened statesmanship for solving a similar problem, in conformity with the loyalties and national sentiments of the refugees concerned.

With such an aggregate of advantages speaking for it, the doctrine of resettlement continues to advance steadily in international favour. Five years ago the representative of the United Kingdom pointed out that:

'The Arab refugees would have a happier and more stable future if the bulk of them were settled in the Arab countries.'

Last year the representative of the United States appealed to Arab delegates to understand 'that eventual solution of the refugee problem lay in a new and stronger economy for the Arab countries, coming to regard many of their refugee brothers as permanent members of the community and co-sharers in the Near East's future'.

Many statements in this spirit are on the record. I do not say that those who have made them are in complete accord with us on the full measure and degree to which this solution should be applied. But it is true, to say the least, that the doctrine of resettling the Arab refugees in Arab countries is not an eccentric notion unilaterally held by Israel. It is the dominant theme of all serious international thought on this subject; and it makes progress in men's minds from year to year.

It is all the more important that the advocacy of resettlement should be wholehearted and candid, and not compromised by illusions. Israel was the victim, not the author, of the war which caused this tragedy. Yet not even the burdens, the preoccupations of self-defence or the herculean labours of absorbing a vast mass of immigration have turned our minds or hearts away from a disposition to bring our contribution to the relief of this distress. I have already referred to Israel's action in completely absorbing the 48,500 refugees who were on our soil when the 1950 reintegration resolution was adopted. With the legalization of entries and the project for the reuniting of families, we have increased Israel's Arab population from 100,000 to 180,000 since the signature of the Armistice.

The United Nations Palestine Conciliation Commission has paid

The Arab Refugees—A Record in Obstruction

warm tribute to Israel's action in releasing bank accounts and deposits to the value of 11½ million dollars in favour of Arab refugees. While our neighbours maintained a ruthless economic warfare against us, we have authorized the transfer of hard currency from Israel to hostile territory.

It is recognized that the payment of compensation for abandoned lands could be an important contribution to Arab refugee resettlement. But, the acceptance of such a burden at any one time would involve our population in a commitment beyond its powers. We were therefore interested in a proposal made recently by the Secretary of State of the United States under which an international loan would be made to enable Israel to discharge this undertaking. My Government has, in recent weeks, responded formally and affirmatively to this suggestion.

It is evident, of course, that a discussion on the payment of compensation would require the solution and clarification of the related problems to which Mr. Sharett has referred in the Knesset. In particular, the Arab governments cannot attempt to stifle Israel financially by blockade and boycott—and at the same time expect Israel to assume heavy financial burdens for this and future generations of its citizens. The Arab governments will one day have to decide whether the pleasures of blockade are more to be cherished than the affirmative duty of enabling the refugees to receive compensation.

These efforts made by Israel in the past, and contemplated for the future, illustrate the earnest concern with which my government approaches the Arab refugee problem. The Committee will, therefore, understand that it is with a full sense of responsibility that I must make it clear that we cannot regard the further repatriation of Arab refugees in Israel as a solution to this problem. Let it not be forgotten that the refugees are members of the Arab world, and fully share the prevailing attitudes of Arab political life. It is enough to read the speeches of the Arab delegates and the representative of the Arab refugees, to reach the ominous conclusion that they are dominated by a passionate hatred of Israel and a desire to see her destroyed. There is, unhappily, every evidence that their sentiments fully reflect the rancours and antagonisms of the refugees. Indeed, one of the Arab delegates gave us to understand that he was speaking for the refugees and on their behalf. It is beyond doubt that the Arab refugee population has been educated for eight years in the sheer hatred of Israel, and certainly not in loyalty and devotion to the Israel flag.

The Arab Refugees—A Record in Obstruction

The proposition that a sovereign state admit into its territory thousands of people who hold its flag, its ideals, its very statehood in profound and passionate disrespect, cannot be seriously entertained.

Two examples of Arab sentiment on this question will illustrate the kind of attitude which Arab refugees would now introduce into Israel. Prime Minister Nasser of Egypt has informed the world through an American newspaper:

'The hatred of the Arabs is very strong, and there is no sense in talking about peace with Israel. There is not even the smallest place for negotiation between the Arabs and Israel.' (14th October 1955)

The Prime Minister of Syria has spoken in even more elevating language:

'Israel is Syria's avowed enemy. The Arabs will not rest as long as this thieving enemy still dwells on holy soil in the very heart of the Arab world.' (20th September 1955)

The Committee will recall the persistent threats of the representative of Syria in this session of the General Assembly indicating clearly and frankly that the object of a refugee movement into Israel would be the destruction of Israel and its so-called 'redemption' for the Arab rule. All statements made by refugee leaders themselves are pervaded not merely by a lack of loyalty to Israel, but by a violent hatred of Israel's very existence.

Here then is our country with its embattled frontiers; the cherished sanctuary of the Hebrew spirit; the focus of so many deep universal sentiments; the product of infinite patience and toil. This small domain of sovereignty is savagely begrudged by a people whose territorial possession stretches out over a whole continent. Cut off from all land contacts; intercepted illicitly in two of its three maritime channels; subjected to blockade and boycott, to siege and encroachment, to infiltrations and commando raids; the object of an officially proclaimed state of war and the target of a monstrous rearmament campaign—this is the picture of Israel's security. No other state in the entire world faces such constant threats to its security and integrity.

Can the mind conceive anything more fantastic than the idea that we can add to these perils by the influx from hostile territory of any number, large or small, of people steeped in the hatred of our very statehood? I do not believe that any responsible conscience will sustain such an idea. There could be no greater unkindness to an Arab refugee himself than to expose him to such an invidious role,

182

The Arab Refugees—A Record in Obstruction

perhaps reproducing the very circumstances which first made him a refugee. Observe another contradiction. On the one hand, Arab representatives tell you that it is intolerable for Arabs to live in Israel. On the other hand, they suggest that thousands of others should be· driven back into this intolerable and explosive tension.

We seek the comprehension of this Committee for this elementary dictate of prudence and security. But above any other consideration, we remind the Committee that Israel is a sovereign state; and in exercise of that sovereignty it must apply its own authority to the question—who shall and who shall not enter its territory. Especially is this so in the present hour of national emergency. All other countries possess and apply a similar sovereign right.

The unreality of the repatriation concept can well be illustrated by reference to the Kingdom of Jordan whose representative addressed the Committee on November 15th. There are 500,000 new citizens in Jordan. But Jordan has gained territory as well as population. It has acquired an area of 2,000 square miles beyond its 1947 limits, and there is no indication that it will renounce a single square yard of it. Now these 500,000 are citizens of Jordan which in this respect has carried out the behest of the reintegration resolution. Many of them have risen to the summit of responsibility in the affairs of the kingdom, and are numbered amongst its Ministers and leading officials.

Can it seriously be suggested that these naturalized citizens of Jordan, who are still on 'Palestinian' soil, are potentially the citizens of Israel—that they have acquired a foreign citizenship and still retain a 'right' of 'repatriation' to Israel? The very idea is full of political and juridical confusion. It is true that their compensation rights exist and that there are grave economic problems resulting from their transference to Jordan. These require a solution with international help. But if Jordan would carry out the General Assembly's resolution of 1948 in favour of economic co-operation, including the common use of ports and highways; or if she would reach a settlement with Israel granting her free port facilities at Haifa, her commercial and financial position would be transformed and the addition of new wealth to new territory and new population would bring about a cumulative economic reinforcement to the benefit of the refugees. The improvement would become even greater if Ambassador Johnston's project received agreement. Here is a striking example of the anomalies of 'repatriation' side by side with the practical advantages of an enlightened resettlement approach.

The Arab Refugees—A Record in Obstruction

The Committee will readily understand in the light of what I have said, why my government cannot approve Ambassador Labouisse's proposal that a procedure of free choice between repatriation and compensation be offered to the refugees. It would, in our mind and conscience, be unmerciful to encourage in the minds of these unhappy people any expectation which could not be fulfilled. Believing as we do that the resettlement of Arab refugees in Israel would hold grave perils both for Israel and the refugees themselves, we cannot in good heart encourage them to opt for frustration, tragedy and war. Moreover, the heavy, emphatic indoctrination to which they have been subjected for seven years, and the complete unlikelihood that we should be invited to the camps to explain Israel's position, rules out any prospect that a genuine freedom of choice is available. Finally, the suggestion is deficient in legal and international principle. It assumes the rights of individuals and completely ignores the sovereignty of States. It is quite improper for the question whether people shall or shall not enter Israel to be dealt with outside the framework of Israel's sovereign consent.

I was frankly surprised to see the Director reach such a conclusion without consultation with the state most directly concerned. The Director's duties in the Arab world during the period of his mission have unfortunately left him no time even to visit Israel. A visit by him to our country would be most cordially welcomed, and would furnish a useful basis for including the Israeli aspect of the problem in any judgment or appraisal of its solution. He would certainly see at first hand that the prospect of Arab refugee resettlement in Israel is remote and full of peril, and that his task should be not to invite requests for such a solution, but rather to confront the refugees and the Arab governments with the necessities and advantages of early resettlement. Progress with the rehabilitation programme; action on resettlement schemes and on water agreements; full co-operation with UNRWA in accordance with its mandate; utilization of the expanding labour opportunities in the Arab world; serious discussion of compensation and related problems—these are the lines on which progress can be made in the coming year, rather than by attempting in these prejudiced conditions to 'poll' the refugees on the question of their repatriation.

I doubt the necessity of commenting in detail on the Syrian representative's proposal for a three-Power commission to devour Israel's territory and force the refugees back into what would remain of

The Arab Refugees—A Record in Obstruction

Israel after the operation. The General Assembly should be treated with more respect than the very submission of such a proposal implies. Of course, no commission, large or small, is going to come to Israel to violate the existing territorial position which rests firmly upon contracts and agreements reached at United Nations behest and witnessed by United Nations representatives. These agreements, including their territorial provisions, are immutable in law and fact, except by procedures and principles of mutual adjustment laid down in the relevant articles of the Agreements themselves, i.e. in Articles VIII of the Syrian and Lebanese Agreements and Article XII of the Egyptian and Jordanian Agreements. Any talk of territorial changes outside the principles and procedures laid down in those Articles rests on unsound legal and moral foundations and is an intervention in the bilateral relations of states.

There is too much unconsidered talk on this territorial question. The present territorial position, resting on firm contractual engagements, is sound in law and justice. There is no juridical distinction whatever between the different parts of the territory within Israel's borders under the General Armistice Agreements. It is for the signatories of these agreements to amend them if they so mutually agree and to do so by the procedures which they have agreed on, or to leave them unamended if they cannot agree to change them. So much for the legal position which deserves more understanding and respect. On the substance of the issue we have great difficulty in understanding why Israel with its 8,000 square miles should be regarded as too big; or why the Arab League states with their 3,000,000 square miles are too small. It seems a highly jaundiced, unchivalrous view, especially when expounded by those who are themselves content to rule vast expanses of territory, either within or beyond their national borders. It will do nobody any harm to leave Israel's 8,000 square miles alone.

These are anxious times for Israel and for the Middle East; and it is perhaps natural that patience sometimes collapses under the weight of concern, making way for slogans or devices for swift cure. But there is no problem in which steady thinking is more necessary than in this question of refugees. For their sake and for the sake of their region, indeed for the sake of peace which hangs in an unsteady balance, the General Assembly should give a strong impetus to the precise fulfilment of the integration programme which it initiated in its memorable resolution of 1950. Nor would it be inappropriate for

the sentiment of this Committee to be heard in loud volume on behalf of peace between the two kindred peoples, Israel and the Arabs,
whose union of hands and hearts could inaugurate a radiant era for
their common region. Can we not take our stand on the solemn
covenants of agreement which we have freely signed, and advance
beyond them to a lasting peace which would honour the traditions of
our past and enhance the opportunities of our future?

CHAPTER XVII

The Perspectives of Science*

M y gratitude goes out to the American Association for the
Advancement of Science, to the National Commission for
UNESCO and to the gracious city of Atlanta, which have
combined to set the scene of this occasion.

I am here to inaugurate the exhibition of Israeli Scientific Publica-
tions. A glance at the catalogue is sufficient to inspire me with a
sense of inferiority. There is scarcely one of the thousand items upon
those walls which does not lie far beyond the domain of ambassa-
dorial comprehension. Indeed, in a gathering of scientists, that is to
say, of men devoted to the pursuit of objective truth, the very presence
of a diplomat requires some explanation.

Let me, then, say that you see on those walls a harvest of seven
years in the intellectual exploration of a small people across all the
fields of natural science and technology. These earnest and pains-
taking investigations have all been carried out in seven years within
a society beset by international and internal turmoil. For the most
part, these efforts have come to fruition in Israel's institutions of
higher learning—the Hebrew University in Jerusalem, the Weizmann
Institute of Science at Rehovoth, and the Institute of Technology at
Haifa.

Few countries have committed their fortunes more ardently than
Israel to the scientific revolution of our age. In our task of reclaiming
a land from poverty and neglect we quickly learned that scientific
progress could do much to compensate for natural scarcities. Synthetic chemistry could find substitutes for scarce raw materials, while
nuclear power and solar energy could compensate for scarcities of
conventional fuels. Thus, a pioneer spirit allied to scientific initiative
could regain the ancient fertility of our land, capture the original
grace of its landscape, and develop standards of material and spiritual
culture worthy of its universal renown. Science harnessed to Israel's
development becomes a potent force in the expansion of a small
country's natural resources.

* To the American Association for the Advancement of Science, Atlanta, Georgia,
26 December 1955.

187

The Perspectives of Science

But there is something here of significance in a far wider sphere. Our region has much to gain from the intensive application of scientific research. The Middle East is not inherently·a poor area, as its glorious history proves. Across its expanses there are ample resources of manpower, skills, natural resources with which to sustain a prosperous civilization. The region has fallen behind the best levels of modern progress through its backwardness in the application of scientific processes, as well as through conflict and divisions which deny the essential truth of our regional fraternity. May we not hope that an end will come to these sterile habits of boycott, ostracism, and hostility; that the barriers which divide Israel from its neighbours will fall; and that the waves of scientific progress will flow across a broader domain between Israel and the Arab world. The people of Israel and of the Arab world have both woven golden threads in the tapestry of scientific history through the Middle Ages down to our own times.

The circle of implications arising from this exhibition reaches beyond the Middle East, and evokes ideas of·universal scope. We are reminded here of the potentiality which lies within all small countries in an age of scientific development. Small countries often ask themselves whether the history of the twentieth century must be written exclusively by the great imperial and continental powers. In military strategy and in economic strength there is little that countries as small as Israel can do to emulate the achievements of their more powerful colleagues in the international community. But in the world of intellect and science we all stand equal. Any country, large or small, which develops a sound scientific tradition, may have something to contribute to the abundance which science has bequeathed to our universal potentiality. It is not an accident that some of the greatest scientific figures of this age have arisen in countries little larger than Israel in their territory and population. We are a small land and shall always so remain. But in intellectual, spiritual and cultural progress we are as free as any nation to soar to the highest peaks available to human effort and initiative. We do not consider that it is the destiny of small countries to be condemned to provincialism. We recall that Israel thousands of years ago was a small country in a barren strip of land between the Mediterranean and the Jordan, surrounded by rich and powerful empires. But those empires have crumbled in the dust, while our small voice has come down across the centuries in constant and undying strength.

The Perspectives of Science

It is natural therefore to find Israel taking an ardent interest in the movement of international co-operation in the scientific field. Our imagination has been powerfully captured by the challenge of the nuclear age. Only a few weeks ago, Israel was privileged to join with the United States and a group of other countries in formulating and presenting for the unanimous consent of the United Nations the historic resolution establishing an International Agency for the Peaceful Uses of Atomic Power. In Geneva in the summer of this year our scientists were able to join with their colleagues of seventy-two other countries in contemplating the awesome challenge of the nuclear age. Two members of our delegation were privileged to preside at conferences of that historic assembly. In Phoenix, Arizona, during the international symposium on solar energy, the inventive contributions of Dr. Henry Tabor to the applied use of solar energy evoked widespread interest.

Now these are amongst the achievements of a small people living in conditions of siege under persistent economic and social stress. Does it not prove the dedication of Israel to constructive and affirmative purposes? Is it not deeply tragic that we are compelled to divert our eyes from our essential mission in order to grapple with the preoccupation of defensive preparedness?

The subjects illustrated in this Exhibition deal mainly with the domains of natural science. An exhibit such as this cannot comprehend Israel's preoccupation with the humanities. But our scientists would be the first to concede that it is only within a humanistic tradition that scientific development can fulfil its higher purposes. In the shadow of atomic destruction, our generation has become acutely sceptical of the fallacies of a scientific rationalism uninhibited by moral restraints. Let me, therefore, recall that the people whose achievement in natural science is illustrated here with such versatile profusion is primarily the bearer of a deep spiritual and humanistic heritage with roots reaching far back in antiquity. For 3,000 years from biblical prophecy to relativity, the Jewish mind has been dominated by one central thought—that the world is not a wild anarchy of incalculable forces but is rather a pattern of order and progress governed by a merciful intelligence and a coherent law. This doctrine of order and progress in human relations lies at the root of Hebrew prophetic thought, while the doctrine of order and progress in the natural world is the central theme of modern scientific exploration. Here we have a bridge on which our religious heritage joins hands

189

with the modern scientific revolution. Is it not moving to find this small people, which alone of all peoples comprehends in its continuous memory three millennia of moral experience, now re-establishing its homeland in the cradle of its birth? Israel's destiny is that of a people small in geography but very great in history. There is something unique in this contrast between our physical dimensions and the unlimited vistas of time and of space over which Israel's mind has ranged. The journey of Israel's mind is not over, but our nation's scientists have erected impressive landmarks on its course.

CHAPTER XVIII

The Nasser Despotism*

It is again my duty to end your deliberations by a review of the political context within which we labour together for Israel's strength and security.

Twelve months ago the scene which we contemplated here together seemed complex enough. But few of us could ever have imagined the sheer violence of the storms which were soon to burst around us on all sides.

Never has Israel's progress been attended by perils so grave, by issues so momentous as those which have crowded in upon us in the closing year.

One year ago this week came the ominous report of the Soviet transaction which transformed Egypt into a military camp, bristling with offensive striking power. Overnight the equilibrium of force upon which our region's security had rested was shattered before our eyes. The Middle East was set, perhaps irrevocably, on a sinister course of competitive rearmament.

At this point the Egyptian dictator, drunk with success, struck out for domination on a continental scale from North Africa to Sudan, from the Arabian Peninsula to the Kingdom of Jordan. In his quest for regional domination, fully proclaimed in his written blueprint, he directed his assaults against the established interests of European powers, against impulses of independence in new Arab societies, against Israel's frontiers; and against the universal rights of the maritime nations.

As this malignant despotism spread through the Mediterranean and the whole of North Africa and the Middle East, the victims of its encroachments began to rally for co-operative defence. There were tripartite meetings. There were consultations in the highest organs of international security. There was the mission of the Secretary General of the United Nations. There was the sudden manifestation of American wrath signified by the withdrawal of the Aswan Dam project.

*At the National State of Israel Bond Conference, Washington, D.C., 23 September 1956.

The Nasser Despotism

Now, all the maritime powers, who have from time immemorial enjoyed an absolute right of free navigation upon and between the high seas, are slowly moving towards habits of defensive association.

Thus today the Egyptian dictator is locked in combat over a very broad field. He is fighting against everybody and everything, except against the poverty, the disease, the illiteracy, the growing economic weakness and political isolation of his people.

Why is it that all the elements of crisis in the international life of our age seem to have found their decisive arena in the lands and the waters of the Middle East? What is the motive force in all this ferment?

The answer lies in the character of Arab nationalism which now commands the resources and the allegiance of multitudes over the vast expanses of three continents.

We could have attended the rise of Arab nationalism with sympathy and goodwill. Who would have failed to be moved by the spectacle of this slumbering people awakening to the assumption of its manifold sovereignty? Who would have begrudged a progressive nationalism the right to establish the identity and the independence of its culture? Who would not have been impressed by any serious attempt to revive the ancient glories of the Arabic cultural tradition? Who would have wished to withstand any serious attempt by this newly emancipated nation to rise to the stirring challenge of an economic and social renaissance? An Arab nationalism dedicated to these affirmative processes would have constituted no danger to Israel and no peril to the peace and the security of mankind.

Indeed, an Arab nationalism thus inspired and permeated could well have been expected to live at peace with the smaller state of Israel, arising to recreate the ancient glories of Judea in an infinitely more restricted domain.

The crisis of the Middle East today lies in the failure of Arab nationalism to vindicate its affirmative purposes. To its tragedy, it has neglected its constructive destinies in favour of a headlong and militant pursuit of prestige.

It has become characterized by several major imperfections: it nourishes the hatred of Western domination long after that domination has passed from the scene and ceased to constitute any threat to the new nationhood in the hour of its early independence. It is distinguished by a complete lack of altruism. It denies the small state

192

of Israel those freedoms and liberties which it so lavishly claims for itself.

It shows disregard of those aspects of national responsibility which look inwards towards the vision of a sound economy, society, and culture, and not merely outwards towards the diplomatic manœuvre and nationalist prestige.

Above all, this is a nationalism which refuses to recognize that its own rights are not the supreme law of the universe, but are qualified by the equal rights of nationhood for others, and by the over-riding interests of the international community as a whole.

These elements of sickness have clung to Arab nationalism and distorted its purpose. That which might have been a bright and healthy impulse has become a morbid and feverish thing. This is the character and mood of the national movement which commands the resources of a vast continent and which has made Israel's downfall the central aim of its collective policies.

What can we do, situated as we are, in the midst of this raging tempest? We cannot change the character of this nationalist movement. Perhaps experience, maturity, even the slow, corrosive force of international opinion, will one day moderate these frenzies and recall Arab national leadership to a recognition of its responsibilities.

But if we cannot change it, one thing we can do. We can survive it. We are determined to define the areas of resistance. Others who are threatened by this tempest can decide for themselves whether they will surrender or resist. For centuries Egypt was a dependency of Western Europe. Today, if Nasser's exclusive control of the Suez Canal is recognized, then Western Europe, the British Isles, France, the great historic communities of the Atlantic alliance, will become the economic dependencies of Egypt; and upon the arbitrary whim of whatever potentate rules on the banks of the Nile will be decided whether the French and the Belgian and the Scandinavian and the British peoples shall receive the commodities for their sustenance and industry.

It is for these powers to determine how they will face this historic turn of fortune. On one thing we are resolved. One of the objectives of this nationalism will be denied. This appetite is not going to be satisfied with the Israeli item on the menu. Empires may sometimes yield while small peoples stand firm.

In 1948, at a time when Arab nationalism was regarded as an irre-sistible force before which great world forces had to bow down in obsequious deference, we proved that aggressive nationalism can be safely and successfully resisted. I say this in a moment of solemnity, when world opinion is awakening 'at last to the expanding ambitions of the Egyptian dictator. In quarters where complacency once prevailed, it is now recognized that a victory by Egyptian nationalism over the maritime powers would be followed by an assault upon Israel. If this is true appraisal, then we are only one contingency away from a supreme test. Nobody who read the papers this morning would assume that this contingency of Nasser's victory over the maritime powers is beyond conception or possibility. Nasser has many targets and he is shooting at them all at once, but this does not mean that he has forgotten Israel which is still the main objective of all the negative and demagogic passions which sweep across the Arab world. The future of Israel is intimately involved in the outcome of the present confrontation between Nasser's Egypt and the Western Powers. It matters nothing whether our interests are directly or indirectly involved in the specific issues of that confrontation. The outcome will determine our destiny.

Should the outcome be the curbing of this rampaging nationalism, the victory of international law over illicit unilateral nationalism, then a revolutionary moment of opportunity will have been created for us.

If, on the other hand, this arrogant Egyptian nationalism triumphs over the world's conscience, over established historic rights, over the law of nations, then again a revolutionary moment will have been created for us in a more sombre and sinister sense.

The question arises: Is he destined to be victorious? Is his triumph inevitable?

All I would suggest in response to this question is that we be not quick or premature in our final judgment. I would recommend to you our traditional Jewish scepticism about the durability of dictators. Look at them as they pass in panoramic procession before the eyes of our memory: Pharaoh and Nebuchadnezzar, Hadrian and Titus, the potentates of the medieval world all the way up to Hitler of accursed memory.

How strongly rooted, how stable, how invincible each of them appeared at the height of his triumphant procession. Where are they now? Say what you like about the Jewish people: in the capacity to survive dictators, we are second to none.

This constancy of history has repeated itself even in the brief national life of Israel. Who is there in this room who could arise and recite the princes, the monarchs, the potentates, the military dictators who have held sway in our neighbouring Arab states within the past eight years?

While our own government has maintained great stability and constancy of leadership—and there are parties in the Knesset who look upon this constancy with less than complete benevolence—one after another of these dictatorships has passed away before our eyes.

Is it to be wondered at then that we in Israel allow ourselves a certain scepticism concerning the reality or authenticity of Nasserism?

I admit that now he rides high on the crest of a wave. A man who chose to leap out of the Empire State Building and have himself photographed in flight would cut a magnificent figure in that isolated moment of time. He might look a little less attractive when he got to the bottom.

All I would say to you, therefore, is: Do not be impressed by the glorious spectacle of Nasser in the moment of flight. Historians will wait for the end of the story.

We who do not have the verdict of history in our grasp must look to the other side of the ledger. Look what deprivations he has brought upon his people, renouncing the aid of friendly countries, alienating those upon whose assistance Egypt's interests depend, losing the potential benefaction of the Aswan Dam, losing access to his sterling balances, losing his entitlement to the American economic aid and technical programmes, losing his assets in France and in other countries of Western Europe, losing even a great part of the normal revenue which would accrue to Egypt from the Suez Canal itself. This is a distinguished performance. It is true that it has been accompanied by much diplomatic pyrotechnics but perhaps the trouble with these military dictatorships in their single-minded concentration on political objectives and their complete disregard of the fundamental issues of the economic and social life is that they do not have Mr. Eshkol[1] at their elbow to teach them that diplomatic glitter is not everything. Man, it is true, does not live by bread alone; but finds it remarkably hard to subsist without it.

But if the final story of the rise, decline and fall of this, our most perilous adversary, remains to be written, we cannot sit back in fatalistic conviction of the certain doom of our foe.

It is easy to believe, and I do conscientiously believe, in the in-

[1] The Israel Minister of Finance, who attended the conference.

evitable decline of Nasser, but it is necessary to survive in order to enjoy the spectacle of that downfall. If history has shown us that dictators inevitably fall, it also teaches us that there is no limit to the havoc which they may wreak in their path.

Could anyone in living memory celebrate the downfall of Hitler when he knew at what fearful price this had been accomplished? These are the considerations which bring us face to face with the central issue of Israel's strength and security as the primary issues of our diplomacy at this time.

The massive rearmament of Egypt announced a year ago was a greater threat to Israel's security than any which we had known before, or have since encountered. We were here confronted not only by the travail and hazard normal to a new society, but by the solemn issue of survival itself. The shadow of physical extinction lengthened over every peaceful home and field in our country. This danger commanded us to seek one overriding purpose, to make Israel stronger; stronger in military equipment and training; stronger in arms; stronger on land and by sea and in the air; stronger in the numbers and in the resolve of our population; stronger in agricultural and industrial production; stronger in scientific and cultural progress; stronger in the trust, the affection and the anxiety of world opinion; stronger in those elements of knowledge, faith and vision without which a nation shall perish.

I tell you that we have, in the past year, become stronger in every single one of these domains.

Full weight and value should be ascribed to Prime Minister Ben Gurion's recent statement that the Israel defence forces have never been as well equipped, or as strongly prepared as today. This authoritative warning should be taken to heart especially in Cairo. If it were my function to counsel Colonel Nasser (I am sorry, President Nasser —he won the election with a majority of 99.6 per cent; neither the Gallup poll nor the Princeton Institute of Research could ever have predicted such a plurality), if I were to counsel him upon the next target of his expansion, I would recommend that he leave Israel alone.

Our efforts to complete our reinforcement are still in full swing. A process such as this is seldom resolved with finality; and the efforts of Israel to increase its military strength in face of new dangers will not cease. But these efforts have not substantively failed. Indeed, amongst the transactions which have made Israel stronger one or two have been publicly announced. We owe appreciation to all the governments whose action, authority, and influence have led us to record new accretions to our defensive strength.

The necessity for our reinforcement has now been explicitly recognized in a large part of the world.

On 8th May 1956 the Secretary of State of the United States of America gave public expression to the belief of the Atlantic powers that wide discrepancies in armed strength between Israel and her neighbours should be removed. This mutually accepted principle has dominated the discussions between our two governments on arms questions in recent months.

From this common ground of principle we have been able to achieve a measure of fruitful co-operation and understanding with the Atlantic powers.

But when the story comes to be finally recorded I shall never understand—and I say this not in recrimination but in anticipation of similar dilemmas—I shall never understand why our embattled people had to undergo the anguish of the first six months following the Soviet transaction; or why we were called upon to live in that fearful circle of danger.

I think that we might have been spared this ordeal. Few peoples would have borne it with such fortitude and restraint. There were other alternatives which were urged upon us; and there is no greater vindication of Israel's statesmanship than the tenacity with which it resisted them.

But the very effort to solve one problem creates another. The strains upon our economy have grown sharply. Nobody here can regret the reasons which have led to that strain.

On the one hand, we have received 51,000 new immigrants in twelve months. On the other hand, we have incurred great expenditures in national security and defence.

Perhaps the most vivid description of this change in the emphasis of our concern would come from a personal reference. The Minister of Defence now rests more serenely at night; but the Minister of Finance is condemned to perpetual insomnia.

The strengthening of our economy and our financial structure now moves to the highest place in our system of priorities. Without a stable, resilient economy we cannot consolidate our progress towards safer margin of defensive strength.

The Nasser Despotism

You who were moved to anguish by the sight of our vulnerability will surely come forward with joyous pride to help us continue upon the road which we have at last ascended.

Nothing is more vital for Israel in the coming months than an increase in all the sources of its financial and economic strength. We refuse even in the midst of our embattled existence to be robbed of our central vision. We cannot build Israel as an armed camp in a desert. No amount of preoccupation with defence can diminish our basic vision of a society, an economy and culture expanding towards broadening horizons of progress.

This is the genius of the movement which gave us birth. Our image would be distorted if we did not possess, beyond the resources for sheer survival, a sufficient surplus of energy with which to carry forward our genuine and authentic mission.

These are the considerations which occupy the great dialogue between the American and Israel governments. The friendship between America and Israel has deep roots in the ideals and the interests of both peoples. I have never believed that either of our governments or peoples really desired to alienate itself from this enduring tradition.

I have a feeling that in recent weeks we may have drawn closer together both in our appraisal of Middle Eastern events and in our estimate of the measures necessary for Israel's strength and prosperity. The preservation of Israel's integrity and independence has been formally enunciated as a doctrine in the foreign policy of the strongest power on earth. From every sector of your public and political opinion we hear fraternal tones of encouragement and support.

I have already alluded to certain principles held in common which have had some influence in augmenting our physical strength. Scarcely less important is the continuing contribution of the United States to Israel's economic and social progress.

In 1955 the assistance which we received from the economic aid programme and the surplus commodities programme of the United States amounted to $55 million. Since 1952 these American governmental programmes have brought $270 million to Israel. Thus, the government and people of the United States have made an incomparable contribution to the development of our economy.

Israel still has many tasks in the fulfilment of which she needs friendly aid. We aspire to the development of our national water resources in order to achieve greater self-sufficiency in food production. We are keenly aware of the unlimited potentialities which nuclear and solar energy open out to all countries which cultivate high standards of scientific discipline. These are two of the fields in which I look forward to the intensification of formal co-operation between our two governments in the coming weeks.

In discussing the tribulations which face us I would not like to underestimate the importance of the great specific issues which now preoccupy the world. Israel is interested on general grounds in the historic confrontation between the universal rights of maritime nations and the unilateral claims of Egyptian nationalism. But we are also concerned with the specific issues of maritime freedom.

Our future prosperity, our capacity to trade freely with new friends in Asia and Africa depends much on our capacity to recapture the seafaring traditions of our Hebrew forebears and to sail freely upon and between the high seas.

Memories have been evoked in connection with this season of Tabernacles. Four thousand years ago our forefathers found an original method of solving the problems of navigation in the Red Sea. We are unlikely to find a similar formula for the Suez Canal.

It is principally against Israel that the Suez Canal Convention of 1888 has been violated for many years without remedy or redress. Those nations which are now so shocked by Egypt's policies in this matter would be wise to recognize one thing. No government is in a good position to assert its own rights if it allows an identical and equivalent right to be denied to others.

There is not one single government or nation which has a right superior to that of Israel to pass freely to and fro in the Gulf of Aqaba and in the Suez Canal. This is an unconditional right belonging to all nations. It is not an act of grace or condescension to be bestowed by Egypt upon those whom she chooses to favour.

Some of the leading maritime powers have confirmed their understanding of this legal situation. They have expressed their conviction that Egypt is in violation of the 1888 convention and in defiance of the law of the United Nations by virtue of her interference with Israeli shipping.

But this violation has been diagnosed by the world powers for many years without remedy being found. It is one thing to recognize an abuse; it is another thing to remove it.

I do not mean that we attach no significance to these assurances of our legal position. I am not prepared to predict that an international system will never, in all historic time, be applied to that maritime waterway. It is important, therefore, that we should confirm the principle of an absolute universality and non-discrimination in the use of a waterway, the founder of which, Ferdinand de Lesseps, dedicated it, 'to open the whole earth to all its peoples'.

It would be extraordinary if this concern by Israel were to be received with anything but understanding and sympathy. We hope that the maritime powers will vindicate the principle of free passage for Israel in any system which they may concert for the defence of their own rights. Israel cannot be expected to acquiesce by word or by deed, by action or by inaction in a situation under which all other nations than herself would exercise their rights of navigation and commerce in the Suez Canal.

Is it not obvious to you that your labours are not a marginal issue for us? They touch the very essence of our destiny. The government and people of Israel send to you, in deep and solemn emotion, their gratitude for your solidarity, especially in times of trial. It is in adversity that a man or a nation estimates the sincerity of his friends.

From the depths of its peril Israel has called unto you, and its voice has been answered. I do not doubt that you will continue to extend your constructive efforts; that you will devote a full measure of your judgment and sympathy to the vigilant scrutiny of our international problems.

And I have another request to you; it is that you intensify your close physical contact with Israel, that you come to Israel more often.

I suppose that it is one of my functions to promote what is called tourism; but I assure you that it is not in those terms that I am thinking this moment. Our ancestors did not talk of tourism when they spoke of physical contact between our people and other lands. They spoke of pilgrimage, of 'Aliyah', of ascent.

Your presence in increasing thousands, quite apart from its economic and financial by-products—and I am glad that Mr. Eshkol is not here to see how cavalierly I deal with that aspect of the problem —is essential in order to manifest to our people that it is not alone but that it has vast hinterlands of trust and affection.

The answers which come to our lips as we face the next year are not simple or dramatic. There is, perhaps, no short answer to these problems. This business of creating Israel calls for the durable qualities of tenacity and patience.

If anyone pretends he has a quick remedy for consolidating Israel, for reconciling it with its neighbouring world, for repairing the great convulsion which its establishment has aroused, you should suspect the sincerity or authenticity of his advice.

The road stretches out before us long and hard. But if the road is hard, surely the prize is worthy of attainment, and almost beyond compare: to restore the broken cycle of Israel's nationhood; to recapture Israel's roots in the most sublime and enduring of all the historic cultures; to gather the scattered debris of the most ancient of peoples and quicken it with energy and compassion into a new birth of freedom; to rescue the most sacred of all lands from primeval desolation; to build a Hebrew society for the perfection of man in the Divine Kingdom; to establish a strong economy as the shield of a vigorous culture; to illustrate for a tormented Middle East the rewards of affirmative progress above the sterile satisfactions of xenophobia; to console the wounded heart of our people for the toll of bereavement which has tortured our memory and experience throughout the past two decades—to do all of these things is, by the grace of history, within the power of your hands.

This is not an enterprise for a small generation. This is a drama conceived in majestic terms and acted in the sight of eternity. If we play our parts in the unfolding of its course, all future Jewish generations will rise up and call our memory blessed.

CHAPTER XIX

The Story of a Blockade*

No examination of the Suez Canal problem is accurate or complete unless it includes the experience acquired by Israel in its efforts to exercise its right of innocent passage in that international waterway.

It is primarily in relation to Israel that Egypt has most consistently violated the 1888 Convention and the Security Council's Resolution of 1951. For other nations, the obstruction of the Canal by the arbitrary action of the territorial power is a grave prospect. For Israel, and for states trading with her, it is an actual experience, enduring without remedy for eight years.

The current debate in the Security Council has underlined the importance of Israel's experience. While members of the Security Council have differed sharply on many things, they have been unanimous on one point. They have again emphasized the overriding validity of the 1888 Convention. They have expressed the view that, under that Convention, all states have the unconditional right, for all time, to free passage for all their ships and cargoes through the Suez Canal. Not one member of the Council has admitted any reservation to that right. Indeed, most members, whether in the current debate or in its recent context, have publicly disputed Egypt's claim to exercise any restrictions against Israeli ships or ships bound to or from Israel.

Today, when the rights of the international community in the Suez Canal are under world-wide attention, Israel finds it necessary to remind the Security Council of the following facts:

First. Egypt has been violating the central provision of the 1888 Convention for eight years.

Second. Egypt is in violation of the 1888 Convention at this time.

Third. Effective measures have not yet been concerted to ensure that Egypt will observe the 1888 Convention in the future.

* To the Security Council of the United Nations, 13 October 1955.

The Story of a Blockade

Fourth. The refusal of Egypt to carry out its international obligations in respect of free navigation in the Suez Canal has already been determined and condemned by the Security Council, in a decision which Egypt has persistently defied.

1. THE EGYPTIAN BLOCKADE IN PRACTICE

A discussion of Egypt's current practice in the Suez Canal requires an allusion to two statements of her legal obligations.

Article I of the 1888 Convention reads:

'The Suez Maritime Canal shall always be free and open in time of war as in time of peace to every vessel of commerce or of war without distinction of flag.

'Consequently, the high contracting parties agree not in any way to interfere with the free use of the Canal in time of war as in time of peace.

'The Canal shall never be subjected to the exercise of the right of blockade.'

On 1st September 1951 the Security Council, having examined an Israel complaint and an Egyptian counter-argument, called upon Egypt:

'. . . to terminate the restrictions on the passage of international commercial ships and goods through the Suez Canal wherever bound and to cease all interference with such shipping beyond that essential to the safety of shipping in the Canal itself and to the observance of the international conventions in force.'

In May 1948, during a military intervention, launched and maintained in defiance of Security Council resolutions for a cease-fire, Egypt established a general blockade against Israel and began to visit and search ships of all nations passing through the Suez Canal. The Egyptian Government established a long list of items, including ships, important categories of goods, and particularly petroleum, as subject to seizure as 'contraband' if found destined for Israel. Vessels transporting or suspected of transporting such goods were detained for visit and search. Cargoes of certain categories were removed and confiscated. These enactments were later formalized in an official decree on 6th February 1950.

In September 1950 these restrictions were enlarged by a decree requiring a guarantee by ships' captains, and, in particular, by captains of oil tankers, that their ships would not ultimately discharge

203

The Story of a Blockade

any of their cargo at any Israel port. Another regulation, still in force, calls for the submission of log books by tankers intending to proceed southward through the Suez Canal. Vessels found to have called at any port in Israel are placed on a blacklist and denied stores, fuel and repair facilities in Egyptian ports, including those at each end of the Suez Canal.

The threat of forcible interference acts as a deterrent to the great bulk of the normal trade which would otherwise pass through the Suez Canal to or from Israel. For example, the hundreds of oil tankers which pass annually through the Canal are allowed transit only on condition that they avoid any destination in Israel. Thus the blockade operates in two forms: primarily, through the deterrent effect of Egyptian decrees and regulations; and secondarily, through active interference with vessels, in the few cases where the regulations themselves have not been sufficient to deter the attempted voyage.

The basic legislation under which the Egyptian authorities obstruct free navigation in the Suez Canal is to be found in the Decree of 6th February 1950, the Arabic text of which was published in the Egyptian Official Journal (No. 36) dated 8th April 1950. Article I reads:

'The searching of ships for purposes of seizing war contraband, shall take place in accordance with provisions hereunder.'

Article III provides:

'Force may at all times be used against any ship attempting to avoid the search, where necessary by firing so as to force it to stop and submit to the search. Where the search subsequently reveals that the ship is not carrying any contraband, it shall be permitted to continue its voyage.'

This language should be compared with that of the 1888 Convention requiring free passage, in time of war or peace, for all vessels without distinction of flag.

Of the Egyptian decree Article IV states:

'If the crew of the ship resists the search by force, the ship shall be deemed to have lost its neutrality by reason of the hostile act. In that event, a ship may be seized even if the search reveals that it was not carrying contraband and the cargo may be impounded for that reason.'

It is instructive to compare the language of these sordid enactments with the lofty terms of the 1888 Convention, consecrating the Suez Canal as an international waterway open to navigation by all ships on the highest level of universality and equality. But the 1950 decrees are not the end of the legislative history. They are followed by other regulations, all tending to aggravate the original restriction.

Thus, an amendment to the decree of 6th February 1950 was published on 28th November 1953, adding the following paragraph to the list of goods liable to seizure as contraband:

'Foodstuffs and all other commodities which are likely to strengthen the war potential of the Zionists in Palestine [*sic*] in any way whatsoever.'

The maritime powers which use the Canal have expressed their revulsion at these arbitrary restrictions. Most of them have protested against them either in the Security Council, or in their direct relations with the Egyptian Government. None of them recognizes any legality in these decrees. But they remain in force. To resist them would require more resolution than the maritime community has yet shown. This becomes apparent when we record the stringency with which these regulations are applied.

The decree of 6th February 1950 establishes a blacklist of ships which, having transgressed or been suspected of transgressing against the Egyptian blockade practices, are to be denied the free use of the Suez Canal. The latest available edition of this list contains 104 ships, inscribed between 1950 and 1955—for the 'offence' of having exercised their rights under the 1888 Convention to trade freely through the Suez Canal. The ships are of British, United States, Swedish, Greek, Norwegian, Dutch, Danish, Panamanian, Liberian, Swiss, Costa Rican and Italian nationality. Thus, all these nations have been deprived of an essential part of their rights under the 1888 Convention. Under an Egyptian law, which constitutes the standing orders of Egyptian officials in the Suez Canal, cargo carried on these ships shall 'be deemed intended for the enemy' and subject to confiscation and seizure, while the ships themselves would be denied the essential facilities necessary for passage through the Suez Canal. The existence of the blacklist is, therefore, the most stringent of the deterrents whereby Egypt has prevented trading with Israel through an international waterway.

As a result of these illicit enactments imposed on the maritime powers, some 90 per cent of the trade which would have normally flowed through the Canal to or from Israel in the past eight years has been effectively obstructed.

The Story of a Blockade

Notwithstanding the Egyptian decrees, some ships have attempted to exercise the rights conferred on them by the 1888 Convention.

On 31st October 1952 a cargo of meat on the Norwegian vessel *Rimfrost* proceeding from Massawa to Haifa through the Suez Canal was confiscated. Under international pressure the cargo was returned in useless condition three months later.

On 2nd September 1953 the Greek S.S. *Parnon* with a cargo of 500 tons of asphalt and a number of Israel-assembled cars, was detained in the Canal under threat of confiscation of cargo and ship. Under intensive pressure by the interested powers the ship was allowed to proceed, having lost twelve days of its journey.

On 4th November 1953 the Norwegian vessel *Rimfrost* was again detained in the Canal and two boats destined for Italy were removed.

On 16th December 1953 the Italian ship *Franca Mari*, with a cargo of meat and hides, was stopped on the way from Massawa to Haifa. The cargo was confiscated. The ship was eventually permitted to proceed.

On 22nd December 1953 the Norwegian vessel, *Triton*, bound from Melbourne to Genoa via Israel, with a cargo of clothing and motor-cycles, was stopped in the Canal and its cargo confiscated.

On 28th September 1954 the Israel freighter *Bat Galim*, bound from Eritrea to Haifa with 93 tons of meat, 42 tons of plywood and 3 tons of hides, was detained in the Canal and exposed to the following treatment: its cargo was confiscated; its crew was thrown in gaol under a fictitious charge of having opened fire on Egyptian fishermen at the entrance to the Canal. False names for the alleged fishermen were fabricated. The Egyptian-Israel Mixed Armistice Commission dismissed the Egyptian story as a total fiction. By this time, the fabrication had been widely published by high officials of Colonel Nasser's government, and had even been proclaimed in the Security Council of the United Nations. Under the influence of Security Council discussions, the Egyptian Government released the crew from prison, transferred them by land to the Egyptian-Israel frontier, and dismissed them across the boundary. The Egyptian Representative in the Security Council then gave an undertaking that the ship and its cargo would be returned. This undertaking was violated. The Egyptian Government appropriated the cargo to itself, and has now commissioned the confiscated ship to the Egyptian Navy.

It is difficult to think of a larger aggregate of offences against international law and maritime tradition than those which Egypt compressed into the single episode of the *Bat Galim*. There is obstruction of free navigation; piratical seizure of a ship in an international waterway; physical violence against the persons of mariners exercising innocent passage; fabrication of charges against sailors in transit; unlawful imprisonment; the bearing of false witness to the highest tribunals of international security; dishonourable non-fulfilment of a pledge given by a member nation at the table of the Security Council. All this was done by a government which claims to be an adequate custodian of universally established maritime rights.

On 8th July 1955 the Dutch ship *Fedala* was detained en route from Massawa to Haifa. Part of its cargo was confiscated and the vessel held against its master's will for three days.

On 25th May 1956 the Greek ship *Pannegia*, en route from Haifa to Elath, was detained in the Suez Canal with a cargo of 520 tons of cement. The crew was not allowed ashore for three months despite the spread of sickness amongst its members. Its water provisions were cruelly limited. In a statement made at Haifa on 10th September 1956 the Greek captain, Mr. Koutales Costa, has given a full account of the inhuman harassments to which he and his crew were subjected.

It will be seen that those few ships which are not frightened off the Israeli route by the deterrent effects of Egypt's blockade legislation have been subjected, at the whim and fancy of the territorial State, to acts of force against their flag, their cargoes, the authority of their masters and the persons of their crews.

Egypt has confiscated and held goods of the value of $5,600,000 seized from ships exercising innocent passage in the Suez Canal.

Not one of the immunities prescribed by the Constantinople Convention has been held in honour by the Egyptian Government in the record of these eight years.

It is legitimate for Israel to invite the Security Council to read the language of the Egyptian blockade laws; to scan the blacklist of ships warned by Egypt off an international highway; to think of the ordeals of the peaceful vessels and crews listed above; and then to ask itself how all this compares with the Egyptian Foreign Minister's quotation on October 8th to the effect that the Canal 'shall always be open as a neutral passage to every merchant ship crossing from one sea to another *without any distinction, exclusion or preference of persons or nationalities*'.

The Story of a Blockade

The ships which have attempted to pass through the Canal to Israel are few in number; but this fact aggravates and does not diminish Egypt's offence. The blockade works principally through the existence of the regulations and their deterrent effects and only secondarily through active assault and confiscation. With tanker traffic entirely intimidated by the inclusion of some 75 tankers on the blacklist and with Israeli flagships confiscated at sight—two categories which would account for the great bulk of normal traffic have been entirely excluded from the waterway. The more traffic passing through the Canal for non-Israeli destinations, and the fewer for Israeli destinations, the more effective and drastic is the blockade proved to be.

2. THE LEGAL POSITION

(a) *Violation of the 1888 Convention*

It remains to compare the current Egyptian practice with Egypt's legal obligations in the Suez Canal. Paramount amongst these is the central injunction of the 1888 Convention providing that the Suez Maritime Canal:

'... shall always be free and open in time of war as in time of peace to every vessel of commerce or war without distinction of flag.'

In subsequent articles the Convention further develops the theme of universality and non-discrimination in the use of the waterway. Embarrassed by the sheer emphasis with which the Convention forbids discrimination, Egypt has sought a slender refuge in Articles IX and X, which empower the territorial state to take measures for the security of its own forces and for the defence of Egypt.

The Egyptian Government has claimed that the security of Egyptian armed forces would have been threatened by the arrival of frozen meat on the *Rimfrost*; of plywood and hides on the *Bat Galim*; of cement on the *Pannegia* and of Australian motor-cycles to Genoa via Haifa. It claims that Egypt's capacity of self-defence would be injured if tankers passing through the Suez Canal were not prevented from depositing crude oil for refining in Haifa, both for domestic consumption and for export to Europe. The argument is without substance, and has no legal basis. Even if the safe arrival of these frozen meats and fuel oils, these hides and motor-cycles were seriously considered by Egypt to be detrimental to her 'security', this would give her no right to deny them free passage through the Suez Canal.

The Story of a Blockade

Egypt's reliance on Articles IX and X to justify her blockade restrictions is decisively closed by Article XI which reads:

'. . . the measures which shall be taken in the cases provided for in Articles IX and X of the present treaty *shall not interfere with the free use of the Canal.*'

Representatives of Egypt in the Security Council, seeking to base their blockade practices on Articles IX and X, have always refused to recognize the existence of Article XI. This Article is a complete refutation of their effort to reconcile their restrictions with the text of the 1888 Convention.

In observations outside this Council Egyptian representatives have fallen back on a new argument. They admit that the 1888 Convention provides for free passage through the Suez Canal even in time of war, and even to 'belligerents'. They go on, however, to assert that this freedom applies only to 'belligerents' who are at war with countries other than Egypt. According to this argument, a user of the Canal at war with any state except Egypt can enjoy the plenitude of his rights; but when Egypt chooses to call itself a 'belligerent', its adversary loses his rights under the 1888 Convention.

There is no foundation for this theory. It is indeed specifically ruled out by Article IV of the 1888 Convention which reads as follows:

'The maritime canal remaining open in time of war as a free passage, even to the ships of war of belligerents, according to the terms of Article I of the present treaty, the High Contracting Parties agree that no right of war, no act of hostility, *nor any act having for its object to obstruct the free navigation of the Canal shall be committed in the Canal and its ports of access . . . even though the Ottoman Empire should be one of the belligerent powers.*'

It is, of course, a truism that in terms of the 1888 Convention, Egypt is the equivalent of the Ottoman Empire.

The conclusion is clear: even if Egypt possessed rights of 'belligerency', she would not be legally permitted to perform 'any act having for its object to obstruct the free navigation of the Canal'.

(b) *International Opinion on the 1888 Convention*

The text of the 1888 Convention is sufficient in itself to disqualify the Egyptian restrictions. If any further argument were needed, it could be found in the view of other signatories to the Convention. Egypt cannot be the sole judge of the validity of its own obligations.

The Story of a Blockade

It cannot unilaterally interpret a multilateral treaty in its own interest.

Not one signatory of the Constantinople Convention has ever been found to uphold Egypt's view that the restrictions against Israel are compatible with the Convention. On the other hand, those signatories of the Convention and other powers who have expressed themselves on the subject at all, have invariably held that Egypt's restrictions against Israel violate the Convention. On 16th August 1951 the Representative of the Netherlands said in the Security Council:

'I now come, briefly, to the Convention of Constantinople of 1888. My government is of the opinion that, even apart from the question as to whether Egypt can claim to be considered as a belligerent, the Egyptian measures of restriction in the Suez Canal are inconsistent with the preamble and with Articles I and XI of the Convention. The rights and duties resulting from the Convention are quite clear. The general principle of the free use of the Canal in time of war as in time of peace, without distinction of flag, determines the language and the meaning of the Convention throughout its contents. The free use of the Canal is the paramount general interest. In Articles IX and X provisions are made to ensure that such free use will not deteriorate into abuse, but even such measures as Egypt is entitled to take under those provisions shall, according to Article XI "not interfere with the free use of the Canal"; not only with the use, but with the free use.

'In the light of this, in our opinion, very clear and unequivocal language, *my government considers that the Egyptian restrictions on the free use of the Suez Canal are undoubtedly incompatible with the Convention of Constantinople of 1888.*'

Similar statements, declaring the Egyptian restrictions to be contrary to the 1888 Convention, were made by the Representative of Belgium on 4th January 1955. The views of the British and French Governments are also on record. Non-signatories, representing many other legal traditions, have similarly found incompatibility between the Egyptian practices and the Constantinople Convention. This was attested by the Representative of Colombia in the Security Council on 28th March 1954; by the Representative of Denmark on 28th March 1954; by the Representative of Brazil on 3rd January 1955; by the Representative of New Zealand on 13th January 1955; and by the Representative of Peru on 13th January 1955.

On 27th September 1956 the President of the United States of America described the Egyptian restrictions on Israeli-bound shipping as 'a black mark', 'most unjust' and as 'not in accord with the 1888 Convention'.

(c) *The Security Council's Jurisprudence*

All the grounds on which Egypt bases its discrimination against Israel shipping and commerce were examined and rejected by the Security Council in its discussions of the Suez Canal problem in 1951, 1954 and 1955.

Egypt has based its alleged right to exercise these restrictions on the doctrine of a 'state of war'. Even if Egypt possessed 'belligerent rights' she would still have no right under the 1888 Convention to obstruct freedom of passage in the Canal to any ship of any flag at any time, in peace or in war. This is stated categorically in Articles I, IV and XI. But the Security Council has determined that Egypt does not, in fact, possess any rights of belligerency in the Suez Canal, or anywhere else. The theory of belligerent rights was the central theme of the Security Council's discussions in 1951. By the time it reached the Council, this doctrine had been rejected by the authorities responsible for interpreting the Rhodes Agreement of February 1949, which defines Egyptian-Israel relations in the aftermath of hostilities. The Rhodes Agreement was concluded pursuant to a resolution of the Security Council in the presence of its representative, Dr. Ralph Bunche. Addressing the Security Council on 26th July 1949, Dr. Bunche interpreted the law of the Armistice Agreement as follows:

'There should be free movement for legitimate shipping and no vestiges of the wartime blockade should be allowed to remain *as they are inconsistent with both the letter and the spirit of the Armistice Agreements.*'

The same matter was discussed in the Egyptian-Israel Mixed Armistice Commission frequently between 1949 and 1951. The United Nations Chief of Staff reported his findings to the Security Council on 12th June 1951. Discussing the provisions of the Armistice Agreement against the commission of 'aggressive or hostile acts', the United Nations Chief of Staff said:

'It is quite clear to me that action taken by the Egyptian authorities in interfering with passage of goods destined for Israel through the Suez Canal must be considered an aggressive action. Similarly I must of necessity consider that the interference with the passage of goods is a hostile act. . . . In my opinion this interference is an aggressive and hostile act.'

The Story of a Blockade

Against this background, the Security Council adopted its resolution of 1st September 1951. A study of that resolution reveals how comprehensively the Security Council put its authority behind the case for the complete cessation of Egypt's restrictions:

In the first two paragraphs of its resolution the Security Council recalled its previous resolution of 11th August 1949, and 17th November 1950, which interpreted the Armistice Agreements as including 'firm pledges against any further acts of hostility between the parties'.

In its third paragraph the Security Council drew attention to the report of the Chief of Staff of 12th June 1951, expressing the opinion that the Egyptian interference with shipping 'jeopardized the effective functioning of the Armistice Agreement'. In the same report, the Chief of Staff had referred to this Egyptian practice as a 'hostile and aggressive act' and as a policy the continuation of which had definitely not been envisaged by the parties when they set their hands to that Agreement at Rhodes.

In paragraph 4 the Security Council noted that Egypt had not complied with the earnest plea of the Chief of Staff that they 'desist from the present practice of interfering with the passage through the Suez Canal of goods destined for Israel'.

In paragraph 5, which constitutes what the representative of France was later to describe as 'the legal foundation of the Security Council's action', the Security Council determined that 'the armistice régime is of a permanent character so that *neither party can reasonably assert that it is actively a belligerent* or requires to exercise the right of visit, search and seizure for any legitimate purpose of self-defence'.

In paragraph 6 the Security Council determined that maintenance of the Egyptian restrictions is inconsistent with the central purposes of the Armistice Agreement.

In paragraph 7 the Security Council disqualified the Egyptian practice on general grounds of international maritime law by defining it as 'an abuse of the exercise of the right to visit, search and seizure'.

In paragraph 8 the Security Council categorically dismissed the Egyptian contention that the Egyptian practice could be justified on the grounds of 'self-defence'.

In paragraph 9 the Security Council condemned the attempt of the Egyptian Government to impose its legislation and its policy of hostility to Israel upon other countries, noting that those restrictions represented unjustified interference with the rights of nations to navigate the seas and to trade freely with one another, including the Arab States and Israel.

Finally, in paragraph 10, the Security Council called upon Egypt 'to terminate the restrictions on the passage of international commercial shipping and goods through the Suez Canal, wherever bound, and to cease all interference with such shipping beyond that required for technical considerations of safety or for the observance of international conventions.

Thus, the Security Council's resolution of 1st September 1951 makes a specific judgment on every one of the issues involved in the case before it. In that discussion, and those which ensued in 1954 and 1955, some eighteen member states of the United Nations, in their capacity as Security Council members, have recorded, by speech and vote, their unreserved condemnation of Egypt's blockade practices. The states thus on record in Security Council debates are: the United States, the United Kingdom, France, Netherlands, Belgium, Denmark, Colombia, Peru, Brazil, Cuba, Ecuador, Turkey, Yugoslavia, Australia.

On the other hand, no member of the Security Council at any time has raised a voice in favour of Egypt's alleged rights to practise these encroachments.

(d) *Further Implications of the 1951 Resolution*

The Security Council's resolution of 1951 gave judgment not only against Egypt's blockade practices, but also against the doctrine of 'belligerency' on which they were based.

In its 1954 discussion the Security Council developed this jurisprudence further. It established the doctrine of Egypt's obligation to allow free passage not only in the Suez Canal but also in the Gulf of Aqaba as well. This was enunciated on behalf of the majority by the United Kingdom who said:

'The second part of the Israel complaint concerns interference with shipping in the Gulf of Aqaba. I have already referred to paragraph 5 of the 1951 resolution, which laid down that "since the armistice régime . . . is of a permanent character, neither party can reasonably assert that it is . . . a belligerent or requires to exercise the right of visit, search and seizure for any legitimate purpose of self-defence". That is a general principle which applies not only in the Suez Canal, but also in the Gulf of Aqaba, and indeed anywhere else.'

The representative of France pointed out:

The Story of a Blockade

'The terms used [in the 1951 Resolution] are obviously intended to constitute a general formula applicable not only to passage between Suez and Port Said, but also in the Mediterranean, the Red Sea and the Gulf of Aqaba itself. Logically, it is not possible to deny Egypt the status of a belligerent in the Canal whilst granting that status in the adjacent areas.'

The representative of the United States and others spoke in similar vein.

In the 1955 discussion on the *Bat Galim* case the question of the right of Israel flagships was considered for the first time. Israel's merchant fleet had only then begun to develop to the point where this subject became of practical importance. The consensus of the Security Council was clearly expressed in conformity with Article I of the Constantinople Convention, which provides for free passage through the Suez Canal for all ships 'without distinction of flag'. It is clear from this Article that the right of free navigation belongs to Israeli flagships, as to all others, on a level of complete equality. This was clearly enunciated by the representative of the United States who said on 4th January 1955:

'Thus we cannot fail to state our view that Egyptian restrictions on ships passing through the Suez Canal, whether bound to or from Israel, *or whether flying the Israel or some other flag*, are inconsistent with the spirit and intent of the Egyptian-Israeli General Armistice Agreement, contrary to the Security Council resolution of 1st September 1951 (S/2322), and a retrogression from the stated objectives to which both sides committed themselves in signing the Armistice Agreement. We cannot fail to state, therefore, that we look to Egypt to give effect to these decisions and agreements.'

On 13th January 1955 the President of the Security Council (Sir Leslie Munro, New Zealand) summed up the *Bat Galim* case as follows:

'It is evident that most representatives here regard the resolution of 1st September 1951 as having continuing validity and effect, and it is in this context and that of the Constantinople Convention that they have considered the *Bat Galim* case.'

The Security Council was clearly aware that if Egypt had the right to commit belligerent acts of its choice against Israel, it would follow that Israel could commit belligerent acts of its choice against Egypt. This was regarded as a specially compelling reason for bringing Egypt's violation to an end.

The United States representative said:

The Story of a Blockade

'The United States is firmly of the opinion that the restrictions which Egypt is exercising over ships passing through the Suez Canal are inconsistent with the spirit and intent of the Armistice Agreement. . . . The result of this hostile act is the engendering of hostility in return which places in jeopardy the peace and stability of the area.'

Three years later, this was echoed by the representative of Brazil:

'Should we accept the Egyptian thesis we should be bound to recognize any measures of reprisal adopted by the Israel Government. It is obvious that in the exchange of hostile acts that would follow we could hardly expect to lay the foundations of a definite solution to the Palestine problem.'

3. The Future

The Security Council has no more urgent task in the Suez Canal problem than to secure the implementation of its existing decision. If the Security Council and the chief maritime powers had shown greater zeal in resisting the violations of the 1888 Convention during the past eight years they would be in a stronger position to defend its integrity today.

Invite the Security Council to consider some of the grave implications which will arise if these abuses are allowed to endure:

If the violation is any longer condoned, it is bound to spread over a larger field. No nation has a greater or a lesser right than Israel to the free use of the Suez Canal. If Egypt is entitled to interfere with ships, cargoes or crews bound for Israel, she is equally entitled to interfere with the ships, cargoes or crews of every other state. This is clear from the fact that any distinction between Israel's rights and those of other states has been specifically repudiated by the Security Council itself. Those who have now understood the dangers of Egypt's policy on navigation in the Canal will, no doubt, agree that no nation can effectively assert its own rights, if it condones the denial of an equal and identical right to other nations.

The Egyptian violations inflict a great injury on Israel, which she is not bound passively to endure. The extent of this injury can be illustrated by one item alone. About 70 per cent of the traffic through the Suez Canal consists of oil tankers. If Egypt obeyed the international law these tankers would be as free to sell their oil at the Israeli port of Haifa as anywhere else. But owing to Egypt's punitive measures, which have put 75 tankers on the blacklist, these vessels refrain from attempting to serve the Israel market. Israel has thus found it necessary to purchase her fuel from other sources than the tanker traffic, and then to convey it without using the Suez Canal. Since the Security Council's Resolution of 1951, it is estimated that Iasrael has paid 44 million dollars more for her fuel supply than she would have paid if a situation of law prevailed in the Suez Canal. This takes no account of the incidental losses to Israel through handicaps inflicted on the petro-chemical and refining industries, the obstruction of Israel flagships from inter-oceanic voyages and the increased cost to Israel of her growing trade with Africa and Asian nations.

Many countries have a much greater fuel import requirement than Israel; and others depend even more than she on the Suez Canal. Israel's experience illustrates the economic outrage to which they may be exposed, and from which they have no present guarantee except the dubious one of Egypt's sufferance.

Israel itself has no obligation to suffer this abuse. Much has been said in the Security Council's debate on the need to base peace on foundations of justice and international law. Such peace as now exists in the Suez Canal is based in large measure on acquiescence in the violation of justice and international law. To endure an injury passively is, in effect, to encourage its repetition and its aggravation.

The Egyptian violations would be serious enough if they deprived only one nation of its rights under the 1888 Convention. When universality is violated in one instance it ceases to exist at all. In fact, however, many nations have suffered encroachments on their sovereignty through the impact of Egypt's restrictions.

In discussing Egypt's practices in the Suez Canal, mention has been made above of some twenty nations whose rights under the 1888 Convention have been violated. A country which desires to trade with Israel through the Suez Canal and is prevented from so doing by Egypt thereby suffers prejudice to its sovereign rights. Egypt herself has a formal right not to trade with Israel. But Egypt has no right to prevent other nations from trading with Israel through the Suez Canal or in any other way. The maritime nations are not colonies of Egypt. Their commercial policies are not subject to Egypt's control. What they sell to Israel, or what Israel sells to them, whether through the Suez Canal or by any other route, is a matter for their and Israel's exclusive sovereign discretion. Thus, so long as Egyptian restrictions persist, all nations are in practice, or in potentiality, deprived of some part of their sovereign rights.

The Story of a Blockade

The Security Council itself observed this fact when in its 1951 Resolution it stated that:

'the restrictions on the passage of goods through the Suez Canal to Israeli ports are denying to nations at no time connected with the conflict in Palestine valuable supplies required for their economic reconstruction, and that these restrictions together with sanctions applied by Egypt to certain ships which have visited Israeli ports represent unjustified interference with the rights of nations to navigate the seas and to trade freely with one another, including the Arab States and Israel.'

It is true that this violation of international law has existed for several years and does not derive specifically from the action taken by Egypt on July 26th. But the long duration of this abuse makes its removal not less, but more, urgent. It would be illogical for the international community to insure itself against future illegalities, while allowing existing ones to continue on their perilous course.

In any new projects designed to ensure and guarantee respect for the 1888 Convention, the Government of Israel claims specific guarantees for its own rights. It has been gratifying in recent weeks to observe a strong surge of world opinion in favour of guaranteeing freedom of navigation in the Suez Canal for the ships of all nations without distinction of flag. But in view of the special experience of the past eight years the general statement of this doctrine is not adequate, unless it is specified that the principle must be applied to Israel as to any other state. Similarly, the experiences of the past eight years conclusively prove the necessity for effective measures of implementation to prevent or correct violations.

Israel's rights are fully established in law and do not stand in need of further adjudication. On the basis of the 1888 Convention, of the 1951 Resolution, and of the overwhelming consensus of international opinion, Israel's right to free passage exists as an axiom and prior assumption in international law. The Government of Israel is at this moment endowed with full legal competence to exercise this right. It does not lie under the onus of proving the legality of its rights either in general or in any particular case. If Egypt desired any relief from the full application of the 1888 Convention the onus would be upon her to seek it, and, in any case, to avoid any interference with navigation through the Suez Canal, whether bound for Israel or anywhere else. It is important that in any future provisions for the adjudication of violations nothing should be done which would throw any doubt

217

The Story of a Blockade

on the existing jurisprudence with respect to the 1888 Convention and the Security Council Resolution of 1951. On October 8th the Egyptian Foreign Minister reaffirmed his government's long-standing declaration stating that the Suez Canal 'shall always be open as a neutral passage to every merchant ship crossing from one sea to another without any distinction, exclusion or preference of persons or nationalities, on payment of dues and observance of the regulations established'. If this declaration is sincere, Egypt cannot continue to maintain its discrimination against Israel in the Suez Canal.

The maritime nations have one obvious method of vindicating their own rights, and those of others, under international law. This would be by refusing to submit to the restrictions which they have frequently condemned. To show deference to the Egyptian restrictions; to refrain meekly from doing lawfully things which those regulations unlawfully forbid; to exclude Israel from normal patterns of trade through the Suez Canal in deference to Egypt's blockade practices—to do this is to become associated, beyond any right or necessity, with Egypt's violations of international law.

The maritime nations, under the 1888 Convention and the 1951 resolution have the right to trade freely with Israel through the Suez Canal. It is surely their legal and moral duty now to exercise that right in practice, and to lay upon Egypt the responsibility for any violation.

On 12th October 1956 the Secretary-General of the United Nations read to a meeting of the Security Council a list of six principles to which Egypt, as well as France and the United Kingdom, had agreed. These principles include the following:

'1. There shall be free and open transit through the Canal without discrimination overt or covert.'

'3. The operation of the Canal shall be insulated from the politics of any country.'

These formulations cannot possibly be reconciled with the continuation, for a single day, of Egypt's overt discrimination against Israel in pursuance of a purely national policy condemned by the international community.

If this statement does not mean the immediate end of discrimination against Israel in the Suez Canal, it means nothing at all.

218

CHAPTER XX

'Embattled, Blockaded, Besieged'*

O n Monday, October 29th, the Israel Defence Forces took security measures in the Sinai peninsula in the exercise of our country's inherent right of self-defence. The object of these operations is to eliminate the bases from which armed Egyptian units, under the special care and authority of Colonel Nasser, invade Israel's territory for murder, sabotage and the creation of permanent insecurities to peaceful life. These are the only military activities for which the Government of Israel is responsible.

Stretching back far behind the events of this week lies the unique and sombre story of a small people subjected throughout all the years of its national existence to a furious, implacable, comprehensive campaign of hatred and siege for which there is no parallel or precedent in the modern history of nations. Not for one single moment throughout the entire period of its modern national existence has Israel enjoyed that minimal physical security which the United Nations Charter confers on all member states, and which all other member states have been able to command.

We meet here under the auspices of the United Nations, a family of sovereign states organized in a system of mutual rights and obligations. Its basic premise is the sovereign equality of all its members. Whatever rights are enjoyed by other members of this Organization belong to Israel without addition or diminution. Whatever obligation any member state owes to another, Egypt owes to Israel and Israel to Egypt. If Egypt denies Israel the plenitude of its Charter rights, then it inflicts deep injury upon Israel, and its competence to invoke the Charter against Israel is seriously compromised and reduced.

What are the obligations which Egypt owes to Israel under the Charter? Under the Charter, Egypt is bound 'to practise tolerance and live together in peace' with Israel as a good neighbour. Under the Charter, Egypt is bound to 'unite its strength' with Israel 'to

*To the General Assembly of the United Nations, 1 November 1956.

maintain international peace and security'. Under the Charter, Egypt is bound to regard Israel as a state endowed with sovereignty equal to its own. Under the Charter, Egypt is bound to respect the 'territorial integrity and the political independence' of the State of Israel, and especially to refrain from the threat or use of force against that integrity and that independence. Under the Charter, Egypt is bound in advance to accept and carry out decisions of the Security Council whenever such decisions are made in favour of Israel as of any other state.

To these broad obligations, derived from the Charter, there must be added to Egypt's account other obligations of a more specific nature, based on the Armistice Agreement of 1949. Under that Agreement, Egypt is bound to respect the demarcation line between Israel and Egypt; to prevent any illegal crossings of that line; to abstain from the threat or use of force from its own side of the line against Israel's side; to regard the Armistice Agreement itself as a transitory measure leading to permanent peace; to respond at any time to Israel's request for a conference to develop the Armistice Agreement into a peace settlement or to amend and review its provisions; and to abstain from any acts of hostility or any acts of blockade or belligerency.

Is there any resemblance whatever between this list of obligations and Egypt's actual conduct of its relations with Israel? Can anyone imagine that, if Egypt had been willing to carry out this system of relations with Israel, we should have been assembled here on this tragic and solemn occasion?

What we confront tonight is a point of explosion after eight years of illicit belligerency. Belligerency is the key to the understanding of our problem tonight. Egypt has practised belligerency against Israel by land. Egypt has practised belligerency against Israel by sea. Egypt has established belligerency as the juridical basis of its relations with Israel. Egypt has held belligerency to be the spiritual and emotional mainspring of its conduct toward Israel. Out of this fourfold belligerency, maintained by Egypt for seven years—but with special vigour and intensity since the rise of the Nasser régime, is born the crisis which the United Nations confront tonight. I would say a word to the Assembly on each of these aspects of Egyptian belligerency.

Belligerency by land took its origins in May 1948, on the very morrow of Israel's emergence to sovereignty. On that date Egyptian forces, joined by the converging forces of other Arab armies, marched into the newly established independent sovereign state of Israel with the avowed aim of its destruction. Alas, the processes which now move so swiftly in Egypt's protection were much slower at that time. It took us eight weeks to secure from the organs of the United Nations the establishment of an effective and stable cease-fire. During that period, every home in Israel stood under the direct shadow of death and extinction.

Our men, women and children fell by the thousands while this wave of aggression threatened to convulse us. At the end of that year, negotiations were held under United Nations auspices which led to the conclusion of the Rhodes Armistice Agreement. This agreement did not promise us an affirmative, trustful and co-operative system of relationships. It did at least, however, promise us immunity from overtly hostile acts. Under the Armistice Agreement, every citizen of Israel is entitled to till every inch of Israel's soil and to navigate every yard of Israel's waters, without let or hindrance by any violent encroachment from the Egyptian side.

Yet, throughout this period of the armistice, our territory has been subjected to constant encroachment. The frontier has not been for Israel a barrier against the sudden leaping forward of violence by day and by night. Our 400 dead or wounded through these incursions tell the story of an armistice frontier which has been violated with consistency, and with special frequency and intensity during the past two years during which the Nasser régime has held sway in Egypt. The toll of dead and wounded has been augmented by countless pipelines blown up, by water supplies demolished, by trees pulled down, by an inferno of insecurity and danger which has raged along peaceful farms and homesteads in the frontier area. Last year to all these torments was added the most penetrating and perilous of all, through the organization and mobilization of the Fedayeen movement.

It may be difficult for nations assembled here, which enjoy a normal security, to understand what has been involved for Israel by this belligerency on land. While much has been said about Israel's responsibility to the United Nations, it is a melancholy fact that since 1948 any Arab state which has ever tried to kill Israelis, to plunder Israel property, to blockade Israel ports, to intercept Israel navigation, has never regarded itself as operating under any effective

221

international deterrent. Thus, the United Nations has not been able to offer Israel the minimum of daily security enjoyed by all its other members in nearly every sector of their national life.

Surrounded by hostile armies on all its land frontiers, subjected to savage and relentless hostility, exposed to penetration, raids and assaults by day and by night, suffering constant toll of life amongst its citizenry, bombarded by threats of neighbouring governments to accomplish its extinction by armed force, overshadowed by a new menace of irresponsible rearmament, embattled, blockaded, besieged, Israel alone amongst the nations faces a battle for its security anew with every approaching nightfall and every rising dawn. In a country of small area and intricate configuration, the proximity of enemy guns is a constant and haunting theme.

These fears and provocations hover over us everywhere, but they fall upon us with special intensity in the frontier areas, where development projects vital to the nation's destiny can be paralysed or interrupted by our adversaries from a position of dominating geographical advantage. In short, it is a small country, where every activity by farmers or citizens becomes a test of physical and moral courage. These are the unique circumstances in which Israel pursues its quest for security and peace.

On innumerable occasions the active defence of Israel life and territory has been compromised in deference to international opinion. We know that Israel is most popular when she does not hit back and world opinion is profoundly important to us. So, on one occasion after another, we have buried our dead, tended our wounded, clenched our teeth in suppressed resentment and hoped that this very moderation would deter a repetition of the offence. But sometimes the right and duty of self-preservation, the need to avoid expanding encroachment, the sentiment that if the claim to peaceful existence is not defended it will be forever lost, prevails in the final and reluctant decision.

This belligerency which assails us by land has its counterpart by sea. In 1948, Egypt established processes of visits, search and seizure; began to confiscate ships and cargoes bound for Israel's ports; enacted restrictive regulations; and applied punitive measures against the shipping and flags of other countries desiring to trade and to navigate peacefully with Israel upon and between the high seas. The flags of fifteen nations, endowed with the unconditional right of free navigation in the Suez Canal, have been abused by unlawful acts of interception. Ships have been confiscated and sold, cargoes have been held and sequestered, sailors have been tormented and wrongfully imprisoned, and all this on the great international waterway consecrated nine decades ago to the universal right of all nations for free commerce and navigation through the Suez Canal.

Thus, classic acts of war by maritime blockade have been added to Egypt's land belligerency in the total pattern of Israel's siege. Throughout the development of this policy during the Nasser régime we have witnessed a constant sequence of aggravation. The blockade and interception have been extended, in the name of belligerency, from the Suez Canal to another international waterway, the Gulf of Aqaba. The State of Israel has had to distort the entire pattern of its economy, to bear illicit burdens running into tens of millions of pounds, in order to compensate for the impact of this piratical system which Egypt has established on a great artery of the world's communications.

Belligerency by land and belligerency by sea are both expressed in a doctrine of juridical belligerency. This doctrine has been discredited by the Security Council of the United Nations, but it continues to be maintained. On 12th June 1951, the Egyptian representative said: 'We exercise our rights of war. We are legally at war with Israel. This armistice does not put an end to the state of war. It will not prohibit Egypt from exercising certain rights of war.'

In the Security Council of the United Nations the Foreign Minister of Egypt declared: 'The Egyptian-Israel General Armistice Agreement will not be interpreted by us as terminating in any legal or technical sense the state of war between Egypt and Israel.'

This jurisprudence continued to be maintained long after it had been adjudicated and rejected. In juridical and legal terms Egypt has cut herself off from her Charter obligations towards Israel, and avows a legal basis for her relationship which makes her appeal to the United Nations highly incongruous. It is strange to declare war against a neighbour and then to complain because there is no peace.

The fourth aspect of this belligerency should be studied in those statements of Egypt's intentions towards Israel which furnish the philosophical background to the belligerent acts which I have described. Here is a typical example of the kind of utterance which bombards the ears of Israel's population by day and by night:

'Wait and see,' says the Egyptian dictator, 'soon will be proven to you the strength and will of our nation. Egypt will teach you a lesson and quiet you forever. Egypt will grind you to the dust.'

On 11th April 1955, celebrating the exploits of Egypt's commando units in Israel, the Egyptian Minister of Religious Properties declared:

'There is no reason why the faithful Fedayeen, hating their enemy, should not penetrate into Israel and transform the lives of its citizens into a hell. Yes, we will be victorious because we are more diligent in death than is Israel in life.'

On 14th October 1955, the Egyptian dictator himself said:

'I am not solely fighting against Israel itself. My task is to deliver the Arab world from destruction through Israel's intrigue, which has its roots abroad. Our hatred is very strong. There is no sense in talking about peace with Israel. There is not even the smallest place for negotiations.'

The press and all the agencies and media of information take up the chorus. A typical example was contained in the leading Egyptian newspaper, *Al Ahram*:

'Israel will not be saved from the Arabs. She will be destroyed under the feet of Arab fighters and the flag of freedom will be unfurled over Palestine.'

There is a tendency in some quarters to underestimate the importance of these pronouncements. I can assure members of the General Assembly that it is indeed a disquieting experience to live in a country surrounded by neighbours which bombard it by day and by night with predictions and menaces for its physical destruction. There is no doubt that these authoritative directives furnish the psychological and emotional background against which belligerency by land and by sea is organized, with growing intensity. But all of these aspects of belligerency together would not of themselves automatically invite a drastic response in self-defence were there not an immediate cause; and I wish to explain frankly and candidly to the General Assembly the special background against which our actions of last Monday took place.

World opinion naturally asks what these Fedayeen units are; what their activities imply for Israel's security; whether their actions in the past and their plans for the future were really full of peril for

'Embattled, Blockaded, Besieged'

Israel; whether the danger was really so acute that Israel might reasonably regard its elimination as a primary condition of its security, and indeed of its very existence.

The Government of Israel represents a people endowed with a mature understanding of international facts. We are not unaware of the limits of our strength. We are among the half-dozen smallest members of this Organization. We fully understand how certain measures might at first sight evoke a lack of comprehension, even in friendly minds. Being a democracy, we work under the natural restraints of public opinion, which compels us to weigh drastic choices with care and without undue precipitation. We are, in short, a government which determines its actions by the single exclusive aim of ensuring life and security for the people whom it represents, while safeguarding the honour and trust of millions linked to it by the strongest ties of fraternity.

In recent days, this Government of Israel had to face a tormenting question: Do its obligations under the United Nations Charter require it to resign itself to the existence of uninterrupted activities to the south and north and east, of armed units practising open warfare against it, and working from their bases in the Sinai peninsula and elsewhere for the maintenance of carefully regulated invasions of our homes, our land, and our very lives? Or, on the other hand, are we acting legitimately within our inherent right of self-defence when, having found no other remedy for over two years, we cross the frontier against those who have no scruples in crossing the frontier against us? Members of the General Assembly may be in a better position to evaluate the choice and to identify themselves with this situation if they hear something of the background of this movement and its place in the total pattern of Egyptian intransigence and agression.

Let it be plain that the system of waging war against Israel by commando penetrations is the product of Colonel Nasser's mind. It is one of his contributions to the international life and morality of our times.

After intensive preparations during the spring and summer of 1955, this new weapon was launched in August of that year, breaking a period of relative tranquillity on the Egyptian-Israel frontier—indeed, coming at a time when Egypt and Israel were engaged in hopeful negotiations with the United Nations Chief of Staff, looking towards

P 225

'Embattled, Blockaded, Besieged'

the integral implementation of the 1949 Armistice Agreement. Between August 30th and September 2nd of last year, the Egyptian Government proclaimed its official responsibility for the new method of invasion. On August 30th it broadcast:

'Egyptian forces have penetrated into the territory of occupied Palestine and pursued the attackers.'

On 31st August 1955 an official communiqué informed the Egyptian people of this new military technique:

'Egypt has decided to despatch her heroes, the disciples of Pharaoh and the sons of Islam, and they will clean the land of Palestine. That we have decided and that is our belief. There will be no peace on Israel's border because we demand vengeance, and vengeance is Israel's death.'

On August 31st another official communiqué stated:

'The Egyptian Fedayeen have begun their activities inside the territory of Israel after the repeated clashes on the border during the past week. The Egyptian Fedayeen have penetrated into Israel's settlements, spread out in the Negev until Beersheba and Migdal Ashkelon, at a distance of 40 kilometres from the Egyptian border and have taught our aggressive enemies lessons that they will not forget. The Egyptian Fedayeen sowed fear and consternation amongst the citizens of Israel.'

On September 2nd the following official statement was broadcast in Cairo:

'The forces of the Egyptian Fedayeen moved towards Israel, approached her capital and caused heavy casualties along the border between Gaza and Tel Aviv.'

These are some of the documents which mark the origin of the Fedayeen movement. United Nations authorities repeatedly condemned these activities, designated them as aggression, held the Egyptian Government responsible for them, and called for their cessation. As one example, I quote a statement at that time by the United Nations Chief of Staff, General Burns. Reporting to the Security Council, he wrote:

'The episode of August 22nd was soon followed by an organized period of attack on vehicles, installations and persons, carried out by gangs of marauders in Israel territory which, according to my information, resulted in the death of eleven military and civilian personnel. . . .

'The number and nature of these acts of sabotage perpetrated well within Israel's territory are such as to suggest that they are the work of organized and well-trained groups.'

That was the opening shot in the Fedayeen offensive in the summer of 1955. In the spring of this year, the activity of these groups took on a new scope and intensity. This was the period during which the arms race initiated by Colonel Nasser, with external help, was running most drastically to Israel's disadvantage. Members of the General Assembly will recall how close we were then to the threshold of general war, while these units came in and out of Israel every day on their missions of murder and plunder, accompanied by the official exhortations of Colonel Nasser and his officials and by exuberant shouts of triumph in all the media of Arab information.

In an address to the Security Council last week, I submitted a detailed chronicle of acts of violence carried out by Fedayeen units between April of this year and a few days ago. Throughout the whole of that period, United Nations officials concerned with security on our frontier were devoting great attention to this problem. On April 8th of this year, the United Nations Chief of Staff addressed a letter to the Foreign Minister of Israel. In this letter, General Burns includes the following passage:

'I will despatch to the Prime Minister of Egypt a protest against the action of the Fedayeen, assuming it to have been authorized or tolerated by the Egyptian authorities, and requesting the immediate withdrawal of any persons under Egyptian control from the territory of Israel. . . .

'*I consider that if Egypt has ordered these Fedayeen raids, she has now put herself in the position of the aggressor.*'

I will not weary the General Assembly with this sordid chronicle in all its details. Suffice it to say that during this period of belligerency there had taken place against Israel 435 cases of armed incursion, nearly 2,000 cases of armed robbery and theft, 1,300 of armed clashes with Egyptian armed forces, 172 cases of sabotage perpetrated by Egyptian military units and Fedayeen in Israel. As a result of these activities, 465 of our people have been killed and wounded. In 1956 alone so far, 28 of our people have been killed and 127 have been wounded.

I have said that this activity is merely the spearhead of Egyptian belligerency. It is a new device for making war and making it with safety. The doctrine is one of unilateral belligerency. The Egyptian-Israel frontier is to be a one-way street. It is to be wide open for these armed Egyptian units to penetrate deeply into Israel to accomplish their mission and to return. It is to be closed in their favour against any offensive response.

It was in these circumstances that the Government of Israel faced the tormenting problems of its duties and obligations under the Charter of the United Nations. We are not satisfied with a justification of our actions in terms of national expediency. There is perhaps no member of this Organization more sensitive to all the currents of international thought, more vulnerable to the disfavour and the dissent of friendly world opinion, broader in the scope and extent of its universal associations, less able to maintain its life on any principle of self-sufficiency or autarchy.

It was within a full knowledge of this fact that we have been forced to interpret Article 51 of the Charter as furnishing both a legal and a moral basis for such defensive action as is applicable to the dangers we face. Under Article 51 of the Charter the right of self-defence is described as 'inherent'; in the French translation it is 'naturel'. It is something which emerges from the very nature of a state and of humanity. This 'inherent right of self-defence' is conditioned in the Charter by the existence of armed attacks against a member state.

Can anyone say that this long and uninterrupted series of encroachments did not constitute the reality of an armed attack? Can it seriously be suggested that we made no attempt to exhaust peaceful remedy? Time after time at the table of the Security Council and in meetings of the Mixed Armistice Commission efforts were made to bring about tranquillity on the frontier. Yet, all this well-intentioned, enlightened and, at certain times, hopeful effort ended without making the life of a single citizen of Israel more secure than it was before.

I have mentioned the problem of opinion. It is, perhaps, natural that a country should interpret its own obligations for the preservation of security more stringently than those who enjoy greater security far away. If we have sometimes found it difficult to persuade even our friends in the international community to understand the motives for our action, this is because nobody in the world community is in Israel's position. How many other nations have had hundreds of their citizens killed over these years by the action of armies across the frontier? How many nations have had their ships seized and their cargoes confiscated in international waterways? How many nations find the pursuit of their daily tasks to be a matter of daily and perpetual hazard? In how many countries does every single citizen going about his duties feel the icy wind of his own vulnerability? It might perhaps require an unusual measure of humility and imagination for others to answer the question how they would have acted in our place. Nobody else is in our place and is therefore fully competent to equate the advantage and the disadvantage of our choice.

The Government of Israel is firmly convinced that it has done what any other nation would have done in our place, with the reservation that many would have done it earlier and with perhaps greater impact of resistance. It is especially moving to us to find that, despite the uniqueness and the eccentricity of our position, something of it is making its way into the general consciousness of mankind. Since this discussion proceeds not merely from the rostrum of the General Assembly, but also against the bar of world opinion, I think it is legitimate to quote an eloquent and cogent passage from one of the great organs of opinion published in this, the home city of our Organization. Yesterday's edition of the *New York Times* stated:

'. . . it would be ridiculous to permit Colonel Nasser to pose before the United Nations or the world as the innocent victim of aggression, or to hold a protecting hand over him. On the contrary, in so far as there is any one man guilty of aggression it is the Egyptian president, for he has waged war against Israel, Britain and France, by propaganda, by gun-running, by infiltration of murderous bands, by stirring up rebellion in French North Africa, by seizing the Suez Canal by force, and scrapping a treaty in the same manner in which Hitler marched into the Rhineland, by blocking the Canal for Israeli shipping in defiance of United Nations orders—finally, by his whole loudly proclaimed programme of throwing Israel into the sea in alliance with other Arab states and creating an Arab empire under his own hegemony which would expand his influence in concentric circles through all Africa and the whole Moslem world.'

In these circumstances, both the position and the attitude of the Israel Government are clear. This attitude is based upon our fundamental concept of reciprocity. If the frontier between Egypt and Israel is to protect Egyptian territory against Israel entry, then it must protect Israel territory against Egyptian entry. We hold it as a self-evident truth that the lives of Israel men, women and children are not less sacrosanct or less worthy of international protection than are the lives of the hired Fedayeen groups, which are the main instruments

229

'Embattled, Blockaded, Besieged'

of Nasserism in its assault upon the peace and decencies of Middle Eastern life.

Beyond these incidents, grave as they are, we discern issues of even greater moment. World opinion must surely choose between two candidates for its confidence: on the one hand, the farmers and workers, the men, women and children of Israel; and on the other hand, the fanatic warriors of the Fedayeen groups. Behind that confrontation there stands the much broader and more significant alignment between Israel and Nasser. A small people builds its society and culture in its renascent homeland. In the early days of its independence it is set upon by the armed might of all its neighbours who attempt to wipe it off the face of the earth. In the following years, its neighbours continue their assault. With warlike acts of their own choice they attempt its destruction by armed intervention. They send armed units into its territory to murder and plunder. They try by every means to ensure that nowhere shall there be tranquillity for peaceful pursuits. They blare forth the most violent threats of Israel's destruction. They accumulate vast armaments for bringing this about. They announce, as they did last week from Cairo, that it is they who will choose the time and the place for the final assault, and that it is for us to wait passively for the moment of their selection. They proclaim that a state of war with Israel already exists. They seize the greatest of the world's international waterways and convert it into an instrument for unilateral national pressure.

Across Africa and Asia, wherever Nasserism spreads its baneful influence, it works actively to subvert all peace and progress and to establish an ambitious and insatiable hegemony. Now, having considered that he has humbled and defeated the international community and the maritime powers, Nasser returns to his first target, Israel, which is to be swamped from three sides with a new wave of Fedayeen violence. The Assembly will recall that the new wave began shortly following the Tripartite Military Alliance concerted ten days ago between the governments of Syria, Jordan and Egypt, under Egypt's control.

While studying with attention all proposals for strengthening security in the Middle East, we must reject with vehement indignation the charges of aggression launched against us here, launched by some states whose own activities in Europe today are well in the forefront of today's international attention.

'Embattled, Blockaded, Besieged'

There is aggression, there is belligerency in the Middle East, but we for eight years have been its victims, not its authors. That is what I mean when I say that world opinion as here represented should decide whom to trust. Shall it be the small free people establishing its homeland in peace and constructive progress—or shall it be the dictatorship which has bullied and blustered and blackmailed its way across the international life of our times, threatening peace in many continents, openly avowing belligerency, placing its fist upon the jugular vein of the world's communications, bringing the Middle East and the world ever nearer to the threshold of conflict, intimidating all those who stand in its path—all except one people, at least, which will not be intimidated—one people whom no dictator has ever intimidated, the people which has risen up against all the tyrants of history, the people which knows that the appeasement of despots yields nothing but an uneasy respite, and that a government which allowed its own citizens to be murdered daily in their homes would lose the dignity and the justification for which governments are instituted among men.

Israel and the Arab states, the region in which they and we must forever live, now stand at the crossroads of their history. An aggressive dictatorship has for the first time encountered successful and glorious resistance. Some elements of its pride have been broken. Those whom it has outraged with impunity have stood up and asserted their rights, and the hope of freedom burns brighter in the Middle East today not only for Israel but for many others in our region who have found ways of communicating to us their deep apprehensions of what Nasser's encroachment means for their own cherished sovereignty. If the power of this tyranny is not artificially revived, our region will again become a place where men of all nations, including Israel, can live and work in peace, where legitimate universal interests will be respected under the sanction of law, where contracts with other lands will be held in respect, where all those in Asia and Europe whose fortune is linked by history and geography with the Middle East will receive justice and respect for their legitimate interests. It will be a region where the great maritime nations will not have to suffer the indignities which they underwent in this building last month, when they had to hang with exaggerated deference on every wave of the hand, on every nod of condescension from the representative of the territorial power, which had converted the un-

231

conditional right of navigation into an act of grace or privilege to be conferred or withheld at will.

Such a Middle East, free from domination and totalitarian influence, will enter, perhaps soon, upon its new birth of freedom. This is the crossroads at which we might soon stand. We could have wished that we had reached it less drastically, with smaller peril and sacrifice. But having reached it, surely we must go forward and not back. This momentous discussion today has made it plain that one thing will not do. It will not do to go back to an outdated and crumbling armistice régime designed by its authors to last for a few months and now lingering for eight years in growing paralysis of function. Least of all can we be satisfied to return to an imperfect armistice, distorted by unilateral belligerency, to a system designed seven years ago as a transition to peace and interpreted for seven years by one of the parties as a continuing state of war.

Israel has no desire or intention to wield arms beyond the limit of its legitimate defensive mission. But whatever is demanded of us by way of restoring Egypt's rights and respecting Egypt's security under international law must surely be accompanied by equally binding Egyptian undertakings to respect Israel's security and Israel's rights under the identical law. Egypt's obligation to abstain from acts of hostility, to liquidate its commando activities, to abolish its illicit discrimination against Israel shipping in the Suez Canal and in the Gulf of Aqaba, is equal and identical in law to Israel's obligation to respect the established Armistice lines.

Our signpost is not backward to belligerency, but forward to peace. Whatever Israel is now asked to do for Egypt must have its counterpart in Egypt's reciprocal duty to give Israel the plenitude of its rights.

Beyond the moment when fire will cease, the prospect must be not one of unilateral claims by one party against the other. The horizon must be of peace by agreement, peace without maritime blockades in the Gulf or in the Canal, peace without frontier raids or commando incursions, peace without constant threats to the integrity or independence of any state, peace without military alliances directed against Israel's independence.

Egypt and Israel are two people whose encounters in history have been rich and fruitful for mankind. Surely they must take their journey from this solemn moment towards the horizons of peace.

CHAPTER XXI

The Tenth Summer

Israel is a people to whom nothing is freely given. Its sovereignty, its narrow land, its scanty water, its capital city, the safety of its homes and lives, its membership in the international family, its commerce with other countries, its maritime access to half the world —gifts which other nations inherit at their birth—are, for us, the fruit of bitter contest. Her difficulties are the only possessions of Israel which nobody has ever tried to take away.

The strife is waged on the scene of diplomacy without respite or repose; and sometimes it erupts into harsher areas. In the sequel to the Sinai campaign Israel's quest for security has held the central place in the preoccupation of the world. For nearly five months the mind of nations was arrested by an urgent dialogue between a small people claiming its minimal tranquillity and a world society which for eight years had let Israel sustain its perils in solitude.

In its international relations, as in other aspects of its fortune, Israel lives in a world of sharp contrasts. 'This people', says a Hebrew tradition, 'is like unto the stars of heaven—and unto the dust of the earth.' There is nothing like the savagery of our neighbours' hatred; but we are also reached by affections of unique tenderness and ardour. Indifference is the only emotion which Israel has never evoked during these unforgettable years of her resurgence.

It is not certain that the second decade will be less turbulent than the first. Arab hostility is the primary cause of Israel's crisis; her other difficulties are secondary results. There are no peoples, and few governments, whose spontaneous attitude to Israel would not be trustful and benevolent, were it not for the competitive bombardment of an Arab rancour which establishes hostility to Israel as the price of Arab friendship. No government of conscience can fully pay this price; but the very disposition to strike a bargain in this invidious market corrupts the true relations of Israel with her neighbours and with the world. Being unable to mitigate the Arab assault, Israel has at least contrived to resist it.

233

The Tenth Summer

Israel's first decade is the story of this resistance; not only of its strains and hazards, but also of its victory. Those who live in siege must either perish or develop attributes to fit their dangers. The assault of Arab violence sharpened Israel's military qualities—a strange result for a people whose nationalism was founded on the Hebrew pacific tradition and on the pastoral liberalism of nineteenth-century Europe. The denial of immigration and settlement inspired Israel to join, and win, the battle for political sovereignty earlier than had once been envisaged. The Arab boycott forced Israel to seek its markets and sources of supply in distant lands. Above all, the daily peril sharpened every impulse of union, caused patriotism to glow with a fervent heat, and thus became the anvil on which the people's inner strength was beaten out like tempered steel. If Israel is truly founded on its own energy of spirit, then Arab nationalism is amongst Israel's architects.

But there is no greater fallacy than that which would speak of Israel's 'isolation'. Against the vehement challenge of the Arab world we have established relations in diplomacy and commerce with the majority of other states in the Old World and the New. Israel's friendships reach into every continent, and make this small land the focus of a universal emotion. Indeed, the aspect of universality is the first amongst Israel's attainments. Wherever the eyes of men fall upon her they are carried beyond the little slice of land and the immediate point of time into a domain of memory where everything speaks of breadth and grandeur. The historic idea extends the frontiers of the geographical fact.

A people poorly endowed by geography will naturally cultivate every inch of its garden with intensity and thrift. New vistas open up for Israel with international recognition of the right of free passage in the Gulf of Aqaba and the Straits of Tiran. A long Mediterranean coastline and access to the Red Sea compensate Israel for her territorial confinement. Uniting the eastern and western oceans across a small strip of land, Israel can become a bridge across which the commerce of nations will flow between the two continental expanses—Asia and Africa on the one hand and Europe and America on the other. The nations of Asia and Europe, in their turn, can be liberated from exclusive reliance on the Suez Canal as the sole link between the Mediterranean and the Red Sea. Israel can emulate other states of small territory which have achieved a measure of strength and eco-

The Tenth Summer

nomic influence through the realization of their maritime opportunities. Three thousand years ago the ships of King Solomon sailed both these oceans—to Tyre and Sidon on the Mediterranean, and to the coasts of Sheba from Ezion Geber, which is Elath. Today, with the opening of its southern window, Israel need not be limited to its predominantly European and American outlook in culture and communications. Clearly this is a supreme national interest—one which Israel will defend to the ultimate point of tenacity and resistance.

The shape of Israel to come emerges only dimly along the road of the future. Much depends on whether our neighbours cease to surround us with malice and rancour. Since 1948 the area of Arab sovereignty has grown in a massive expansion which makes nonsense of this perpetual, avaricious envy directed against Israel's meagre portion. But there is no sign that the tempest will abate. It is better, of course, that Israel should flourish in peace with her neighbours; but nobody should underestimate her capacity to flourish in any case.

The tenth year is still embattled, but its vision is not without radiance. The twentieth will find Israel with its third million of population, with the Negev and Galilee abloom, with Jordan waters carried southward to the dry places. The pulse of commerce will beat strongly between Elath and the eastern continents, while the links grow tighter between Israel and her own Mediterranean world. Nuclear and solar energy will bring freedom from the servitudes of imported oil, and give Israel a horizon as broad as its scientific disciplines can reach. The Hebrew faith and tradition will gain new strength everywhere through the emanation of Israel's example.

These achievements are all within Israel's power. Peace, the final gift, is in the hand of others, although its pursuit is still amongst the first laws of Israel's policy.

The first decade hands on the unfinished tasks. But it will never be eclipsed in Israel's memory; for in the eyes of an aged weary people it rekindled the splendour of a youthful dawn.

CHAPTER XXII

Sinai and Suez—A Retrospect

Stillness has brooded over Sinai for most of recorded time. But now and then a spasm of violence shakes the wilderness. The interludes of human strife and habitation leave their mark, not on Sinai itself, but on everything around. With their passing, Sinai sleeps again; but the course of history seldom flows unchanged.

The events of last winter in Sinai are of this history-making dimension. Nowhere in the world could men or nations escape a shock which some deemed salutary and others perilous, but of which none could deny the primary impact. Three nations arose in force and wrath to resist the Nasser tyranny. Their compulsions sprang from different points of emotion and interest, and none held any purpose in complete identity with another. But they were alike—and not as alone as they often seemed—in regarding Nasser's excesses as an outrage to the rights of nations and to the law and conscience of the world. Nor was the common adversary their only link. These were the three peoples who, two decades before, had been placed by history in the vanguard of resistance to the Hitler assault. The national memory of each had learnt, by ordeal of pain, that an aggressive despotism can only be withstood too late—never too early. Because this truth was not more swiftly seized less than a generation ago, the Jewish people had been engulfed in hideous agony, France humiliated and overrun, Britain brought to its greatest peril since the Napoleonic wars, and the light of goodness all but extinguished forever from the world of men. In the annals of resistance to tyranny these are three peoples of special lineage and experience. But beyond this broad affinity, the merits of their actions in the winter of 1956 must be weighed on separate scales.

2

Like water into which a stone is cast the consequences of October

Sinai and Suez—A Retrospect

1956 continue to ripple outwards in ever-widening circles. But even the first results were of universal scale. A dictatorship learnt, to its surprise, that the patience of free peoples has its inexorable term. Israel taught that those who lay siege to their neighbour must ultimately count on their victim breaking out, rather than co-operate in his own strangulation. The Soviet Union saw the fated and predictable results of the spectacular rearmament of Egypt. Europe awakened through months of fuel scarcity to seek a better economic future than a life of uneasy breath with Egyptian fingers on its jugular vein. The Commonwealth was torn by the diversity of interests in its midst. The United States arrayed itself against the three nations from which its own spiritual, cultural, linguistic and political legacy was wholly derived; but thoughtful American minds soon began to wonder if the judgments which demanded this strange alignment could be without flaw. The United Nations seemed to have become a forum of vigour and decision. But it became so only because the United States and the Soviet Union were in agreement, and because its recommendations were addressed to democracies, not to dictatorships—to Israel and not to the Arab States. Since it still has no victories in matters disputed by the two greatest powers, and has never been able since 1948 to modify Arab policies conflicting with the Charter, its successes in the winter of 1956 must, with sorrow, be ruled as episodic, not substantive. Moreover, the international bodies which organized such power and authority to contain the explosion had not shown the same zeal in preventing it. Sinai has caused men everywhere to ask the great questions about the United Nations. The great answers are yet to be found.

3

A literature of remorse has sprung up in Europe around the Suez and Sinai expeditions. Some of this writing has the speed and profusion, but also the transience, of a mushroom growth. In Britain the remorse of the writers is for having begun the expedition; in France, for having ended it before its work was done. But the criticism all hinges on the allegedly 'abortive', unfinished character of the enterprise. The implication is that it solved and clarified nothing, and that its only fruit was sacrifice and woe.

These retrospects may turn out to have been premature. Separated by a full year from the immediate memory, we can already

Sinai and Suez—A Retrospect

proclaim one thing in full conviction. Whether Sinai is applauded or not, it cannot, with any truth, be described as abortive of results. On the contrary, it emerges as a potent event, dividing the past of the Middle East from its future by a series of sharp and radical transformations. And the critics of the process are often the champions of the results. Those who castigated the means cannot forbear to applaud some of the ends.

Foremost amongst these is that the legend of Nasser's military dominance perished in the desert sands. So did the legend of his magnetic appeal to an affectionate Arab world; for in Egypt's peril not one Arab bullet was fired in her defence. On the debris of these shattered myths new alignments arose in the Middle East, in sharp dissociation from Nasser's hegemony. A balance between Egypt and Israel was restored, not so much physically as in the more crucial sense of qualitative estimate. After Nasser's defeat, Arab régimes which chose to defy him discovered the valour of which discretion is the better part. It is easier to hurl defiance at a neighbour when one is separated by a garden fence as sturdily resistant as Israel had shown itself to be. Within a few months of the Sinai campaign, the Egyptian dictator, presiding over a ruined economy and deserted by half the Arab world, was arresting opponents seeking his destruction and fulminating in Abidin Square against a 'conspiracy launched by the United States' for his undoing. He still gloated over Soviet largess in weapons and his mastery of Europe's supply line. But the once dominant voice now had a desperate ring: and the truculence was that of a man at bay. If this generation is, in Nasser's flamboyant words, 'in search of a hero', it is not conscious of having found its quarry on the banks of the Nile.

Those in the west, who take consolation from this readiness of the same northern Arab States to strike loose from Nasser's yoke, are, however inadvertently, relishing the fruits of Sinai. They are endorsing a spirit of independence and separatism which would never have arisen but for Nasser's defeat and would never have survived if there had been territorial contiguity between Egypt and the northern Arab world. Without the intervening wall of Israel territory, Egypt, with its preponderance of arms and population, would have little difficulty in establishing its dominance over the States of the Levant and the Fertile Crescent. Thus, by a paradox of fortune, Israel's territorial integrity is the surest guarantee for the independence of the northern Arab States. This reflection does little credit to the outworn concepts of 'territorial adjustments' which, by bringing the Egyptian frontier into contiguity with Jordan, would have established the Middle East as a domain of Egyptian hegemony rather than as the abode of its separate independent sovereignties. Instead of confronting an Egypt and Syria open to totalitarian control, the west would have found the whole Arab world arrayed against it.

4

The new equilibrium between the countries of the Arab world has been attended by changes of equal scope between the Middle East and the west. The United States became committed far beyond its previous intention to the preservation of the independence and integrity of all Middle Eastern States. Tens of millions of Americans saw and heard their President pledge his honour to the pursuit of greater tranquillity for Israel and her neighbours, and to the mobilization of 'firm action by the society of nations' if Israel's legal rights were violated again. The Gulf of Aqaba was proclaimed by the United States and the other maritime nations as an international waterway open to all ships bent on free and innocent passage; and within a few weeks it had seen the first movements of a commerce more varied and promising than in all the years before. The United Nations, under Canadian initiative, developed new symbols and agencies of its authority; and its Emergency Force sealed up two of the danger points in the Egyptian-Israel conflict. Above all, world opinion arose, in a swift transition, to look upon Nasserism with a disillusioned severity, and to surround Israel with a new comprehension of the unique problems and choices which beset her security. In the shelter of this respite Israel advanced in another spurt of her consolidation. The year since Sinai has brought more strength to her sinews than many years before.

These, together, are profound changes in the Middle Eastern landscape. They must be compared with the brooding, thunderous air which sat heavily upon our region in October 1956; and the comparison is a vital part of any historic judgment on the decisions of that crucial month.

5

But recourse to arms requires a deeper justification than safety of outcome. The issue of conscience depends not on whether Israel was fortunate, but on whether she was right. Here, too, the passing months bring calmer appraisal. Israel has no cause to renounce her claim to vindication in terms of rectitude, as well as of utility.

Sinai and Suez—A Retrospect

Never has a nation more embattled than Israel risen up against an assailant more menacing and aggressive than the Nasser régime. The Israel forces were tactically on the offensive—but within the framework of a nation's self-defence. Egyptian forces were tactically on the defensive—but in the context of an essentially aggressive design. Failure to see the truths of aggression and defence in their general and, therefore, their true perspectives explains the confusion which seized the United Nations and its leading Powers in October, and the slow contrition which brought the curtain down on a different scene in March.

The issues are whether Nasser deserved to be resisted; and whether those who resisted him were righteous and lawful in their decision.

The first of these questions finds unity of response even amongst those who differ sharply on the second. The Egyptian régime had been attended at its birth by universal sympathy and goodwill. It seemed to promise a new vision of Egypt's society, and an era of moderation in her international relations. But soon after its triumph in securing the evacuation of British forces, the Nasser régime turned aside from the road of labour and social reform towards the allurements of xenophobia and the dream of hegemony. It suppressed all diversity and dissent in order to establish Egypt as a police state of ruthless uniformity. It violated its obligation under the treaties and decisions requiring free passage in the Suez Canal. It fomented strife and rebellion in North Africa. It sent its attachés and agents into all Arab lands from Morocco to Jordan in an effort to subvert them into Egyptian satellites. Its radio transmitters filled the air of Africa and Asia with strident abuse of the democratic world. It repelled efforts to bring about a settlement with Israel. It imported a torrent of Soviet weapons to institute a perilous and explosive race in arms. It converted the Middle East into an arena of rivalry between the Great Powers, amongst which it manœuvred and bargained in an overt campaign of extortion. It announced Israel's destruction as the central aim of its national policy. It organized the Fedayeen groups for brutal murder and violence on Israel's soil. It concerted a pact with a subservient Jordan and Syria, and dedicated the alliance to Israel's forcible extinction. Wherever its influence spread it actively undermined all peace and progress and filled the Middle East with an anxious air of peril and intimidation.

The comparison with Hitler flatters and exaggerates Nasser's power. But it does not misrepresent his spirit or intention. In the

Sinai and Suez—A Retrospect

wide scope and frank egotism of his ambitions, in his refusal to be inhibited by the interests of other countries or by the restraints of universal law, he entered the lineage of the historic despots who have dreamed of power on a continental scale at the expense of other nations' freedoms—and, in this case, of another nation's very existence. When retribution fell upon him, an eminent newspaper which opposed the Sinai and Suez expeditions wrote with clear insight that 'it would be ridiculous to permit Colonel Nasser to pose before the United Nations or the world as the innocent victim of aggression, or to hold a protecting hand over him. On the contrary, insofar as there is any one man guilty of aggression, it is the Egyptian President . . .'.[1] In similar vein, an implacable critic of the British and French actions writes: 'Nasser was a Hitler-like menace to Israel but not to anybody else.'[2]

In London, the Labour leader, Mr Hugh Gaitskell, had warned his countrymen on 2nd August 1956 that the pattern was 'very familiar. It is exactly the same that we encountered from Mussolini and Hitler in those years before the war.'

Another critic of the Suez expedition has written a graphic account of Nasser in the public act of seizing the Suez Canal. This description will raise vivid memories in all who remember the Fourth decade of this century:

'The same evening, at a mass meeting in Alexandria, Nasser announced the news to a screaming, hysterical crowd of 100,000 Egyptians. Sweating under the arc lights, gripping a microphone with both hands, he spoke for two and a half hours reviewing the whole of Egyptian foreign policy since the régime came to power, and screaming as the climax of his speech:

' "Americans, may you choke to death on your fury! The annual income of the Suez Canal Company is $100 million. Why not take it ourselves!—And it will be run by Egyptians! Egyptians! Egyptians!"

'The crowd swayed and chanted with frenzy. "It was like watching", said one observer, "a dæmonic sorcerer conjuring up from the bowels of the earth the legions of hate and fury." '[3]

It is remarkable how often the Hitler imagery arises on the lips and pens of diverse commentators when they seek to convey a picture of Nasser's personality and actions before Sinai. Is it difficult to

[1] *New York Times*, 30th October 1956.
[2] *Middle East Crisis*, by Wint and Calvocoressi, p. 84, London, 1957.
[3] *The Suez War*, by Paul Johnson, New York, 1957, pp. 8–9.

imagine the apprehensions, and the consequent spirit of resolve which welled up amongst a neighbouring people saturated with agonizing memories of the havoc which a rampant dictatorship can perform even on the road to its own appointed doom?

6

In explaining the official American attitude to the Suez and Sinai expeditions, President Eisenhower acknowledged on 30th October 1956 that the nations resisting Nasser 'had been subjected to grave, repeated provocations'. The question of provocation has special relevance to the one nation to whom 'Nasser was a Hitler-like menace'. An appraisal of Israel's choice must include an effort to imagine a small nation separated by twelve minutes' flying time from an adversary equipped with aggressive strength of unknown potency, proclaiming an active 'state of war', practising a blockade in two out of three available waterways and establishing an encircling alliance designed to strike the final blow. The counsel that 'it would have been better for Israel to have waited' is perhaps too facile when uttered from positions of safety thousands of miles away. Nobody who believes that Nasser's momentum was driving relentlessly towards Israel's destruction can dogmatically wish that its full impact had been awaited; and it is significant that the critics of the Anglo-French action are so often forced to reserve judgment on Israel's decision. Israel does not have the continental expanse of an America which could reel under Pearl Harbour and gather its strength for the retaliation. She is not even a France or Poland whose territories were broad enough to allow them to bear the first assaults of the two world wars and rally to summon aid from within and without. To bear the first blow might have simplified Israel's international posture; but the nation might well have celebrated its virtue posthumously.

There are some who interpret the United Nations Charter as meaning that if your neighbour advances against you with a sharp knife announcing his intention to cut your throat, you must not move until he has made the first incision. This version, which bestows the initiative on the aggressor as a matter of right, can more easily be reconciled with the letter of the Charter than with its spirit. When the issue is one of survival every people must make its decision in solitude of responsibility. When the United Nations Charter acknowledges to every nation the 'inherent' right of self-defence, it implicitly places this judgment in the individual domain and, at least in the first instance, outside the range of majority decisions. The leading authority on the Charter faces this problem lucidly:

'Article 51 . . . states that nothing in the Charter impairs the inherent rights of self-defence "if an armed attack occurs against a Member of the United Nations" and "until the Security Council has taken the measures necessary to maintain international peace and security". Presumably, it is the right of each Member . . . to decide when, and for how long, conditions exist which justify the exercise of this right. To this extent *the Article clearly opens the way* for action which may be regarded by other Members as inconsistent with the purposes and principles of the Organization.'[1]

It should be remembered that Israel had been under blockade as well as under intermittent armed attacks for nine years. Thus while the case for Israel's resistance is primarily moral and political in nature, it has a more solid foundation in formal legality than its critics have acknowledged.

It was the strength of this case which brought international opinion to favour—and, indeed, to establish—different arrangements in Gaza and the Straits of Tiran than those which prevailed on the eve of October 29th. If Egyptian policy had not been aggressive in each sector, it would scarcely have been necessary to assume a new international responsibility in both. Gaza and the Gulf of Aqaba were important not only intrinsically, but as symbols of a purposeful belligerency by land and sea. To have evacuated them unconditionally, and thus to make way for the renewal of the explosion, would have convicted both Israel and the United Nations of startling irresponsibility. The decision to withdraw came as soon as it seemed that Israel forces would bequeath Gaza and the Gulf to a system of internationally supervised order, not to an Egyptian-controlled belligerency. The three Israel decisions of the crucial six months—to resist; to hold out in Gaza and Tiran; and to withdraw—are not contradictory with each other. They form a unitary pattern of which the central theme is change from belligerency to security, if not, as was originally hoped, across the whole range of Egyptian-Israel relations, then at least in the two main centres of potential conflict. The immediate sequel to Israel's withdrawal found the Negev, north and south,

---

[1] *The Charter of the United Nations. Commentary and Documents*, Goodrich and Hambro, p. 299.

Sinai and Suez—A Retrospect

liberated for development and navigation where previously there were chronic insecurity and blockade.

7

Sinai and Suez plunged American policy into a tangled dilemma. The ideas which set its early course were simple enough to be understood even by those who were injured through their application. In America, as elsewhere, there were many who perceived that the crisis might not have arisen at all if the European powers had felt more consistent support against Nasser's seizure of their life-line, and if Israel had not been frustrated for over six months in her efforts to restore the terrifyingly swift change in the balance of arms. In examining the American orthodoxy in opposition to the use of force, it is only just to recall that the western hemisphere contained no state, like Israel, which was in direct peril from a belligerent neighbour; and no continent like Europe which found its very line of sustenance seized by a tyrant's hand. Remoteness is not always an aid to judgment, and history will never know how a similar peril west of the Atlantic would have been met. But, in any case, as the United States became more intimately engaged, its position evolved beyond the mere opposition to force into a recognition that causes of real substance and authority had dictated the resistance to Nasser. This development was too gradual to bring a constructive solution in the Suez Canal, which the United Nations cleared of physical and political obstruction—and then handed back, incredibly, to Nasser's unilateral national control. It was astonishing in Israel eyes that the Anglo-French position in Port Said was not exchanged for an internationally controlled freedom of passage in the Suez Canal under the auspices of the United Nations Emergency Force. On the other hand, Israel's tenacity for over four months gave time for an advancing American position to assert itself. By February 1957 this position was formulated in terms of clear support for free passage in the Straits of Tiran, under the surveillance of United Nations forces, and for a maximal assertion of international responsibility in Gaza. In the Gulf of Aqaba the practical solution of stationing United Nations forces was enriched and deepened by Mr. Dulles' memorandum of 11th February 1957 proclaiming the legal and political principle of international navigation and advocating means of securing it. When all the leading maritime powers endorsed

244

Sinai and Suez—A Retrospect

this doctrine, an important milestone was reached in the history of the Gulf as a recognized international waterway. Historians will, in fact, discern two elements in the United States approach; not only opposition to the military initiative of three friendly countries, but also a recognition that a return to the *status quo* of blockade and frontier violence must be averted. On 3rd November 1956 the United States representative in the United Nations had enunciated this second theme with great emphasis:

'Let us stop the futile process of patching up previous agreements and understandings, which but serve to provide new pretexts for further provocations. Let us face up to our responsibilities under the Charter. Let us work together for lasting settlement of what has become a dangerous threat to the peace of the world.'

This implicit promise of a 'new deal' for the Middle East was not sustained in the United Nations against powerful Arab-Asian pressures. But it did find a partial, if localized, fulfilment in the commitments which the United States undertook, together with France and other countries, on the eve of Israel's withdrawal. These commitments are clearly established in the public minds of both peoples, and there have been perceptive American definitions of them, two of which aroused special interest in Israel and throughout the world. The first was a review published after Israel's withdrawal, pointing out that President Eisenhower:

'. . . is more committed than the United States perhaps originally intended to a peaceful and prosperous Israel in the Middle East. When the President of the United States goes on the air to say what the United States is prepared to do to see that the Israelis do not have to face the same aggression again from Egypt, this amounts to more than sounding words of sympathy.'[1]

In similar vein and with greater precision an American political commentator wrote on 1st April 1957:

'The honour and good faith of our Government and of the President himself are directly involved in the Israeli-Egyptian crisis. This is because Israel withdrew from Gaza and the Sinai Coast of the Gulf of Aqaba only after receiving certain assurances, or pledges from the United States. Without them it is a practical certainty that Israel would not have withdrawn from positions so important to its national existence.

'These assurances were examined and developed by the two

[1] *Time*, 11th March 1957.

245

Governments over a period of several weeks. The explanation which Mrs. Golda Meir, Israel Foreign Minister, made to the United Nations General Assembly on March 1st . . . was written in full collaboration with our State Department. Indeed, the original draft was extensively altered at the request of the State Department. . . . Thus Mrs. Meir's statement was actually a joint document. . . . It may be said that in some respects our assurances were only statements of our own policies and not guarantees that we could get the United Nations and other nations to go along with them. But we cannot escape our obligation . . . our honour and good faith are at stake.'[1]

Thus the dialogue between America and Israel—at times the most painful but also the most intimate in which they had ever engaged— ended with the charting of paths along which both nations felt able to journey together.

8

For several years the critics of the United Nations clamoured for more action and vigour. But the case in which the United Nations displayed its most vigorous action has become the most acute source of disquiet about its future. It is no small matter to find the first President of the General Assembly constrained to write the following words:

'Never before has the insufficiency of the United Nations as at present constituted stood out so clearly. In spite of its apparent success I believe that it has never come so near to the brink of failure. In the present United Nations setup, which is not what its founders wished and hoped it would be, everything short of war is allowed. Treaties may be violated, promises can be broken, a nation is licensed to menace its neighbours or to perpetrate any sort of trick on it, just as long as there is no actual war. The attitude of Egypt during the last few months is a case in point. While Egypt denied transit through the Suez Canal to Israeli ships, sent death commandos on to Israeli soil, violated the Treaty of Constantinople, sent arms to be used against the French in Algeria and made preparations to attack its neighbour, the United Nations was powerless to intervene. Such intervention would not come within the scope of the Charter as at present interpreted. But let Israel in desperation send troops into the Sinai

[1] Ernest Lindley: *Newsweek*, 1st April 1957.

Sinai and Suez—A Retrospect

Peninsula, and let Anglo-French forces land at Port Said, and they are sure to be condemned. Meanwhile, those who are looking on impassively at the brutal repressions of the revolt in Hungary could not find words harsh enough to damn them. . . .

'This brand of justice is nothing but a caricature. Such an interpretation of principles amounts to *rewarding any nation which is audacious enough to accomplish the most reprehensible act but which very cleverly stops short, not of violence, but of open war*.'[1]

Months later an even greater voice expressed a similar anxiety. Sir Winston Churchill's phrase was: 'Hit-and-miss justice.'

There is a double criticism here—not only discrimination between the Hungarian and Middle East crises, but also an even more serious discrimination within the framework of the Middle Eastern case, between the Egyptian provocations which the United Nations did nothing to restrain, and the consequent resistance, which the United Nations did everything to liquidate. In the end, the resistance was eliminated, but the capacity of provocation was restored, albeit inhibited by the presence of the United Nations forces at two explosive points. Even with this reservation, the end of the drama was played out in a cold, harsh light. After all, the dual source of conflict had been Egypt's claim of belligerency against Israel and her assertion of an exclusively national jurisdiction in the Suez Canal. Suppressing a revolt against both these abuses, the United Nations left each of them intact. Unilateral belligerency and unilateral control of the Canal were actually restored to Egypt's hands. Egypt, more than any other state in history, had received the aid of the United Nations in its adversity—and had then reasserted the very anti-Charter attitudes which had brought her into need of aid. 'Insufficiency', 'brink of failure' and 'hit-and-miss justice' are heavy words when used by men of eminent lineage in the careful art of speech. But it will be difficult to challenge this sorrowful verdict until the United Nations evinces for Israel's security and for international rights in the Suez Canal at least a fraction of the zeal which it devoted to the salvage of Egypt's position in the winter of 1956. Equality is the first condition of justice; and a justice which is not equal is not justice at all.

The preponderance of Arab numerical strength is making it increasingly difficult for justice to be done when it conflicts with any

[1] 'The West in Disarray', Paul Henri Spaak, *Foreign Affairs*, New York, January 1957, pp. 185–6.

Sinai and Suez—A Retrospect

Arab claim or position. A shift of power has taken place from a veto-locked Security Council to a General Assembly in which there is no equilibrium between Asia and Europe, and still less between the Arab world and Israel. But the numerical anomaly is only a part of the crisis. No less perilous are habits and attitudes which are becoming crystallized through lack of informed and vigilant criticism. There is a 'fire brigade' approach which is content to put out the flames without pondering too much on how the combustion arose. There is a reluctance to follow a chain of violence to the first link from which it takes its origin—usually in some provocation which 'cleverly stops short not of violence but of open war'. To cut off a nation from its normal maritime access to two-thirds of the world is a case in point. What people is there who would suffer this for eight years amidst United Nations inaction? The United Nations also needs to overcome the procedural faults such as haste and lack of due notice in formulation, to which Prime Minister Menzies of Australia has called attention. All in all, the workings of our international mechanism during the crisis of last year must lead, not to slogans of complacency and triumph, but to efforts at improvement, readjustment and repair.

9

History has not spoken the last word on this swift and drastic episode. There is room for faith that the Middle Eastern future belongs to national independence, not to dictator-ridden hegemony; to freedom of the seas, not to squalid blockades; to respect for the rights of all, and not of Arab nationalism alone. If this faith is vindicated across the unfolding years, its true defenders will of a certainty include those in Israel who, in resisting tyranny, hallowed the Sinai desert with their sacrifice.

Jerusalem,
August 1957

Highlights of Events

1947

Nov. 29th   The United Nations recommends the partition of Palestine and the establishment of a Jewish state.

Nov. 30th   Arab attacks on Jews begin throughout the country with the assistance of 'volunteers' from neighbouring countries.

1948

May 14th   The establishment of the State of Israel is proclaimed.

May 14th   United States Government recognizes Israel.

May 15th   Regular armies of Egypt, Iraq, Jordan, Lebanon and Syria invade Israel.

June 11th   First truce for 30 days is proclaimed.

July 8th   Arabs resume hostilities.

July 18th   Second truce begins.

1949

Jan. 20th   U.S. Export-Import Bank grants $100 million loan to Israel.

Feb. 14th   Israel's First Knesset (Parliament) opened in Jerusalem by President Chaim Weizmann.

Feb. 24th   Armistice Agreement with Egypt signed on the Island of Rhodes.

Mar. 23rd   Israel-Lebanon Armistice Agreement signed.

April 23rd   Israel-Jordan Armistice Agreement signed.

May 11th   Israel admitted to membership in the United Nations.

July 20th   Israel-Syria Armistice Agreement signed.

Sept. 12th   Free and Compulsory Education Law passed by the Knesset.

Highlights of Events .

1950

May 25th   United Kingdom, France and the United States issue the 'Tripartite Declaration'.

Sept. 24th   Operation Magic Carpet, which brought 47,000 Yemenite Jews to Israel by air, is completed.

1951

March   Syria uses force in an attempt to halt the Huleh Swamp Drainage project.

May   Prime Minister David Ben-Gurion visits the United States and launches the State of Israel Independence Bonds Issue.

May 18th   U.N. resolution authorizes Israel to continue Huleh drainage work.

July   Air transfer of 110,000 Jews from Iraq to Israel since 1950, is completed.

Sept. 1st   The Security Council calls on Egypt to terminate her blockade practices against Israel.

Oct. 10th   United States Congress grants $65 million as Mutual Security Aid to Israel.

Nov. 4th   Israel announces readiness to pay compensation for the abandoned lands of the Arab refugees.

1952

May 7th–14th   International Symposium on Desert Research, organized with the co-operation of UNESCO, is held in Jerusalem.

June 13th   Israel Atomic Energy Commission is established.

Sept. 10th   Israel-West Germany Reparations Agreement signed at Luxembourg. West Germany to pay Israel $715 million worth of goods on account of Jewish property confiscated and plundered by the Nazis.

Oct. 9th   Israel agrees to release blocked accounts of Arab refugees in Israel banks.

Nov. 9th   Death of President Chaim Weizmann.

Dec. 1st   Israel submits to the United Nations a 'Blueprint for Peace in the Middle East', proposing direct peace negotiations with the Arab states on all aspects of Arab-Israel relations.

Highlights of Events

Dec. 8th	Knesset elects Mr. Itzhak Ben-Zvi, President of Israel.

1953

January–June	Situation on the Israel-Jordan border deteriorates with increased sabotage and murder by Arab marauding bands.
Sept. 2nd	Israel starts work on hydro-electric project on the Jordan near B'not Yaacov. Syria protests before the Security Council.
Sept. 16th	Israel is elected to Vice-Presidency of the U.N. Eighth General Assembly.
October	Ambassador Eric Johnston, President Eisenhower's special envoy, arrives in the Middle East to work out a plan for the joint use of the Jordan waters by Israel, Jordan, Lebanon, and Syria.
October	Further outbreaks of marauding activities across the Jordan-Israel border.
Oct. 27th	The Security Council asks for temporary suspension of the work near B'not Yaacov.
Dec. 8th	Israel Premier Ben-Gurion resigns. Mr. Moshe Sharett heads the new Cabinet.

1954

Jan. 22nd	Western draft resolution at the Security Council, which would have authorized the U.N. Chief of Staff to permit the resumption of work on the Jordan hydro-electric plant, is vetoed by the Soviet Union.
Mar. 20th	Draft resolution in the Security Council, calling on Egypt to comply with the 1951 Resolution on the Suez Canal blockade, is supported by majority of members of the Security Council but vetoed by the Soviet Union.
Oct. 6th	Israel offers before the U.N. General Assembly to conclude 'Non-aggression treaties' with the Arab states.

1955

Jan. 4th–13th	Security Council calls on Egypt to release Israel ship *Bat Galim* which was seized by Egypt on September 28th at the entrance of the Suez Canal.
February	Egyptian Fedayeen (suicide squads) penetrate deep into Israel territory, carrying out espionage and murder.

Highlights of Events

Feb. 13th   Four Dead Sea Scrolls acquired in the U.S. are returned to Israel where a 'Shrine of the Book' is to be built in Jerusalem to house them.

June   Completion of the 65-mile Yarkon-Negev water pipeline to carry irrigation waters from Yarkon River north of Tel Aviv to new farmlands in Negev.

Aug. 26th   U.S. Secretary of State Dulles outlines American foreign policy in the Middle East.

Sept. 22nd   Oil is struck in Heletz, Israel.

Sept. 27th   Announcement of Egyptian-Czechoslovakian military agreement whereby Egypt obtains vast quantities of Soviet arms.

Oct. 11th   Egypt informs Ambassador Johnston that the Arab League has decided to defer decision on the Jordan water plan.

Oct. 18th   Israel Premier Moshe Sharett appeals for a security pact with the U.S. and for permission to buy arms from the Western Powers.

Oct. 22nd   Moshe Sharett leaves for Geneva to discuss the Middle Eastern situation with the Big Four.

Nov. 1st   U.S. Secretary of State John Foster Dulles promises sympathetic consideration of an Israel arms request.

Nov. 2nd   David Ben-Gurion returns to Premiership, presents his Government before the new Knesset; offers to meet with any Arab leader to discuss peace.

Dec. 6th   Israel protests to the U.N. Security Council on continued Egyptian aggression.

1956

Jan. 16th   Premier Nasser announces a new Constitution for Egypt; pledges to reconquer Palestine.

January–February   Egyptians attack Israel patrols and convoys throughout the Negev.

April 9th   President Eisenhower outlines American foreign policy in the Middle East.

April 11th   American Ambassador to Israel, Edward B. Lawson, praises Israel for her remarkable restraint 'in face of Arab suicide squad terrorism'.

April 26th   Cease-fire agreements between the Arab states and

Highlights of Events·

Israel arranged with U.N. Secretary-General Dag Hammarskjold.

May 29th Egyptian Premier Nasser announces that he himself organizes and supervises Fedayeen activities.

August– Renewed wave of Fedayeen attacks.
September–
October

Oct. 22nd Egypt, Jordan, Syria announce the conclusion of a unified military command, 'the principal concern of which is the war of destruction against Israel'.

Oct. 29th Israel forces occupy the Sinai Peninsula and the Gaza Strip in order to destroy Egyptian Army and Fedayeen bases of attack against Israel and to ensure free navigation in the Gulf of Aqaba.

Nov. 2nd United Nations General Assembly urges a cease-fire in Egypt; withdrawal of British, French and Israeli forces; reopening of the Suez Canal and restoration of freedom of navigation.

Dec. 31st Refugees from Egypt and Hungary bring up the number of immigrants into Israel in 1956 to 55,000.

1957

Jan. 23rd Having withdrawn her forces from the Sinai Peninsula, except for the coast of the Gulf of Aqaba and the Gaza Strip, Israel makes withdrawal from these areas dependent on adequate guarantees against renewal of Egyptian belligerency.

February Negotiations between the governments of the U.S.A. and Israel lead to agreement on completion of withdrawal, freedom of navigation in the Gulf of Aqaba and occupation by U.N.E.F. of the Gaza Strip.

Mar. 4th Israel announces to the United Nations her decision for full and prompt withdrawal from the Sharm el-Sheikh and the Gaza areas. Israel's expectations for free navigation in the Gulf of Aqaba and occupation and administration of the Gaza Strip by the United Nations are approved as reasonable by the United States and many Western Powers.

Mar. 14th In spite of Israel's protest, the UNEF Command fails to prevent return of Egyptian administration to Gaza.

253

Highlights of Events

Mar. 18th   Joint communiqué issued by U.S. Secretary of State Dulles and Israel's Foreign Minister, Mrs. Golda Meir, expressing Israel's concern over Egypt's return to Gaza, and reaffirming United States' declared policy on free passage in the Gulf of Aqaba and U.N. responsibility in Gaza.

April 6th   First tanker, American *Kern Hills*, arrives at Elath on Gulf of Aqaba with crude oil to be pumped through newly laid pipeline to Beersheba.

April 24th   After investigating Syrian complaint against building of bridge by Israel across the Jordan River in the demilitarized zone (of the Huleh swamp area), Acting Chief of Staff of the U.N. Truce Supervision Organization reports his satisfaction that the bridge was intended to facilitate the completion of the Huleh reclamation project.

May 21st   The governments of Israel and the United States exchange statements on Israel's support for the purposes of the Eisenhower Doctrine.

May–July   Tension increases along the Israel-Syrian border, following repeated shooting and shelling by Syrians, resulting in a number of Israeli deaths and casualties.

July 22nd   The Rothschild family of England makes available £1·6 million for the erection of a new Knesset (Parliament) building in Jerusalem and transfer the holdings of their colonization organ in Israel (PICA) to the national institutions.

July 23rd   Israel-bound Danish cargo vessel, *Brigitte Toft*, allowed, after delay, to pass through Suez Canal, but an Israeli seaman aboard was arrested and forcibly detained by the Egyptian authorities.

INDEX

Index

Index

R   257

Index

258

Index

Index

Index

East, 239; and withdrawal from Gaza, 245–6; with France, on issue of Jerusalem's interim government, 40–1; the 1949 loan, 73, 249; and 'security aid', 250

Uranium and coal compared, 104

U.S.S.R., 16, 108; and Egypt, 191, 237, 238; and Israel's application for U.N. membership, 23; and Jerusalem Statute, 42; and Jordan hydro-electric plant, 251; and Nasser arms, 191, 252

Vergani, Msgr. Antonio, 124

Wailing Wall, Jerusalem, 49–50
Walled City, Jerusalem, 48

War as 'natural state' idea, 127

Water resources, 94

Weizmann, Chaim, in 1915, 115; and deserts, 94; Institute of Science founded by, 99, 106, 107, 187; and synthetics, 105, 106; tribute to, 77–8; *see also* 249, 250

WHO, work of, 99

World Bank, 99

Xenophobia, *see* Nasser

Yarmuk-Jordan rivers projects, 177, 252

Yemen, 15, 169; Jews leaving, 179

Zionism, 65–6, 115–16, 128, 136, 137, 138, 139

261

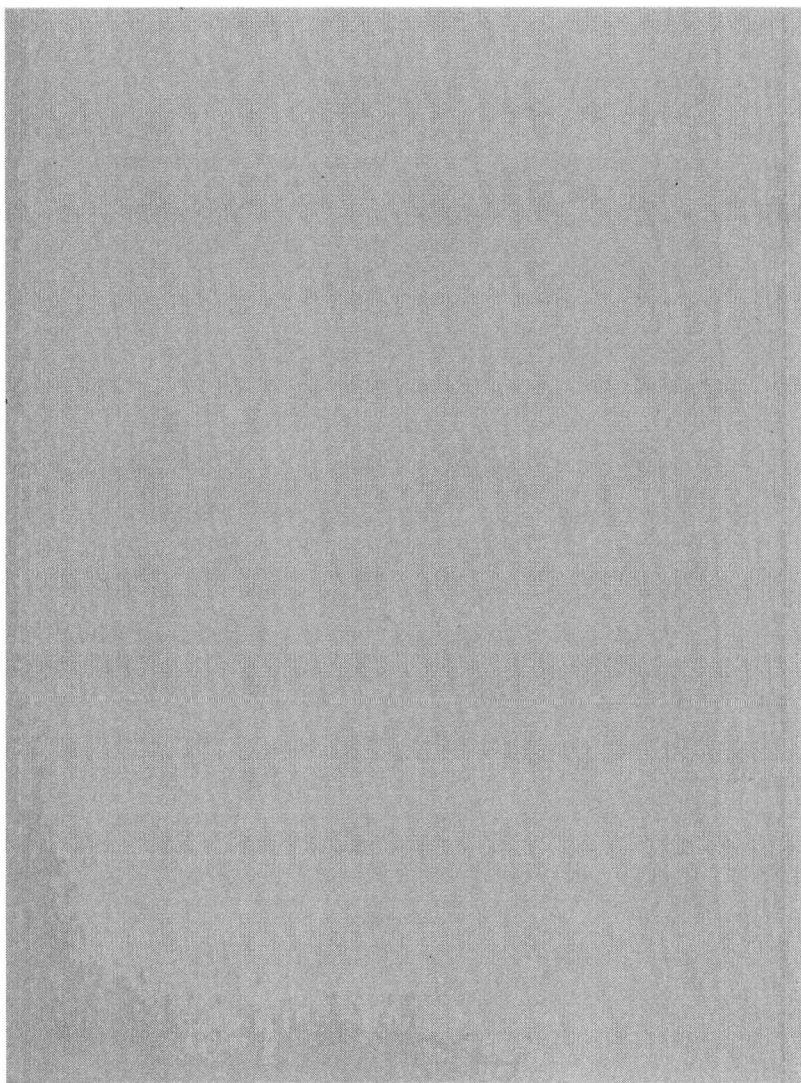

DATE DUE

MY 2 0 '68			
GAYLORD			PRINTED IN U.S.A.

Printed in the USA
CPSIA information can be obtained
at www.ICGtesting.com
LVHW020032311223
767812LV00012B/738

9 781014 415776